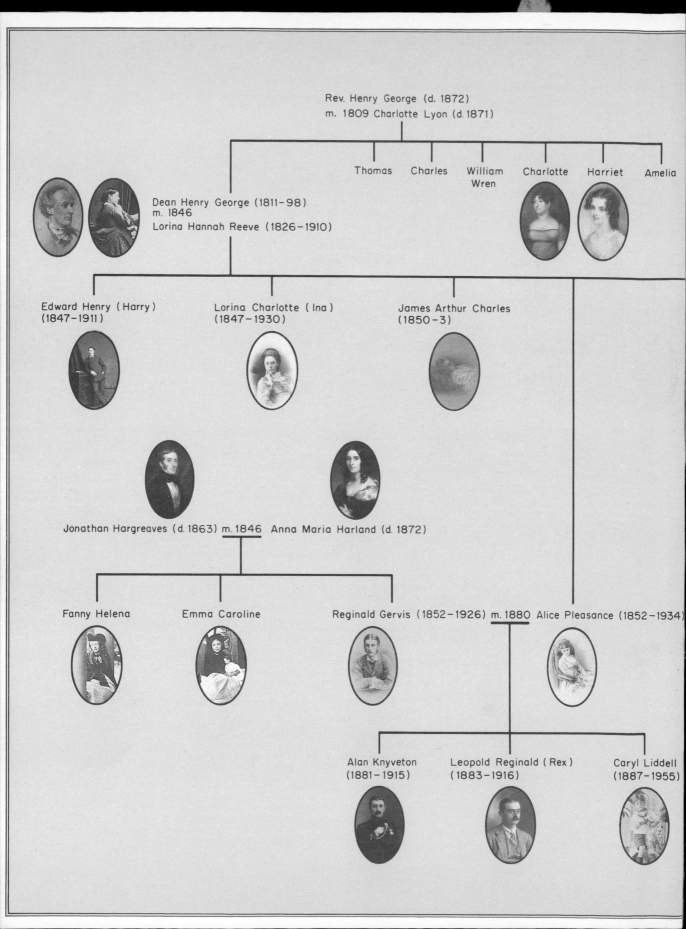

Rev. Henry George (d. 1872)
m. 1809 Charlotte Lyon (d. 1871)

Thomas | Charles | William Wren | Charlotte | Harriet | Amelia

Dean Henry George (1811–98)
m. 1846
Lorina Hannah Reeve (1826–1910)

Edward Henry (Harry)
(1847–1911)

Lorina Charlotte (Ina)
(1847–1930)

James Arthur Charles
(1850–3)

Jonathan Hargreaves (d. 1863) m. 1846 Anna Maria Harland (d. 1872)

Fanny Helena

Emma Caroline

Reginald Gervis (1852–1926) m. 1880 Alice Pleasance (1852–1934)

Alan Knyveton
(1881–1915)

Leopold Reginald (Rex)
(1883–1916)

Caryl Liddell
(1887–1955)

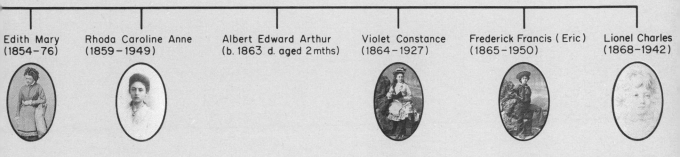

Edith Mary
(1854–76)

Rhoda Caroline Anne
(1859–1949)

Albert Edward Arthur
(b. 1863 d. aged 2 mths)

Violet Constance
(1864–1927)

Frederick Francis (Eric)
(1865–1950)

Lionel Charles
(1868–1942)

THE LIDDELL AND HARGREAVES FAMILIES

CONTENTS

INTRODUCTION

Judging by the number of beds in this country allegedly slept in by royalty, the monarchy has been for centuries a pretty lethargic institution. Or perhaps we just hanker after the slightest contact with the famous – even if that amounts to no more than clutching the merest gewgaw they brushed against. The instinct is a passionate one: it drove hysterical teenagers to near suicide at an auction of hotel linen soiled by the Beatles. And it extends to all classes: for fifty years Cecil Beaton treasured a faded rose kissed by Greta Garbo; and Viscount Leverhulme cherished a death mask of Napoleon. Whatever the motive, our lust for relics of the mighty ensures a commerce in memorabilia steady enough for them to be relied on as an investment. So shopping lists and *billets-doux* acquire more lasting value than hard currency.

In a three-day sale at Sotheby's in July 1935, thirty lots were offered for sale from the estate of Mrs R.G. Hargreaves. They included eleven copies of the same book, a biscuit tin and some plaster figures presented to her on her eightieth birthday. In all, the lots made £180. The lots sold *because* they were owned by Mrs Hargreaves, but not one of the purchasers was interested in the real Mrs Hargreaves.

She died on a chill November day in 1934 at The Breaches in Westerham, Kent – the kind of village which newspapers say 'nestles sleepily'. This unremarkable event disturbed Westerham's rural somnolence as surely as the death of the village's famous son – General Wolfe, whose heroic exploits at Quebec two centuries before earned him a posthumous statue on the green. Had Mrs Hargreaves been no more

Opposite page:
The Breaches, Westerham.

Westerham.

than plain Mrs Hargreaves, then even local reporters might have been hard put to it to make a story out of her death, except by saying, "Woman dies in house leased from man married to cousin of Rider Haggard". But just as the house overlooked Wolfe's statue, so Mrs Hargreaves' fame overshadowed his; news of her death was for a while to eclipse any of Westerham's lesser claims to fame. Mrs Hargreaves' son and sister, Caryl and Rhoda, knew well that they would have to share their private grief with a more showy and sentimental public sorrow. When they lost a sister and mother, the world mourned for her alter ego, as the most famous little girl in English Literature: "Alice is Dead".

Mrs Hargreaves was born Alice Pleasance Liddell, daughter of the Headmaster of Westminster School and soon to become Dean of Christ Church College, Oxford. On Friday, July 4th, 1862, when Alice was ten, she and her two sisters, Lorina (or Ina) and Edith, were rowed from Folly Bridge, Oxford, the three miles up river to Godstow for tea in the shelter of hayricks on the banks of the Thames. The oars were manned that afternoon by the Reverend Robinson Duckworth (Fellow of Trinity College) at stroke, and at bow Charles Dodgson, thirty-year-old mathematics tutor at Christ Church, with a penchant for little girls and a singular fancy for Alice. The year after he first met Alice, Charles Dodgson spun himself a *nom de plume* with the help of the editor of a comic magazine, *The Train.* He juggled with "Dares", "Edgar Cuthwellis" and "Edgar U.C. Westhill", but rejected them in favour of "Lewis Carroll" (from his middle name, Lutwidge, and the Latin for Charles, "Carolus"). It was this name that would be on the world's lips, but Alice always knew him in real life as "Mr Dodgson". As an old lady, Alice recalled Mr Dodgson's awkward appearance and demeanour: the stammer, the upright carriage "almost more than upright, as if he had swallowed a poker", and his white flannel trousers flapping over black boots.

Dean Liddell, from a drawing by George Richmond.

Folly Bridge, Oxford, 1854.

Godstow, the Old Bridge (before 1883).

Charles Dodgson.

En route to Godstow on that "golden afternoon", according to Dodgson, the "cruel Three" importuned him to tell them one of his nonsense tales. This extempore romance, in which Charles Dodgson sent his heroine "straight down a rabbit-hole to begin with without the least idea what was to happen afterwards", and told merely "to please a child I loved", burgeoned afterwards into one of the most famous children's books in the world – *Alice in Wonderland*. In that sense the afternoon was indeed golden; and in the memories of the protagonists they had weather to match: twenty-five years later Dodgson recalled "as clearly as if it were yesterday, the cloudless blue sky above, the watery mirror below, the boat drifting idle on its way"; and seventy years after the event Alice corroborated that – "blazing summer afternoon with the heat haze shimmering over the meadows". Objective record is more dreary: the London Meteorological Office reports the day as "cool and rather wet".

The success of *Alice in Wonderland* guaranteed Alice immortality, adding her name to those notable Dark Ladies who brought poets agonies and ecstasies. Had he known what was to happen to his book, it would not have been arrogant of Charles Dodgson to append to the manuscript two lines for his "onlie begetter":

> So long as men can breathe and eyes can see,
> So long lives this and this gives life to thee.
> (Shakespeare, Sonnet 18)

Certainly her role in the book bestrid Alice's life. In her later years it made her a public property, and the press kept an eye on her almost daily doings. So the bleak newspaper headlines announcing the death of Mrs Hargreaves came as a sudden shock to no one.

Alice had lived, as it were, with her immortality for over seventy years, praise for labours not truly her own, and performed in a quite separate, fictional role. But her vicarious fame through Lewis Carroll's book made it hard for the world to think of Alice as having an independent life outside Wonderland, or even to realise that she did not *really* tumble down a hole to meet the White Rabbit. Many people, encouraged by the press, were happy in this fantastic confusion between Alice and "Alice". The real-life lady told the story of a young child who met her for the first time, only to depart wailing, "But she hasn't got a long neck". If the newspapers were right in their obituaries –

"she will never be anything to the English-speaking world but the long-haired little girl of ten whom Tenniel drew" – then there is sad irony in that: Sir John Tenniel's model for the original woodcut illustrations in *Alice in Wonderland* was not Alice Liddell, but (if anyone of flesh and blood at all) Mary Hilton Badcock. Alice, quite adamantly, always wore a *fringe*.

Alice Liddell, however, was more than the long-haired little girl whom Tenniel didn't draw. Her claims to remembrance go beyond giving soul and title to at least one of Lewis Carroll's books. Alice was the talented daughter of an egregious family, whose historical roots lay in soil rich enough to be detailed in *Burke's Peerage*. (This august volume is, in one respect, tantalising for those digging into families' pasts: it observes the old-fashioned courtesy of never disclosing ladies' ages. All their dates of birth are rigorously excluded, as if they were delicate creatures outside time, like butterflies caught in amber.)

The Liddell line can be traced in *Burke's Peerage* under the title "Ravensworth", the name of the family castle in Country Durham, acquired in 1607 in the reign of James I. The Liddells were staunch Royalists, and were rewarded for their loyalty when Charles I created the first baronetcy of Ravensworth in honour of a stout defence of Newcastle against the Scots during the Civil War. Thenceforth the Liddell line is studded with MPs, high sheriffs and peers. By a further gesture of royal benevolence Sir Thomas Liddell became Lord Ravensworth at the coronation of George IV. Sir Thomas was Alice's great-uncle.

Those chapters of the Liddell saga which house Alice's immediate family are rather more than a continuing tale of hereditary privilege. Alice's father, Henry George, had inherited to the letter his father's (and grandfather's) names; but that was all he inherited, and there was no chance of growing fat on a name alone. By a sad mischance, Alice's grandfather was denied any part of the family estate by the carelessness of his father; he died – prematurely that is, before making his intended disposition of the property. Sir Thomas, eldest son, took the lot, three seats to his younger brother's none. The latter, Alice's grandfather, denied wealth in this world, looked to the next: he entered the Church, traditional haven of later-born sons.

Alice's grandmother, born Charlotte Lyon, was also nominally well-connected, but that again put nothing into her purse. As fourth daughter of Thomas Lyon (brother of the eighth Earl of Strathmore) she aspired to one of the two family seats in the event of her older brothers' dying without heirs. Somehow, both orb and sceptre eluded her grasp; neither the absence of heirs nor the confused will of her father proved sufficient, and Charlotte was left, almost literally, out in the cold. Alice's grandfather provided the modest shelter of his rectory and connubial bed.

Had fate and the vagaries of the Liddell forebears decreed otherwise, Alice would have been daughter of a country squire, idling out his days in the North East, beggared by the depreciation of landed property and bewailing the heavy charges on his estate. Denied these questionable advantages, Alice's father had to rely on his wits to prove the truth of the family motto: *Fama semper vivit* ("Our reputation lives for ever"). He proved it by making his way to the Vice-Chancellorship of Oxford University and Domestic Chaplaincy to the Prince Consort; among his children he could number a JP, Fellow of All Souls College and Counsel to the Speaker of the House of Commons, and a Consul at Lyons and Copenhagen. Alice, too, inherited her family's ability and was expected to use it, though brought up in an age which often condemned intelligent women to remain desert – or drawing-room – roses.

Families such as the Liddells leave their mark in official histories. But their real vitality radiates more from personal memoirs – letters, journals, notebooks and pictures. Alice's family were fervent correspondents, compulsive diarists and competent artists. No holiday of theirs was complete without journals and sketches, and no relationship or friendship brooked separation without a 'craving for epistles'. Alice acted as a magnet for these records and, when she died in 1934, her house had become a depository of family chronicles and pictures. Her son, Caryl, inherited the monument and consigned it to an attic. On his death it moved

Dean Liddell and his family, c. 1885.

house, but lay largely undisturbed and unkown for another quarter of a century.

The route that took me to that collection and into the lives of Alice and her family was a gradual one: from a rather haunting early memory of *Alice in Wonderland;* then enjoying it more as an adult (the real test of great children's books). Years later I learned that Lewis Carroll and *Alice in Wonderland* were subjects of near-fanatical devotion, studied by some with a perfervid pedantry I thought reserved only for Shakespeare and cricket. At a conference of teachers of classics I met an extraordinary man who reminded me of the White Knight (Alice met him through the looking-glass; he continually fell off his horse). With his sugar-loaf hat, flamboyant moustache and irrepressible enthusiasm, my man was quite as eccentric as Lewis Carroll's creation. And one lunchtime he earnestly explained how his research had been instrumental in establishing exactly *which* Victorian Latin primer had been used by Alice's brother. The actual identification turned on a complex pun on the word "mouse", or "muse" – or both. (In Wonderland Alice addresses the mouse in the pool of tears, "O Mouse" – remembering the declension, "A mouse, of a mouse, to a mouse, a mouse, O mouse", in her brother's Latin primer.)

Two months after this strange encounter, I drove to Tetbury in Gloucestershire to meet Alice's granddaughter, who now owned the family collection of documents. She had decided to make public what she called her "Alice memorabilia". I arrived to find a house on a manorial scale, guarded by three dogs – long, short and tall – and a parrot, which kept a wary eye on me as I gazed over the vast central hall. Its decor and furnishings were a sumptuous tribute to the style of the eighteenth-century local landowner, Thomas Cripps, who had the place built for his new bride before he was twenty-six. This one room, at once opulent and severely classical, from its blooming orchids to its egg-and-dart friezework, ran up to a height of two storeys in the middle of the house. There was nothing of Alice here, however; her quiet niche was more remote, on the top floor, in the

The house at Tetbury.

playroom, appropriately enough, among the detritus of other children's lives. In climbing the oak staircase, I ran the gauntlet of the gaze of family worthies, whose portraits loomed over the stairwell. Behind their mute pigments their spirits may not have been sanguine at the imminent exposure of the Liddells' past.

At first glance, the playroom had a vaguely nautical air, with its porthole windows (more properly, I later learned, called Baroque *oeils-de-boeuf)*, though they looked out on a sea of green grass and the waves of rural Gloucestershire.

Metaphorically, I might have called the room Aladdin's cave, or, better, Merlin's room as it appeared to young Arthur in *The Sword in the Stone.* Remember the odd antiquarium that greets Arthur's gaze: "an astrolabe, twelve pairs of boots, a dozen purse nets, three dozen rabbit wires, twelve corkscrews, some ants' nests between two glass plates, ink bottles of every possible colour from red to violet, darning needles, a gold medal for being the best scholar at Winchester, four or five recorders" – and so on, to include "the fourteenth edition of the *Encyclopaedia Britannica* (marred as it was by the sensationalism of the popular plates)" and "a complete set of cigarette cards depicting wild fowl by Peter Scott". Over the next few days my rummaging through the cardboard boxes, chests of drawers and bookcases in the playroom served only to confirm that fiction is no stranger than real life.

The first cupboard I opened was crammed with a library, singular in two senses – over two hundred and fifty different editions of *Alice in Wonderland:* in German, French, Japanese (with illustrations by Arthur Rackham), Czechoslovakian, Portuguese, Bulgarian, Spanish, Polish, Dutch, Swedish, Italian, Russian, Gaelic, Esperanto, Braille and in shorthand. There was Alice in Latin *(Aliciae Per Speculum Transitus Quaeque Ibi Invenit),* Alice abridged, set to music, dramatised and "told mostly in words of one syllable". There was a facsimile of the first edition, signed by Charles Dodgson and presented to Alice. All the other books were either signed by Alice or had pasted on the inside covers letters from her, culled at random from her correspondence. They spoke of the varied minutiae of her life. The first letter I saw, written only months before her death, recommended "Winston's Marlborough – I think it is a book to have", ordered two dozen bottles of white wine and a "sovereign's worth of what you call your cheap tulips", and cast mild aspersion on a recent engagement: "They say the girl is very nice, quite very nice, even if her parents are rather common. (This must not be said out loud.)" Among the trivia and the tittle-tattle appeared more interesting moments: one letter from Alice, written a couple of years before her death,

ALLEN'S MARVELLOUS CHOCOLATE
Manufactured by F. ALLEN & SONS. LONDON
Five Prize Medals Awarded
ALICE IN WONDERLAND
THE NURSERY "ALICE"
GUINNESS CARROLLS for 1935

hinted at her weariness at living in the shadow of her fictional counterpart: "poor little Alice, I am quite tired of that little lady, slightly ungrateful on my part, I admit."

In most of the drawers and boxes there was little sense of order, and interesting things turned up arbitrarily in odd places. A *billet-doux* to Alice's younger sister, Violet; a party invitation to her from Benjamin Jowett, Master of Balliol College and one of the most famous of Victorian scholars; two letters from the infant Alice (one with a reference to Charles Dodgson which would have alarmed Alice's mother); and two letters from Charles Dodgson – all these fell into my lap from between the leaves of a birthday book, itself a present from John Ruskin. All around there appeared big people doing the small things of which even notable lives are compounded. Charles Dodgson, for example, writes to Violet with a wry charm, enclosing a present of a brass pencil sharpener (April 28th, 1888): "It is the invention of a friend of mine: so I am bound, if only to my position as his friend, to make his invention known to any whose exhaustive knowledge of Dynamics (here I do not allude to you), or whose miserly craving for anything bright and metallic (here I do not allude to you), or whose artistic pursuits rendering the sharpening of pencils an hourly necessity (here I allude to you) fits them for it." (One of 98,721 letters written and filed by Dodgson between 1861 and his death in 1898.)

A detailed inventory of the riches of the playroom, compiled over several days, eventually ran to over twenty pages, and some single items in the list were a compendium in themselves – such as, "Anna Maria Hargreaves' diaries, 1850s and 1860s". The scale of the cache was in itself quite daunting. Anything, but anything, it seemed, with even a remote bearing on the real-life or fictional faces had found its way into the room: Alice's prayer book and cheque stubs; "Alice" floor tiles and cigarette cards; Alice's spectacles, fan and silver buttons; an "Alice" biscuit tin (containing three different Alice in Wonderland card games); Alice's necklace (another present from John Ruskin) and one of her milk teeth mounted in a gold ring. Some items were simply

Alice's possessions.

baffling; it was impossible to say what part they play in the story of Alice and the Liddells. What does one make of the battered diary of an anonymous sixteen-year-old boy of "dwarfish stature", compelled by mysterious circumstances "to leave all dear relations and friends", to make his way in the navy; sailing at first (appropriately in view of the conditions he endured) in *HMS Perseverance* for the Mediterranean in 1859? Floggings (usually two or three dozen lashes), courts martial, fallings overboard, crashings to the deck from the rigging or backwards into open holds – all these the author escapes, closing his diary with a cry of blessed relief: "The long-hoped-for day, the day on which terminates the commission of *HMS Avarice;* Thanks be etc."

Some of the drawers and boxes contained quite startling miscellanies; it was like being faced with the challenge of several jigsaw puzzles, their pieces mixed up. One box alone contained among its hundred or so items: a copy of the will of the Right Honourable William Pitt in which he acknowledges debts of over £13,000; a newspaper story of apparitions of Alice's father on the walls of Christ Church College; and a poem, "Hermits of the Blockhouse", written during the Boer War.

An oil painting of Alice by her sister, Violet, stood sentinel outside the playroom, as if to show how her person dominated the collection. But she had attracted items, too, which would otherwise have been lost or destroyed, and which show how rich in relationships were the lives of the Liddells. The family's status and varied talent put them in touch with great events and great people. The neglected playroom, therefore, looks out on fascinating vistas. To list the room's real treasures at this stage would pre-empt the excitement; each chapter of this book will start on a shelf, in a drawer or a cupboard, and move away in time and place to explore the lives of people, known and unknown, all of whom left vivid records – both of their daily routines and of what made their hearts beat faster. What binds the whole together is the remarkable Liddell family and the allure one of their daughters held for a young Oxford don, who loved trains, wire puzzles and little girls.

Sandown, watercolour by Anna Maria Hargreaves.

1 LITTLE WORTH REMEMBERING

Alice's grandfather narrowly escaped being a god – and a supremely classical one at that. To unravel the truth of that curious assertion let us start with an old engraving (culled from a book) among Alice's possessions at Tetbury. It shows a group of men in formal garb around a miniature windmill, with the intrepid air of posing for a trophy picture, as if they've just shot a tiger or climbed a virgin peak – though they're obviously not dressed or equipped for either venture. What really dazzles the eye in the picture, however, is the low sun on the horizon, reducing the men to awestruck observers. But who the men are, on the face of it, is a mystery. If they act out the climax of a tale, their frozen tableau is bleakly shorn of narrative.

That engraving, however, so easily slighted as a freak survival, teaches the first lesson of Alice's huge miscellany at Tetbury: never neglect the flimsiest item; it may turn out to be like one of those annoying jigsaw pieces, all abstract design and garish colour, which seem to belong to a quite different puzzle, but which eventually drop in like a key stone. So with the picture: its secrets were revealed by a tattered black exercise book which turned up later, filled with the spidery handwriting of Alice's father, Henry George Liddell.

He begins by deterring the irresolute reader: "I have little worth remembering to record." But the next one hundred and sixty pages give the lie to his modesty. Pestered by Alice and his other children to leave some memorial for "when I am no longer here to tell the tale", Henry finally succumbed in 1887 at the age of seventy-six. From time to

Dean Liddell in retirement.

time over the next six years he sat quietly in his study, looking out to the horizon of his life, before the battle of Waterloo. Events which changed the course of English life slip almost unnoticed past the eye: the first penny post, in 1840, which Henry laboriously detailed for his sister Charlotte in Rome ("a letter may go from Land's End to Johnny Groats house for the small sum of a penny"), and the "temporary" sixpenny income tax "in all its obnoxiousness".

And so to the puzzle of Alice's grandfather's "divinity" and the sun picture. Both are explained in Henry's portrait of *his* grandfather, Sir Harry Liddell of Ravensworth. He was decidedly an oddity, with ample means to live a life of dissipated ease. Sir Harry could and did indulge whims which otherwise might have been crushed under the tedious necessity of earning a living. As it was, drunken revelry probably drove him to a comparatively early grave.

One piece of Sir Harry's bravado was casually to wager, while alcohol pricked him on to adventure, that he would see the midnight sun in Lapland before he died. He won his bet, returning with several trophies – two or three Lap girls, some reindeer and a sledge, and a picture. The girls soon pined for home (whither they were duly despatched), the reindeer died of a surfeit of rich English pasture, the sledge languished for want of snow; all that remained was the picture.

Ravensworth Castle in the early nineteenth century.

The site of Binchester, from Bishop Auckland.

In another of his drunken bouts, Sir Harry vowed to bestow on his next son the questionable boon of being called "Jupiter". The intended victim (Henry's father, Alice's grandfather), born soon after, was duly offered for baptism. To his credit the vicar, Caleb Dixon, had the temerity to ignore the proffered name and, at the crucial moment, substituted *his own* father's names – Henry George. Shorn of divine status, the baby grew up happy enough with his extemporised names to pass them on to his own son (Alice's father). Nothing, however, could quell the persistent rumour that Alice's grandfather was really called "Jupiter".

With a father who so narrowly avoided deification at baptism it seems fitting, if not downright inevitable, that, in digging up his early experience for his exercise-book autobiography, Alice's father should strike classical roots. He was born at Binchester in County Durham – "a good, square, stone house, placed on an eminence, facing the Bishop's Palace at Auckland and distant from that town about a mile". Binchester, Henry explains, with a mind tuned to etymology, stood on the site of an old Roman station – Bina Castra. (The bishop later bought it and pulled it down; perhaps it blocked his episcopal prospects.) That

The Old Orchard, Binchester.

fragment of history lived on as more than abstract fact: in an adjacent field were subterranean vaults supported on brick piers – ruins of a Roman hypocaust (a kind of underfloor central-heating). Here, exploring and lost in the dark, the infant Henry Liddell learned his first, if mundane, lesson in classical research – always carry plenty of candles and matches. Thereafter, Binchester became the focus of phobias and fantasies: of meeting a Bengal tiger on the terrace or of being embraced in bed by a skeleton.

The day of Henry's second classical lesson became a landmark in his memory, one of those moments when his life took on distinct purpose and which he recounted with a proper sense of awe. It was on his sixth birthday, an event he anticipated with rare excitement: his father (then rector of Boldon) had promised him a "great honour and reward". What dreams crowded Henry's head before the great day? And as he tripped in the shadow of his father into the study what new toy did he hope to be clutching on exit? Alas, his father had in mind less an indulgence than a ritual; he took a well-thumbed book down from the shelves and inducted his son into the mysteries of the Eton Latin Grammar. Henry left the room a sadder, if wiser, young man: "I fear that, as I went on from day to day, I did not regard the honour so great as I did on the first day."

If nothing else, the routine learning of Latin irregular verbs and, later, the chanting of arithmetic to a "dull and patient" village schoolmaster drummed into Henry that he could not ride to success on his family pedigree but only by dint of hard work. As he grew up, a lowly offshoot of Ravensworth stock, he saw richer relations variously go wild or run to seed.

The faces of Henry's giddy forebears stare from the pages of family albums which later passed into Alice's hands. But the pages give away no secrets: erratic great-uncles and aunts, goggled-eyed and frozen, are subdued to flatness, as still and as dull as the cardboard pages that entomb them. The early Victorian camera was too blunt an instrument to record nuances of the moment. Bombazined or bewhiskered, not even relaxed enough to say "Cheese", the Liddells might be pillars of soot for all the life in their

pictures. But these grim aspects belie their true selves as they were caught, warts and all, in the pages of Henry's autobiography.

One of the most remarkable in this family gallery was his father's eldest sister, Aunt Bessie ("Titchie"). There were few saving feminine graces in her: uneducated, indulged and abrasive, she treated the world like a tyrant. She and her husband were as miscible as fire and water, and quickly agreed to live apart. (The family did not mourn his departure: he was not regarded as a very 'creditable acquisition'. He eked out his indigent latter days at Boulogne, in refuge from his creditors. His one contribution to young Henry's education was to object testily to his confusing 'lie' and 'lay' – as Northcountrymen still do today.)

Bishopton Grove School.

Bessie lived on at Ravensworth, where she resolutely cut the image of a man, dressed always in buckskin breeches under her riding habit, and wearing her red hair cropped very short. Once she was actually assaulted by a jealous husband who mistook her for his wife's lover. Bessie was famous for her feats on horseback: refusing to pay the toll on the Gateshead road, she simply leaped the gate; and to save an eight- or ten-mile ride from Ravensworth via Newcastle bridge to Bradley Hall (on the opposite bank), she and her horse swam the river. Outspoken and with a ready anthology of blunt oaths, she did the rounds of her friends and relatives. They all dreaded her coming, since she was predictably critical of their food and their houses. She ended her days at Ravensworth, "blind and deaf, a burthen to herself and to others".

Henry's memories of Tyneside embraced less wayward family friends – like Mr Shaw of Usworth, a fat and good-humoured Irishman, with a large and riotous brood of boys and girls, which a French governess tried, in vain, to curb. At Usworth, out of reach of the stern Gallic eye, Henry climbed the cherry trees to gorge the fruit until his hands and face were black with juice. He once fell from the summerhouse roof and broke his arm (it was never straight again).

Early in life Henry left the vagaries of his family and the vicissitudes of Tyneside, though he was at first a reluctant traveller, and his destination held fresh and equal terrors of its own. He recorded with what sense of desolation at the age of eight he and his younger brother, Thomas, were abandoned at a school near Ripon in Yorkshire:

In the course of a long life I have not escaped several sharp and severe sorrows . . . but I do not think that any sorrow of youth or manhood equalled in intensity or duration the black and hopeless misery which followed the wrench of transference from a happy home to a school . . . I remember as if it were yesterday, the sinking of heart, the utter despair, the wish that I could die on the spot, when my kind and loving father parted with us in the Master's study and, passing out of the green gate of the little garden in front of the house, disappeared from sight.

For four years Henry languished under the baleful care of the master, Mr Weidermann, cadaverous and dark-complexioned, habitually squinting through gold-rimmed spectacles and clad in a bright, tartan dressing-gown. His regular and violent fits of passion the boys explained away as the result of an illness during which his brains had been removed and washed in salt water. Two ushers abetted Weidermann in his malpractices: Snowdon, sandy-haired and lanky, with legs of unequal length; and Patchett, short, square-built, much pitted with smallpox and very ready with the cane. Violence, in fact, was in the very fabric of the place. Older boys blew little pins in balls of sealing wax through pea-shooters to fix small boys' ears to their heads. During this ordeal, the victims were expected to sit still in rows with their hands over their eyes.

Charterhouse School.

After four years of unrelieved adversity, in the course of which Henry Liddell remembered nothing of quality either in the teaching or in anything else, he was removed further south to Charterhouse. Although the school was then under the great Dr Russell, this move only prolonged Henry's wretchedness for another six years. At Charterhouse, Henry's "home" – almost his entire world – was the seventy-foot "Long Room", low, dark and dirty, and where, in communal squalor and accumulating filth (there was only one towel), the boys ate, worked, played and fought. The only object in the place which Henry could call his own was a small locker. George Atkinson, a Tyneside compatriot, secreted in his locker a snake, which he would push under boys' arms during lessons or wrap round their necks. Officially, boys had a share of the open fire, though the younger ones saw little of it.

Dr Russell's "revolution" at Charterhouse had introduced a system where senior boys (*praepositi*) taught the juniors – and tried to keep them in order. For boys without physical or mental muscle the task was a sore trial and a complete waste of time for their charges. Henry Liddell in letters home from "Beastly Charterhouse" regarded the scheme as "worse than slavery". But while it wasted time, effort and talent, the system saved the school the expense of hiring enough masters to do its job properly.

Charterhouse put self-mortification high on its list of essentials for pupils, punishing or humiliating those who made flamboyant or even normal gestures of independence. Henry remembered "Tilly", who sported a pale green, cutaway coat with metal buttons, being pilloried by a master, Andrew Irvine (later vicar of a parish in Leicester): "Stand up, you, sir – you vulgar-looking boy in a green baize coat." Henry's own banner to the cause of personal identity was a crimson silk watchguard, which passed round his neck and meandered down his waistcoat to the fob. His housemaster, "Old Watkinson", made of it a metaphorical noose to hang Henry with: he caught Henry's form seated when they should have been standing (under school rules governing regular change of posture). "You, sir," he shouted, "*you* know not the time? You who make more show with your watch than any other boy in the school!" Generally, the regimen at Charterhouse discouraged self-esteem. Dr Russell, ignoring promise but confident in the future, told Henry that he was as lazy as he was long and would bring down his father's grey hairs to the grave. (After his brilliant degree at Oxford, Henry returned to Charterhouse where he was paraded by the new headmaster before the boys as an example to them all. Henry avoided the boys' opprobrium by asking for a school holiday.)

Henry had an equally low opinion of Dr Russell: he was "a good, very good, not to say admirable schoolmaster, but then he is only a schoolmaster". He felt that, if anything, Russell hindered his progress and might therefore actually be responsible for his father's grey-haired interment. "We have to sit for hours hearing him hackering on to try if he can beat into the heads of those at the bottom by constant reiterated repetition what we knew perfectly by once going over; which of course renders what we do very little."

Dr Russell, Henry Liddell's headmaster at Charterhouse.

William Makepeace Thackeray.

One short part of Henry's sojourn at Charterhouse was a relative Elysium. Those who had survived the lower school and proved themselves worthy of a place in the Sixth (by a prodigious effort of rote learning all the Odes and Epodes of Horace) earned the title, *emeriti,* and waited for a vacancy. In the interim they were expected to sit in rapt attention, "drinking in the knowledge displayed by the Head Form". Henry and his peers limited themselves to a mere show of attention, so that when they were called upon to show their learning, "great was the consternation, grievous the display of ignorance, and vehement the wrath of the Doctor".

Among the *emeriti,* Henry squandered his time beside another destined to be famous despite ignoring the headmaster – William Makepeace Thackeray. Together Henry and William busied themselves drawing; Henry envied his rival's skill in caricaturing scenes from Shakespeare – Macbeth and his lady as a butcher and his wife "brandishing two reeking knives". (After Charterhouse, Henry and William parted, only to meet seventeen years later in London on regular rides in Rotten Row. There Thackeray told Henry's wife: "Your husband ruined all my prospects in life; he did all my Latin verses for me and I lost all opportunities for self-improvement." *Vanity Fair* was being published at the time in monthly instalments and Thackeray would discuss possible developments in the story. Mrs Liddell suggested that Dobbin should marry Amelia.)

An added deprivation for Henry at Charterhouse was not being able to escape the rigours by seeing his family at weekends or sometimes even in holidays. In pre-railway days travel was tedious and expensive. London to Newcastle was still a four-day journey by coach and a chilly seat on the outside cost £4 7s 6d. "Going out" from Charterhouse on Saturdays and Sundays into a more welcoming world was a privilege precious enough to incite boys to forge notes of invitation. The alternative for those forced to stay in was a grim penance served on the cramped and tiny backless seats of the chapel, or wandering aimlessly around the playground. It seems somehow symptomatic in such a place that even moments of hilarity were subject to

Watercolour by Alice.

Watercolours by Henry Liddell.

Pulteney Street, Bath, c. 1820, from a painting by David Cox.

forfeit: the boys' library committee forbad laughing among its members on pain of a sixpenny fine. At one meeting Henry had an uncontrollable (and expensive) fit of giggles, which cost him eleven and sixpence.

Henry's contacts with the outside world during terms at Charterhouse were few and therefore all the more golden. Regularly at Whitsun he stayed with two of his father's sisters, Aunts Charlotte and Anna in Bath. Like the blunt and masculine Bessie, they had their whims and caprices, but after the enormities of school, life at Bath was a glorious release.

In her long life Anna had undergone a sort of Pauline conversion. In her youth she had a penchant for the outdoors and late hours. She would insist on changing after balls into boots and stockings to go fishing. But in old age, settled in Bath, she stayed in bed till the afternoon, and developed a morbid dread of fresh air, keeping every window clamped shut. She went out rarely: occasionally to the theatre – but she minimised her exposure by insisting on being carried there in a sedan chair. (Henry remembered being indulged in this "ancient and luxurious mode of conveyance".) Anna's only other motive for venturing out was to see her old friend, Salmani, the printseller, to whom she paid high prices for a large collection, which on her death was valued as worthless. Lack of fresh air may have hastened her end; also her immoderate faith in huge quantities of Morrison's Pills.

Of all the relations that Henry brings back to life in his memories, Aunt Anna and her doings are chronicled with the greatest affection:

Methinks I see her now in her broad-brimmed white beaver hat, and an immense shawl, slowly pacing along with her hands behind her, stopping ever and anon to look into a shop window. Like her sister, Bessie, she was extremely fond of snuff and blew her nose with a trumpet-like sound on a vast Indian silk handkerchief, which she carefully arranged before use with a sort of cushion. Another curious trick she had of turning round several times before settling herself into a chair, much like a dog upon a hearth-rug . . . She was a Tory of Tories. One chief object of her vituperation were the railways. I believe she never trusted herself to this novel mode of locomotion, and constantly declaimed against the wickedness of devoting so much fertile soil to these barren iron roads. She found it hard to forgive my father for allowing my brother Charles to be apprenticed to Stephenson and take part in executing these nefarious works. But she had a kind heart . . .

By comparison, Henry's portrait of Aunt Charlotte is mere silhouette, but she played an important part in developing talents in Henry that he was later to pass on to Alice. Before she became a cripple with "rheumatic gout", Charlotte's two loves (she was never expert in either) were music and drawing. Henry used to sketch with her, and took lessons with her from Benjamin Barker, brother of the better-known Bath artist, Thomas.

These sorties to Bath and local diversions in London made Henry's life at Charterhouse less intolerable. In July 1829, he turned his back on the place for the last time as pupil, with a great sense of escape: "Never did pilgrim departing from an inhospitable mansion shake off the dust from off his feet with more hearty satisfaction than I did on quitting the noble foundation of old Thomas Sutton. It grieves me now (1890) when I see how differently boys regard their old schools, to think how cordially I hated both my own places of education." Disillusionment in his own schooldays was one spur to a lifelong commitment to educational reform.

From Charterhouse Henry Liddell's aspirations turned towards Oxford, though, if he thought it a promised land, he was destined to find there acres of more wilderness. Much of the university still slumbered idly in the mists of the eighteenth century, trailing wispy clouds of medieval glory. The poet, John Keats, saw the place (in 1819) as a green siesta for clerics:

There are plenty of trees,
And plenty of ease,
And plenty of fat deer for parsons.

Oxford, from the Henley Road, 1849.

Acrimonious debates that were to lead to reform were beginning to stir the languid air in a few torpid common rooms. The leaders of the great Oxford Movement – Keble, Pusey and Newman – were already ensconced in their colleges, thundering from the pulpit of St Mary's, the University Church, at once alarming and entrancing congregations over the devil's deeds in Oxford. Within three years Newman was to write the first of the famous *Tracts for the Times*, embarking on a spiritual journey that would lead him, and others, to Rome. Although never a Tractarian, Henry Liddell was to fall under the spell of Newman and hang upon his sermons – "bolt upright in the pulpit, with spectacles on nose, with arms, as it were, pinned to his sides, never using the slightest action except to turn over the leaves of his sermon, trusting entirely for effect to the modulation of voice".

However, real reform of the university was to be delayed for a generation or more, in the face of implacable opposition from diehards such as Dr Martin Routh of Magdalen College, whose standard response to proposed change was, "Wait, sir, until I am gone!" He died in 1854, aged one hundred, but change could not wait on his tardy demise. The railway came to Oxford in 1844; Routh outdid Henry's Aunt Anna and refused to recognise its existence. His college proposed a rule forbidding dogs; Routh simply called his "cats". In 1850 the government set up a commission of enquiry into the universities at Oxford and Cambridge (Henry Liddell was one of its members); its report brought snarls of resentment from a sleeping dog that would rather be let to lie. The Duke of Wellington (Chancellor of Oxford University from 1834) was said by his housekeeper to have taken to bed with him on the night he died a copy of the royal commission's report "with a pencil in it".

Oxford, St Aldates from Folly Bridge, 1811.

But that is to anticipate the cold wind of change. When Henry Liddell first reached Oxford in 1829, the teaching focused exclusively on classics. In effect, the curriculum asserted that in the pages of Homer and Vergil lay all ye know on earth and all ye need to know, not only for some abstract ideal but also, quite simply, to "get on". Thomas Gaisford, Dean of Christ Church College (where Henry Liddell knocked for entry), did not mince words at the end of a sermon to students: "Nor can I do better, in conclusion, than impress upon you the study of Greek literature, which not only elevates above the common herd, but leads not infrequently to positions of considerable emolument." Truth, Beauty etc. are all very well in their place, but the world must be served, must it not?

Such thinking was ironically partly the result of the university's being a limb of the Established Church. Of the 25,000 undergraduates enrolled between 1800 and 1850, 10,000 took holy orders. Many would unthinkingly have echoed Dr Philip Shuttleworth's plea to the Goddess of Learning:

Make me, O sphere descended Queen,
A Bishop, or at least a Dean.

The goddess showered her worldly gifts on some tutors quite lavishly. In 1837 a Senior Fellow at Brasenose College held a stall in Hereford Cathedral and two livings in the diocese which brought him eleven hundred pounds a year, while he was actually living in Paris.

The devil set before these professedly poor and pure prelates a constant temptation in the guise of "gentleman commoners", a privileged class of undergraduate students, who took up their places at the colleges as of right, with no pretensions to brains or intention ever to work. They treated the university like a gentleman's club, strutting down the High in their gold-tasselled caps and velvet-sleeved gowns. For this prerogative they paid double fees, and the university, for its part, condoned the farce, by making few demands on the idle clique's time, setting ludicrous exams which, for example, looked for only a

Oxford, from the Meadows, early nineteenth century.

cursory knowledge of Cressey's *Fifteen Decisive Battles of the World*.

Henry Liddell first approached this flawed paradise in the summer of 1829 and found himself turned away. His schooling had made him expert in the fundamental skill of reading Euripedes, but left him unable to meet even the trifling entrance requirement in simple arithmetic. His ignorance was so profound that hc could not say what was a third of a quarter. So Henry was ignominiously despatched back to the obscurity of the North-East, where in nine months his father's curate initiated him into the arcana of Euclid and algebra, differential calculus and analytical geometry. At Easter 1830, failing a summons, Henry returned to Oxford to demand his rooms at Christ Church, confident that he knew more maths than students who had been there two years. He felt none of the diffidence of Dr Johnson who as *servitor* (the poorest rank of undergraduate) was ashamed to go through the gates of Christ Church because of the state of his shoes. However, Henry found himself lodged in a squalid refuge, with furniture worth only a couple of pounds. He was, on his own admission, wretched, shy and lonely – knowing no one except one old schoolfriend, and bruised by the current etiquette of resolutely-turned cold shoulders. A contemporary manual on behaviour advocated a general air of taciturn superiority – "It will impress strangers with a very high notion of your consequence." Such was the humble establishment of the Liddells at Oxford.

The story from these quiet beginnings, through a forty-pound scholarship, to a double-first degree is one of awesome dedication to studies, which precluded even visits home. Holidays Henry spent in Oxford or with friends, where (unlike home – to his mother's chagrin) the atmosphere was conducive to reading. Nine hours a day seems to have been the norm, with breaks for walking, cricket and bathing. Three years after taking his degree, Henry outlines the regimen: "I get up at six, or a little after and take a walk, sometimes diversified by a bathe, before breakfast. The effect is excellent. I find myself able to sit at my books from nine thirty to five without any inconvenience, and I never was better." Henry was at the time responsible for tutoring students, while also furthering his own French, German, classical studies, divinity and scientific studies; in his spare time he kept pace with "the reading of the day, without which no gentleman can go into society". At the same time he was amassing entries for the great Greek lexicon.

This fat dictionary would have immortalised the name of Liddell even if *Alice in Wonderland* had never been written. Actually, the lexicon perpetuated two names, since it was a joint project of Liddell and Robert Scott, a student friend at Christ Church. For generations of schoolboys since, it has been a classical bible, ultimate arbiter on matters of ancient Greek vocabulary. It takes its place with the English Dictionary and the *Dictionary of National Biography* as one of Oxford's definitive publishing ventures, the more amazing since it is the work of two young men. The story goes that, if discussion arose later in Liddell's presence on the accuracy of the lexicon, dual authorship gave him the chance to blame Scott for any mistakes. The apocryphal libel is compounded in an epigram (composed by a Westminster schoolboy):

Charlotte Liddell.

Two men wrote a lexicon, Liddell and Scott;
Some parts were clever and some were not;
Hear, all ye learned, and read me this riddle,
How the wrong part wrote Scott and the right part
wrote Liddell.

The lexicon was nine years in the making. Some of Henry's letters suggest the enormity of the undertaking. His sister Charlotte gave him, in effect, a correspondence course in the theory of music: scales (diatonic and chromatic), sharps,

W. E. Gladstone

flats, keys and chords litter the pages. "And now you ask me what I can want all this for in a lexicon?" Henry's answer was simple. The Greeks, as they say, had a word for it, and he needed to know the English equivalents. If Henry had any doubts over the value of the drudgery, sales figures dispelled them. Within a week of publication in 1843 Henry could report the lexicon "selling like blazes". Nearly nine hundred copies sold before the university term started, and the print run of three thousand already looked meagre. Within a year a second edition looked a certainty, and this monument to scholarship took on the aspect of bestseller: "Unprecedented success – Extraordinary Novelty – Rare Attraction – as the showmen shout in the streets". A new edition of six thousand copies appeared in 1845. Thereafter, revising, correcting and enlarging it occupied Henry Liddell's spare moments until the end of his life (Scott died in 1857). By 1897 the lexicon had reached its eighth edition and Henry had found so many inaccuracies in the German model they used as a basis that it would have been less time-consuming to have started from scratch at the beginning. As it was, the initial reading was prodigious: one undertook to scour the whole of Herodotus, the other Thucydides, before moving on to earlier historical and philosophical writers, tragedy, comedy and so on. Nightly during term Liddell and Scott would meet in Liddell's rooms in Great Quad, working from seven to eleven, one clutching the pen, the other scrutinising texts. In the summer holiday before publication Henry describes the lexicon routine to his sister: "I get up at five every morning, work hard till about six thirty or seven, have a cup of coffee and a bit of bread, work hard till about eleven, have breakfast, work hard till two . . ." and so on until bed at nine thirty. How Henry Liddell continued throughout his life to find time for the lexicon among his myriad responsibilities is a mystery.

As important as this silent devotion to books in Henry's early years in Oxford are his louder moments in the company of men who were to become lifelong friends and whose names became public property. They included William Gladstone, whom Henry met first as co-member of the WEG Essay Club. Monthly they sharpened the edges of their minds on blunt issues; in consecutive debates they preferred poetry to philosophy, affirmed their faith in phrenology ("feeling bumps"), dismissed modern drama as pernicious, grudgingly acknowledged, by only four votes to three, that the poems of Tennyson (newly appeared in a first slender volume) showed "considerable genius". Many undergraduate clubs were the preserves of the rich and well-bred, sating their expensive tastes in dining and dressing. With more modest means, Henry could only join clubs where moderation was the rule – or, at least, where extravagance was limited to ideas and opinions. One such group, united by the desire to talk and save money, called themselves "The Tribes" (meeting in Tribe, the tailor's, house). They talked grandly and sipped wine minutely: in four nights the ten of them drank less than four bottles of wine. Henry felt privileged to be admitted to this august band; the original ten members numbered among them two future bishops, one archdeacon, four fellows of All Souls College or professors elsewhere, and one Governor of India.

There was, too, kudos attached to Henry's roots in the North-East. In many a southerner's eyes he had the aura of a Marco Polo, or any travller who could spin fantastic tales from his safaris beyond the fringe of civilisation. Gibbieson, a compatriot of Henry's, laid it on thick; on a journey to Guildford, Henry recorded,

Gibbieson told me many curious things. Among others, it seems, he takes no small delight in hoaxing Mr Pye, the butler. Mr Pye is a Devonshire man and has never been near the North Country. So Gibbieson telleth him of divers wonders that are there, as that the cabbages grow to a height of twelve or fourteen feet, and that the turnips are so large that the sheep eat their way in and then three or four creep into the hollow and put up there for the night. This naturally staggers Mr Pye's credulity. Whereupon he goeth to Mrs Currie (who is also a Northumberland woman) and asketh her whether Gibbieson hath told the truth. And she, nothing doubting, putteth on a grave face and saith, "Oh yes – and when we want to boil a turnip, we are obliged to get a pot so big that, if you tap on one side, a person on the other cannot hear you." Poor Mr Pye was so dumbfounded by this that he went out declaring that he would go and ask Mr Liddell.

Henry was happy to embroider the fiction.

He added several cubits to his student stature in Oxford in another curious way – by being recognised as an authority on cholera. On a Christmas visit home in 1831 he found Tyneside ravaged by the disease, imported by the crew of a foreign vessel. The streets of Newcastle were "almost deserted except for the dead carts, and the chance persons I met seemed as if they expected to be stricken down". This fear infected the South as far as Oxford, where students took to carrying a note in their pockets, which, in the event of their developing suspicious symptoms, advised the first person who found them to summon Henry Liddell for a definitive opinion.

Henry does not say how many fellow students he thus condemned to early graves, but he later made a decision

Henry Liddell, aged twenty-eight, from a portrait by Cruikshank.

which would enable him to offer a cure to their souls: in 1836 he took holy orders. This decision, if not automatic, was at least obligatory for anyone intending to make a career at the university. However, Henry did not take the step lightly; it was "so important, and – for me – so awful a change in life". But in later life he knew that, had he been thirty years younger, a student in Oxford freed from its clerical yoke, he would probably not have been ordained.

With a degree and in holy orders Henry was qualified to nurture minds and care for souls. Christ Church appointed him tutor. For a while the old self-consciousness returned – "I was meditating over the air, tone and gesture to be assumed when my first lecture enters the room . . . circles of reverential youths look to my nod, as of great wisdom". With this uncertain rehearsal of his new role as teacher, Henry moved into the university sancta – the senior common roms – haunts of those legendary eccentrics, whose quirks leavened the dough of routine studies and made good anecdotes for Henry's letters home. Unreformed Oxford gave plenty of elbow room to cranks. To those who bewail a modern world with room only for anonymous dullards, it may come as a relief to hear one of Oxford's nineteenth-century fogies, Moses Griffiths, himself lament that the "queer old fellows" of his youth were no more. "Impossible! Impossible!" he cried, when Dr Macbride of Magdalen suggested that he and Moses might themselves be seen by young men as "curious". Although distance lends comic enchantment to them, their vagaries were often frankly obnoxious. Griffiths so disliked undergraduates that he used to spend the whole of the term outside Oxford at Bath, only returning for the vacations. Even then his solitude was disturbed by the odd undergraduate but, finding himself dining with a student in hall, Griffiths asked for a screen to block out the offending prospect.

One of Henry's letters catches the very timbre of Griffiths' voice:

There is a Fellow of Merton – very odd, old man, Moses Griffiths (commonly called "Mo") by name. He detests the name as much as you do Hannah. "What do you think, sir," says he, "the parent deserves who christened their son *Moses?* What, sir, indeed?" Today I met mad Talbot with this worthy individual, who insists on being called Edward, has his name so printed in the Oxford Calendar, and quarrels with anyone who calls him Moses . . . I took off my hat and bowed profoundly. So did he. "Not the first time I have seen Mr Liddell," said Mo. "Sir, I have seen you – more than once – in the pulpit, seen you, yes sir, and heard you, too – not what one could say one would wish to say, sir, of every man." I bowed. "Sir, you are very good." . . . "One would be glad to hear every word you say, sir. May I recommend you to speak a little louder, sir . . . Pray, sir, are you not to be the Christ Church proctor next year?" "I believe so, sir," I said. "I congratulate you, sir, on your office." "Why, sir," I said, "I do not know that I contemplate the office as a matter of congratulation." "No, no, sir, horrible – horrible the office, but (tapping his pocket) the money, sir, – *ipsa pecunia* [i.e. the ready money], sir. Good morning." And we bowed and departed. He is the queerest little round fish, with the strangest manner in the world.

Dr Richard Jenkyns was another of Oxford's legendary characters with whom Henry rubbed shoulders – or, to be accurate, nether parts of the anatomy. Dr Jenkyns, for thirty-five years Master of Balliol College, was a squat little man, literally overshadowed by his imposing wife. Once a footman announced the stumpy master and consort as, "Mrs Jenkyns and Master Balliol". Henry Liddell once shared a coach with him, returning from his aunts in Bath:

Dr Richard Jenkyns.

When I got into the coach, who should be opposite me but Dr Jenkyns, a little important man, who thinks a great deal of matters of form. 'Ah, Mr Liddell, he said, 'I am delighted to have so good a companion' – of course I bowed and looked pleased and muttered something about – you know what as well as I do. But in truth I was very sorry indeed to find so great a little man opposite me – for he has a very outgrown *forepart*, so that my knees came to about the middle of his waistcoat, and I could not move without agitating his inside, and, as there were two goodly females in the other two places, my situation was not what I should have chosen, had I been asked.

Henry had to endure the rigours of travel by coach for several years after this close encounter with Dr Jenkyns. The railway finally puffed into Oxford in 1844, to the dismay of prurient dons, who saw it as a visitation of the devil, a steaming and smoking demon ready to whisk innocent students away to the satanic delights of London. Some objectors carried on just as before, such as Dr Routh, who pretended trains didn't exist, even when they delayed his students. One intrepid speculator built a flimsy house in the track of the proposed line and insisted on compensation for its removal. All the excitement and alarm proved ill-founded: the earliest trains took even longer to reach London than the coach – seven hours instead of six (for a journey of sixty miles). And on Henry Liddell's long journey from the North-East, trains merely brought their peculiar brand of annoyance, which he suffered with glum resignation:

> I sit down dutifully to let you all know that I had a very prosperous journey and arrived at Oxford at about half past nine on Friday morning, going round by London and having abode nearly an hour at Fallowfield and Harwell, just an hour at Hartlepool, three-quarters of an hour at Stockton, the same time at York, thirty-five minutes at Derby and one hour in London (in all the stopping being more than five hours in twenty-three) and having changed vehicles eleven times. So ill-managed is railway travelling at present.

One other lifelong friend Henry Liddell first met at Oxford, though unaware that this noteworthy youth, three years his junior, was to develop a sonorous voice and a florid pen to command the attention of thousands. In the eyes of many (including himself) he was to become in matters of art and social reform little short of a prophet. The story of his long friendship with the Liddells emerges from a neat parcel of letters spanning forty years, and wrapped in pink ribbon, as if love letters or a barrister's brief. In a sense they are both –

by turns affectionate and respectful, or acrimonious and resentful. They trace the thwarted progress of a bruised idealist, from his youthful zeal, through a world-wearied middle age, to a fragile senility. He walked with his head in the clouds of utopia, while stubbing his feet on the stones of brute facts. The letters all bear the signature of John Ruskin.

Henry Liddell first noticed him as a student at Christ Church, carrying the burden of an ambitious father who expected more for his son than the sherry trade he himself worked in. In John Ruskin's own words, his father had high hopes of his entering high society, winning prizes, taking a double first, then marrying Lady Clara Vere de Vere, writing poetry as good as Byron's and becoming Primate of England before the age of fifty. Certainly Ruskin stood apart at Oxford, if as somewhat of an oddity; there cannot have been many undergraduates whose mothers joined them in lodgings to keep them company. Henry Liddell recognised Ruskin as different from the run-of-the-mill gentleman-commoner, rather as one might catch sight of an orchid among thistles:

John Ruskin, 1842, from a portrait by George Richmond.

(1837) I am going to see the drawings of a very wonderful gentleman commoner here who draws wonderfully. He is a very strange fellow, always dressing in a greatcoat with a brown velvet collar, and a large neck-cloth tied over his mouth and living quite in his own way among the odd set of hunting and sporting men that gentlemen commoners usually are . . . Ruskin tells them that they like their own way of living and he likes his; and so they go on, and I am glad to say they do not bully him, as I should have been afraid they would.

Bullied by bad health, John Ruskin fell short of his father's hopes at Oxford; trailing few clouds of glory, he made an enfeebled exit in 1840, without a degree, but with memories of Henry Liddell whom, half a century later, he remembered as 'the only man among the masters of my day who knew anything of art' and who taught him all he knew about art.

Three years later, browsing in a Birmingham bookshop,

Henry Liddell happened upon a crusading volume *Modern Painters*, without knowing its authorship. It was to make Ruskin's reputation; and it opened Henry's eyes (and later those of his family, too): "It was like a revelation to me, as it has been to many since. I have it by me, my children have read it." After the second edition the following year, Henry Liddell and John Ruskin cemented their friendship in an abstruse correspondence which climbed the dizzy heights of theoretical questions about art. Coyly and reluctantly, Ruskin dropped the formal address, "My Dear Sir"; thereafter they met as equals on "agreeable and interesting reunions" weekly in London, until events in Oxford years later spiced their friendship with sweet and sour.

With his elevation to the rank of tutor, Henry Liddell's scribbled manuscript abruptly ends. In a sense, much of the rest is public knowledge, but it was not the fear of repeating an old tale that gave Henry pause. He had evoked memories of the first great sorrow of his life. In 1838 his sister Harriet,

Harriet Liddell.

already engaged to be married to one of Henry's closest friends, Stephen Denison, died. Eight months later Henry wrote to his father:

> It is but lately that I have been able to turn my mind to our lost treasure with any degree of callousness and satisfaction to myself. For before that, all seemed a dream; even at Easington, I could not bring myself to believe that she was gone for ever – in this world, and not once only have I actually looked up, expecting her to enter the room. Nay, one night her name was on my lips. And then, when the reality came upon, it made me so wretched that I could not bear to think of her, or aught connected with her, much less to talk or write of her. Therefore, if you found me less what I ought to have been, less of a comfort and assistance, I am sorry for it, and simply confess that I was aware at the time it was so, but could not rise from the apathy.

Harriet's loss was the first in a series of family tragedies over the next forty years. The last of them Alice could not bring herself to speak of even fifty years afterwards. Together they show that intelligence, talent, wealth and success could not push any Victorians far beyond the reach of sudden death.

Watercolour by Henry Liddell.

2
THE INTRUSION OF A STRANGER

One box of yellowing and speckled old letters at Tetbury seemed for some time irrelevant – the more so since they were drably signed "Smith", and there were reams of scripts bearing the name "Liddell". But the writer of these slighted missives turned out to be rather less unprepossessing than her name – a remarkable character, in fact. Her letters for thirty years from 1845 are rich in themselves and as a window into the lives of the Liddells. She laughed and wept with the family; she saw Henry's children grow up, marry and tragically die.

Lady Pleasance Smith was already seventy-two when the Liddells first knew her, but she lived on for another thirty-two years. By half a century she survived her husband, James Edward Smith, the botanist, who beat the Empress of Russia and Gustavus III of Sweden in the scramble to buy the famous Linnaeus natural history collection. That Lady Smith lived at all was a triumph over heredity: three of her four older brothers and sisters died at birth, while she lived to nearly one hundred and four. She died in 1877, her mind alert, her pen busy, and her only frustration failing sight, which in the end reduced her letters to near-illegible scrawls: "I long to write to you, but cannot much and yet I think the more"; "my mind and heart are full of a thousand things I could say but my imperfect sight forbids." Her mind, however, could still argue nice points of moral philosophy and detail a critique of the Temple of Diana at Ephesus. A few days before her death, she recited most of Gray's *Elegy* by heart. Her letters are a kaleidoscope of ideas and events, by turns moving, amusing and

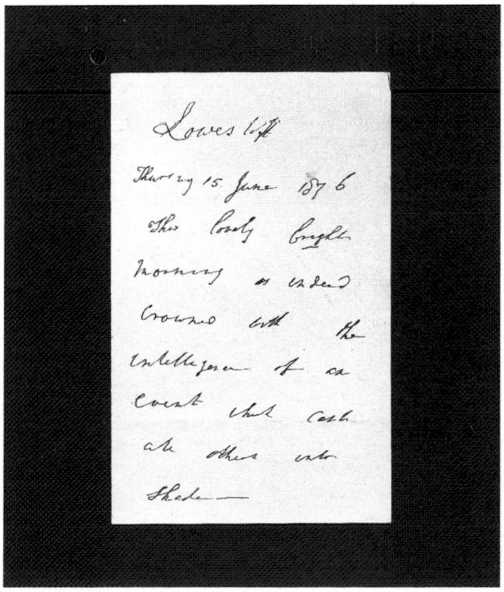

Lowestoft
Thursday 15 June 1876
This lovely bright morning is indeed crowned with the intelligence of an event that casts all others into shade —

Letter from Lady Smith, aged 103.

provocative; yet they all date from the old age of one who was already well in her teens at the French Revolution and whose father, at the time of her birth, heard John Wesley preaching in the streets to "turn the mob proselytes".

Lady Smith would have approved of using her letters to draw her picture; she distrusted conventional portraits as omitting the warts or etching decline too deeply. Already seventy when photography was invented, she looked on its early wonders with apprehension. The only image of herself she approved was a painting of her in incongruous gypsy garb two years after her marriage, done by the "Cornish Wonder", John Opie, who became the darling of London society in the 1780s. Another happy picture was painted in the words of William Roscoe, a Liverpudlian of many parts (historian, patron of art, abolitionist MP, botanist, banker and author of a nursery classic, *The Butterfly's Ball and the Grasshopper's Feast*), in a letter to his wife: "He who could hear and see Mrs Smith without being enchanted has a heart not worth a farthing." Her letters are equally a test of the heart's value.

'Seaview' would have more than a hopeful hotelier's boast as a name for Lady Smith's house. She lived close enough to hear the boom of the breakers, to be flooded at abnormally high tides and to be plagued by sand piling up in the garden. It was the best of places and the worst, lit by the glories of the Aurora Borealis but fetid with the "*stench*, I can use no other word, from the herring pools", which made it impossible to open a window.

Lady Smith as a fortune-teller, 1794, from a portrait by John Opie.

Though a native of Lowestoft all her life and imprisoned there by old age, Lady Smith sat in the centre of a world with far-flung mental horizons. She did not, could not rely on smoother ways of travel to make her journeys. On the contrary, she viewed the coming of the railway with distinct apprehension – it would disturb her "perfect seclusion and rural beauty", turning it into a "scene of business and the busy hum of men". Although in 1853 (at the age of eighty-one) she still planned hopeful itineraries ("my passion just now is for the middle of Spain. When I make my text tour . . ."), it was through books and the Liddells that Lady Smith left Lowestoft.

Lowestoft, the High Street, 1784, from a painting by Richard Powles.

Lowestoft, the Fish Market.

Books were at once Lady Smith's solace, stimulation and company; they proved to her the truth of the maxim, "never less alone than when alone": "for I seldom find solitude irksome, if that can be called solitude when, without fear of interruption, I can open volumes and converse with the thoughts, the affections, the hopes, the fears and adventures of men long ages since departed and whom one wishes to meet more intimately". Thus she travelled in biography, science, philosophy, history and poetry. She hero-worshipped Macaulay and breakfasted with Addison (digesting an issue of his *Spectator* each morning).

Letters and newspapers, almost exclusively *The Times*, brought remote events and big people into Lady Smith's drawing room, under scrutiny of her sharp eye and ready wit: "The alterations in the cabinet [under Lord Palmerston] remind me of a whirlwind taking up a pile of leaves and replacing them almost in the same spot they were before. However, 'tis better than a Derby or Disraeli whirlwind which would have blinded us and choked us with dust." Again: "There is a story in circulation that Princess Beatrice has had her mind distressed about the pillar of salt into which Lot's wife was turned, and has written to Dr Stanley on the subject – she wants to know if it is the same salt she eats."

Lady Smith had lived long enough to see pendulums swing and wheels turn full circle several times; so she gazed coolly

Lowestoft, the Royal Hotel.

on passing fashion: the crinoline "extension" was to her "beyond all nature". But she took greater alarm at less transient changes – such as the Industrial Revolution she lived through: "I see another dreadful occurrence from machinery. Let me entreat you never to let your children see Wheels at Work. The dress of woman is almost sure to be entangled."

As the wheels of the Industrial Revolution turned dizzily ever faster (trains at *twenty* miles an hour), Lady Smith clung to one fixed and still point – her faith in the traditions of the English aristocracy. To her social graces were not just the frills but the fabric of life itself. She would have agreed with Mrs Beeton, that high priestess of the Victorian kitchen, that dining (as opposed to merely eating and drinking) was both the privilege and the index of civilisation. Lady Smith would measure the stature of a nation in part by the girth of its diners; any decline in cuisine she lamented like the end of the world: "You observed perhaps in *The Times* some remarks upon the usual fare at second-class dinners – 'the dim soup, the cold fish, the evil side dishes, the mutton and the boiled chickens'. These remarks do not apply to you (Mrs Liddell) who have a professor in your kitchen . . . but I hope they will put English Ladies upon improving their dinners [details here of a menu served in 1616] . . . here is a beautiful simplicity, no gout or dyspepsia lurking in the treacherous composts of our modern dinners." Foreigners, of course, could not be expected to compete; and wars were for Lady Smith as much a clatter of cutlery as a clash of weapons. In a long letter during the Crimean War she animadverted on the insanitary state of Russia, where, she had heard, the servants spat on the plates to clean them, where the soup contained "living victims in distress", where visitors were assailed by vermin and where "the horrors of the kitchen are inconceivable and there is not a bed in the whole empire which an English traveller, aware of its condition, would venture to approach".

At the Last Trumpet, however, a nation's blood would count for more than its stomach; Lady Smith saw one route to salvation in good breeding, though her faith occasionally wavered: "I have faith in blood, though perhaps it is

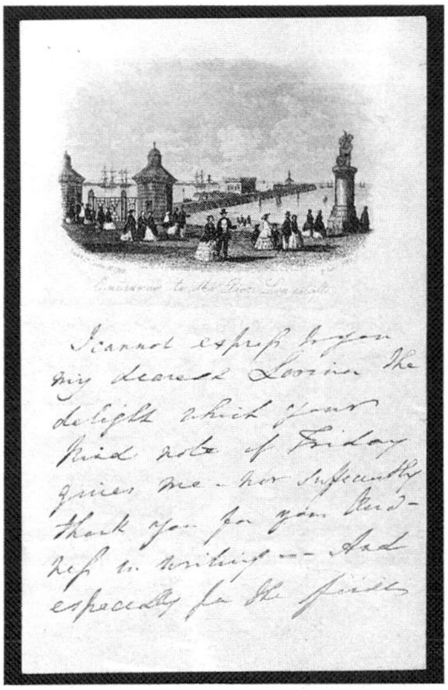
I cannot express to you my dearest Lorina the delight which your kind note of Friday gives me – nor sufficiently thank you for your kindness in writing – And especially for the

16 November 1864

My dearest Lorina

Your letters always welcome to me, & last not least so, gives me the more pleasure that the news it contains throws a bright beam of joy on

Letters from Lady Smith.

training. One sees such deviations that there is no calculating – Cain was Eve's." Nothing, however, sent such a tremor through Lady Smith's establishment as the evolutionary theories of Charles Darwin. From an early age Lady Smith had loathed anything simian – especially gorillas. "There was a good figure of a gorilla in *The Illustrated News* – a horrible, fearful monster and when I saw another figure of a poor fellow torn in pieces by one of those ferocious beasts, I wished some enterprising person would lead a well-appointed regiment, well-armed with gunpowder and shot, and extirpate the whole race. Old Nick himself would quail before these demons." Lady Smith therefore saw it as effrontery that Charles Darwin should, as she believed, uproot her family tree and seat a monster in its branches:

As far as I can understand Mr Darwin's theory, it seems to make the Great Artificer a bungling workman, leaving creation to be completed by an accident of an accident, and leading, one would think, to endless confusion and monstrosities – I cannot say I should like to consider myself the grandchild of an ape – for of all the animals the monkey, though in figure approaching human form, in intellect how inferior to several others in teachableness, in agreeableness of temper and in companionableness. The dog, the horse, the elephant – how much more sagacious are they, and though an elephant is somewhat allied to a hog, yet I would rather have had an elephant for my grandsire than a monkey.

Despite these rash incursions made into her tidy world by such wild thinkers as Darwin, Lady Smith clung firmly, if blindly, to the traditional virtues of home and family. She took exception, especially, to two of the great Dr Johnson's cynical maxims on marriage: "50,000 marriages would be as happy, or more so, if they were made by the Lord Chancellor, without the parties having any choice in the matter"; and, "A lady will take Jonathan Wild, as readily as St Austin, if he has threepence more, and, what is worse, her parents will give her to him." Lady Smith's faith in the more romantic marriage had recently been fortified by the

Mrs Liddell (née Lorina Reeve).

perfect match between her niece, "Lil", Lorina Reeve and a man, who, "notwithstanding his unbecoming whiskers", was in Lady Smith's eyes less a rake than a saint. He was Professor of Moral Philosophy at Oxford, no less, and his name – Henry Liddell. It was the engagement of Henry and Lorina that first urged Lady Smith to take up her pen and write herself into the lives of the Liddells.

In Henry Liddell's "official" biography, published in 1899, his wife Lorina (née Reeve) appears on the scene like a character summoned up by an author to enliven the story and rouse the flagging reader. She enters pat on cue from nowhere, her trousseau complete. It was, however, more than neglect on the biographer's part that omitted the human details of the story; his reticence was quite deliberate: "It would be unbecoming to dwell at length upon this occurrence and all that it involved." He felt that characteristically Victorian reverence for a man's marriage, home and family as not only his castle, but also a walled garden where to pry would be to trespass. John Ruskin elaborated the sentiment: "This is the true nature of the home – it is the place of Peace; . . . so far as it is a sacred place, a vestal temple, a temple of the hearth watched over by the Household Gods . . . so far as it is this, and the roof and fire are types only of a nobler shade and light . . . so far it vindicates the name and fulfils the praise, of Home."

Modern eyes, however, are not content with pious façades, and modern ears like to hear the blood pounding in marble breasts. But Henry Liddell is himself almost silent on the story of his early love – or loves. His childhood and adolescence were dominated by men – at home, school and university. In the pages of his autobiography his mother is a mere name, and the only other women are aunts who cosseted or diverted him. His academic life at Christ Church pointed the way to sober celibacy. When did the rustle of petticoats, then, first enkindle in Henry more than filial affection?

There is a solitary glimpse in the collection at Tetbury of young Henry Liddell's private, romantic emotions: it takes the form of a poem – one of three surviving pieces of verse by Henry. The less interesting pieces (though quite proper to the public man) are a hymn, *Miserere Domine*, and a turgid sonnet extolling the virtues of a Madonna by Raphael. The other, penned in October 1844, was inspired by flesh-and-blood beauty; it is an elegy, lamenting the end of a seven-year romance:

Ah me! They tell me thou art doomed
To be another's bride!
Ah me! and I must throw all hopes,
All dreams of bliss aside!

Henry's grief ran to twenty-four verses; in them he mourned the loss of one who would have made the perfect wife.

An Elegy, October, 1844.

Ah me! They tell me thou art doomed
To be another's bride!
Ah me! and I must throw all hopes,
All dreams of bliss aside!

Seven years are flown since first I seemed
To know thee as thou art;
Since first the flame arose that soon
Burnt hot within my heart.

It was not only that thy Soul
Was filled with Sympathy,
And Love for all things beautiful
On Earth, in air, and sea;

Not only that a lively Wit
Had made thy mind its home;
And shot with arrowy flight o'er ways
Where others slowly clomb;

Not only that a love for Art
And poesy was there;
And all thy heart's chords seemed to thrill
In harmony with mine;

It was not these alone that filled
My soul with love for thee;
For then, perchance, the flame had died
And left me fancy-free.

But when by its first storm of grief
My bark of Life was tost;
When all my fond hopes, wishes, dreams
In one blank void were lost;

When one – the fairest, sweetest, best,
That e'er bore Sister's name,
Was ta'en away and left me in
This world of sin and shame;

Oh, then to see thee weep, when I
Had no tears left to flow;
To feel thy hand's kind pressure, and
Thy sympathy to know,

'Twas this that bowed my heart to thee,
And made me feel indeed,
That Love is not an empty name,
No youthful dream, no lambent flame,
But a true friend in need.

And then, within my heart of hearts
I built a Temple fair
And pure, as mortal fane may be,
And set thy image there.

And there each morning when I rose
My orisons I made;
And there each night when I lay down
My vows I duly paid.

Ah, say not 'twas too fondly done –
They err who deem that Love
Is all of earthly mould, and draws
The soul from God above.

True love lifts up the heart to heaven,
Sets free from selfish care,
Lends purity to every thought,
Reality to prayer.

'Tis this that on the student's desk
Still sheds its cheering ray;
And lends a beacon-light of hope
To guide his lonely way.

Yes – when I've sat till midnight hour
Mid books on books high piled;
Oftimes, methought, thy image fair
Stood by in bodily presence there,
And on my labours smiled.

And if, at times, the praise of men
Came flattering on mine ear,
'Twas for thy sake that flattery pleased,
For thee that praise was dear.

For oh! methought, could I have e'er
Won honour fortune fame,
To lay them at thy feet, and dare
My hidden Love proclaim,

Couldst thou have known my Truth, and felt
To me as I to thee,
That had been worth a world of pain,
A world of toil to me!

And yet so frail the hope, so long
The time, that oft I strove
To quell those thoughts; and sometimes deemed
That I could cease to love.

But now the veil is torn; and now
Too well I know the power,
The soft unconscious influence
That reigned in every hour.

Ah me! and now – those thoughts, those hopes
I must throw all aside;
For thou art doomed (oh misery!)
To be another's bride.

Well – God be with thee! only thus,
Thus only may I dare
To breathe thy still-loved name, and thus
Remember thee in prayer;

So – God be with thee; send thee peace,
And length of days to see;
And make thee happier than I
Can ever think to be.

H.G.L.

Despite Henry's fears, "all dreams of bliss" were not cast aside; the void left by his Dark Lady (no clue to her identity) was soon filled by another – Lorina Reeve of Lowestoft. Henry, "Dearest Hal", was for her "that indescribable something which makes anything everything"; she was to him "My Own Perl", "mia carissima". However perfect their bliss, it was not Lorina's image that Henry had worshipped in the temple of the heart. He met her when unrequit hopes made him vulnerable, and in circumstances that made him aware of his loneliness. There is a single allusion to the first meeting in a letter to Alice nearly forty years later, among a catalogue of deaths: "First there is your dear uncle. It was at his marriage that I first saw your dear mother and the sad thoughts carry me back through a long and varied vista to that happy time." (He was referring to an earlier link between the Liddell and Reeve families: Henry's cousin married Lorina's elder sister.)

Although most other records have nothing to say about "that happy time", Lady Smith followed its progress with

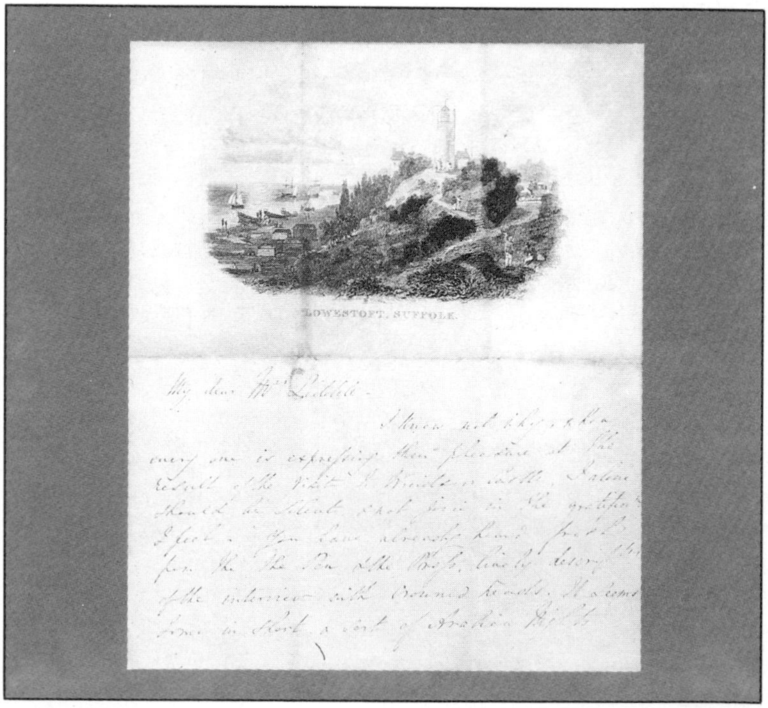

Letter from Lady Smith.

breathless excitement. Lorina's affairs of the heart were to her matters of moment; winning Henry Liddell outdid her expectations – he would deliver Lorina from the clutches of lesser, "fast" men. So Lady Smith sang her joy in a letter to Henry's parents. This, her first entrance, is beguilingly humble: she asks Mr and Mrs Liddell to "pardon the intrusion of a stranger", before enlarging on her niece's good fortune: "I had anxiously wished that such a lot might be hers, but as anxiously feared the chances were not in favour of her meeting and attaching such a man as Mr Liddell – yet I know her to be deserving of a better fate than the common herd of sporting, tandem-driving men could ensure."

Henry and Lorina were married in July 1846, and Lady Smith trumpeted her approval with a fervour more quaint than enraptured: "I delight in the plenitude of your mutual felicity." At a penny letter's remove, she followed their first ecstatic steps on honeymoon, from Bath, through the Wye Valley and much of Wales, to Liverpool. En route Henry and Lorina climbed what were, after all, modest hills – Plinlimmon, Cader Idris and Snowdon – but for Lady Smith distance did not lend them enchantment, only horror – as if the young couple had looked over the edge of the world: "I should fear to look into the awful crater from the summit [of Snowdon]." It was for the Liddells the beginning of a fascination with the wild places of Wales.

The more misogynist dons at Oxford did not concede, at the time of Henry's marriage, that it was possible for the Professor of Moral Philosophy at once to embrace the concepts of Plato and a beautiful young lady. In fact, dons were officially denied connubial bliss until the 1880s – except for Heads of Houses and professors (like Henry) who could display their consorts in public. Dean Thomas Gaisford of Christ Church (he who advocated Greek literature as a ladder to "get on" in life) was a married man himself and confided in Dr Bull that he found "love and lexicography were not incompatible". However, Henry Liddell was anxious to move on, possibly impelled by Lorina's ambitions – or apprehensions; she, after all, would run the gauntlet of celibate dons, such as Dr Whately with his sour definition, 'A woman is a creature that cannot reason and pokes the fire

Dean Thomas Gaisford.

from the top." (He managed himself, by guileful strategem, to avoid calling on woman's services even for domestic drudgery, sticking black plaster to his calves to save darning his stockings.)

Henry already knew how high Lorina had set her sights, and he had warned her that the way to the stars was not only arduous but an alluring path to damnation:

Once more I must repeat my warning. Be not ambitious. Desire not high place for me. We shall be far, far happier in a private station, with a competency, than with dignity and wealth. I feel it to be so from the bottom of my heart. Cares, occupations, troubles, business, all sorts of things will interfere with the placid and happy enjoyment of life. Wish not for it, Dearest. If ever I was serious, I am here on this point. However, we will not anticipate what may never happen. I cannot help praying God that it may not.

Perhaps Lorina prayed the opposite and God inclined his ear her way; in a few weeks He spurned Henry's orison spectacularly and beckoned him to high places. All was secrecy at first: Henry's letters allude darkly to "the thing", to "the affair you know of", to conversations "with another Person this morning, who gave me information on another authority". To these nameless informants Henry added Lord Canning, Sir Robert Peel and the Queen's Domestic Chaplain, all of whom pointed him "the way that I should go". In the middle of May 1846, Henry revealed all, though in words not calculated to enlighten the layman: "It is now publicly known that I am Archididascalus Westminasteriensis elect." More plainly, he was about to become Headmaster of Westminster School. Despite his protestations of lowliness, one of the main conditions he laid down was that the job should guarantee him at least a thousand pounds a year – not enough, perhaps, to have raised the eyebrows of Jane Austen's Mrs Bennett, but a sufficiency, nonetheless. One can feel the pressure of the invisible hand of Lorina.

The job was no mere sinecure; it can only have been a modicum of missionary zeal that prompted Henry to take his

Dean's Yard, Westminster, watercolour by Sidney Corner.

new bride to that forbidding pitch. Westminster School, whose list of Old Boys reads like an historical *Who's Who*, had declined by the 1840s to a point where it was surprising that any parents who loved their offspring should choose to send them at all. Few, only a few, did. The names of the great men who had survived the school (including Ben Jonson, George Herbert, John Dryden, Sir Christopher Wren, John Locke, Matthew Prior, Samuel and Charles Wesley, William Cowper, Edward Gibbon, Jeremy Bentham, Lord Raglan, Lord John Russell) – all these proved insufficient recommendation set against the bullying, idleness and squalor that prevailed in 1846. The job of headmaster had fallen vacant after a complaint by a parent to Sir Robert Peel; as a result, the captain of the school was expelled and the headmaster, Richard Williamson, resigned.

As the new headmaster, Henry Liddell dressed himself in the mixed metaphor of knight errant and besom: "I shall have to make myself many enemies. But nothing can be done without this . . . I shall boldly throw down the gauntlet and make a clean sweep." He sacked the whole staff, bar one, and, on the model of Dr Arnold at Rugby, set about ensuring that the boys developed healthy minds in healthy bodies, even though in some of the new buildings the Dean indulged his unlovely penchant for corrugated iron and whitewash, and in the new day rooms the windows were set high and glazed opaquely to deprive boys of a view. "Rigorous" best describes the new regime, in both good and bad senses. Henry Liddell was reputed only to punish lying, but that mercilessly, never again trusting the offender. Flogging continued: both public handings (with a rod on the back of the hand) and, for more serious misdoings, beatings on the bare backside in the privacy of the library. One boy arrived home with his hands such a mess of cuts from a beating by Liddell that he hid them in kid gloves for two days: "It was the fashion to smile when receiving, as if you rather liked it. I never heard a boy make any exclamation."

One victim of the new austerity was "Boots", a grimy, stuttering and idiotic vagrant, who had previously prowled round Dean's Yard. He suffered attacks of epilepsy, when he would roll on the ground, shrieking and foaming at the mouth. He sold ferrets and white mice to the boys and for a few pence he would sing a ditty, "Rise up, William Riley". Boys on the sick list gave him their medicine (which he drank with indiscriminate relish), instead of pouring it out of the window. "Boots" was swept away by Liddell's new broom, a scrap of debris from the past.

There are few smiles on the stern public face of Henry Liddell; but what of the family man, the husband and new father, behind the private doors of 19, Dean's Yard? To this questionable haven Henry brought Lorina in 1846 from the healthier air of Lowestoft. Here over the next nine years were born the first five children (including Alice) in "The

Westminster, 1851.

Metropolis of Great Britain and Ireland, the Mart of the World and, according to Sir John Herschel, the centre of the terrestrial globe" (as Murray's *Guide to London* boasted in 1851). In fact, Alice's birthplace was a sprawling and unhealthy leviathan: already London tried to house over two and a quarter million people, swarming the streets on 3,000 omnibuses, 3,500 carriages (excluding private carriages) and 40,000 horses, bustling along narrow and ill-maintained channels, dimly lit by 360,000 gas lights. In Westminster the gas company often left the road unmade after laying the pipes. The people of London burned three million tons of coal a year, with a smoke so dense that at times it prevented astronomical observations thirty miles away. Nine and a half million cubic feet of refuse thrust its way daily down the sewers in a kind of painful peristalsis, to the Thames. The river gave off heat and stench enough to drive Members of Parliament from their chambers. But London took pride in being the sovereign city: there were thirty-seven King Streets, twenty-seven Queen Streets and twenty-two Princess Streets. As if to symbolise, however, that its huddled populace were not quite sure where urban progress was taking them, whether to hell or utopia, the numerous North, South, East and West Streets meandered arbitrarily to all points of the compass.

In the official memoir of Henry Liddell, Lorina is reduced to dutiful appendage, only relevant when engaged on school business. She stands literally backstage as seamstress for the school play and coach to boys saddled with female roles: "restraining their stride within feminine limits and teaching them the management of their arms". The annual Latin play, indeed, was a major, even royal, occasion, perpetuated by a statute of 1561 (*De Comoediis et Ludis in Natali Domini exhibendis*), and an event of the "season" for London's aristocracy. Mrs Liddell acted a part not confined to the wardrobe: as hostess she placated a pernickety audience and whimsical servants: "The plays went off with considerable approbation and the dresses were much praised; nineteen to think of and arrange was no joke, but the fastidious Old Westminsters were satisfied. Bultitude as butler pro-tem officiated so well that we did not feel Watson's absence – he was so steady and punctual and clean – and kept our plate and glass in first-rate order – but then he was disagreeable in manner and his temper quite unbearable."

Later the page-boy "gave trouble", deadly offence in an employer's eye. He stole Mrs Liddell's watch (a present from Lady Smith) and hot-footed it to Leamington where he sold it for six pounds to a gullible jeweller. To compound the villainy, the boy filled his pockets with trinkets before leaving the shop. Caught, the miscreant begged forgiveness; the jeweller relented and there was no prosecution. The young thief joined the Mormons and set off for Salt Lake City – "a very *nice* disciple", as Mrs Liddell wryly observed.

Mrs Liddell's aspirations, however, ran to more than sewing costumes, planning menus and keeping a watchful eye on light-fingered servants. She wanted a role in London society, and her position as Henry's wife secured her an entrance. She dined and danced in company where, it seems, the real criterion of success was the outright rank of the guests: "the party was not very large but very elite" (including the Duchesses of Gloucester and Cambridge, and Princess Mary). Rubbing richly-apparelled shoulders with the pedrigreed made Lorina distinctly finicky about the company her daughters later kept and those who sought

Watercolour by Henry Liddell.

their hands in marriage. At Westminster she rarely showed deference, even in the highest circles: she approved of Lord Canning's china, but reserved judgment on his cellar – "no port wine after dinner, only claret and sherry – neither to my taste, but the correct thing no doubt". At the Cannings, too, Henry savoured a very rare dish – one Miss Stuart: "and for the future I must say that all the beauty I have ever seen in flesh and blood is as nothing by the side of hers. She is quite peerless. I am sorry to say that I did little else than see her."

The Cannings had been friends since Henry's student days in Oxford. They provided two wonderful anecdotes, the first in a letter from Henry to his sister Charlotte in 1841:

> Lady C. showed me a long and amusing letter from Canning who is with his yacht in the archipelago. Among other curious things he says that Mt Athos is covered with monasteries, inhabited by monks of so staid an order, that they never allow females to land on the promontory. Lady Canning wished much to land, for it is very beautiful. So Canning went to see the Patriarch of the Mountain, more, however, from curiosity than from any hope of succeeding. The old man stroked his long white beard, and explained to C. that no disrespect was meant to him, but that the rules of the society were so strict, that not even a feminine bird or beast of any kind was tolerated in the Holy Precincts – so much so that if a stray bird lighted by chance within them, the brethren made a point of shooting it, for fear it should be a hen. Canning, having heard that they lived mostly on eggs, asked how they managed matters, and the old man gravely protested that they all came from the mainland. C. is very sorry that he did not recommend the Ecalerbion or Steam Hatching Apparatus.

The second Canning story, in a letter to Lorina in 1845, also points to the quaintness of foreign places:

> I found Lord Canning here when I came in from church. He tells me that in Belgium people are quite mad – poor things – for want of potatoes. And they have got hold of the strangest superstition. They are Roman Catholics, you

Charles Canning, 1851, from a portrait by George Richmond.

know, dear; and they believe that Pontius Pilate danced over the tomb of our Saviour, and that the dance he danced was – the polka. Therefore they believe that this is a cursed dance and that it is gross impiety to dance it. And they believe that the present scarcity of potatoes is owing to people having danced the polka too much. And the people of Namur have sent to the richer set and told them that if they have any balls this winter, their houses shall be burnt. It is sad to think of the ignorance they must be in and of the distress which they must be in to make them catch at such delusions.

Mrs Liddell kept Lady Smith in touch by letter with her ennobled social round, summarising parties and people with a brevity that made and marred reputations in every phrase: "Elizabeth looked very handsome, quite a striking girl, she is so much improved – the Honourable Henry in high good humour and figuring about immensely – Lady Hardwicke resplendent in diamonds – Lady B. in pearls – Adolphus rather aged – and father George grown (we thought) rather ugly – Mrs George ditto, and such a curious toilette, with very little left for the imagination – Lady Constance Grosvenor looked very pretty – Lady L. very uncomfortable and as if the heir was momentarily expected – Disraeli *cleaner* than usual, but speaking to no one and no one to him – Lord Normanby wonderfully made up, with a most masterly constructed perruque [wig] . . ."

Lorina seems herself to have cut an image in society which turned envious and ogling eyes in her direction. After the Queen's Ball in June 1847, Lady Smith heard from her "old friend", Lady Elizabeth Spencer Stanhope, that Lorina had been "decidedly, if not the *very* prettiest, certainly one of the loveliest and most beautifully dressed of the guests there, as she was also voted to be at the drawing room . . ." Gratifying as these communal royal occasions must have been, they could not match the prestige of a personal royal summons.

Royal chambers were first thrown open wide to Henry in January 1846. "Soapy Sam" Wilberforce was offered a mitre at Oxford, thereby vacating the position of Domestic

Chaplain to Prince Albert. Offered the post, Henry Liddell was as much flattered by fulsome royal notice as by the terms of the job:

There is no pay. Still, it is an honour, and the offer is conveyed in very handsome terms . . . [it] says the Prince is anxious to attach to his person "one who has kept the even tenor of his way amid the perils by which his path at Oxford was beset". So I suppose I may consider it a sign that my name is not unknown or unnoticed in high quarters . . . Also that he (the Prince) wished sometimes to have personal communication with his chaplains – yet that the duties would not be of such a kind as to infringe on my time. So all that is very well.

Henry then awaited the summons to Windsor. There, on Sunday, April 19th, he preached his first sermon in front of the Queen in the small, dark, octagonal chapel.

Relaxing after the ordeal among "all the splendour and luxury", his thoughts turned to Lorina, hungry for the slightest crumb from the royal table, and he penned the minutest details of the blue-blooded weekend: the ornate setting, the patrician company (the Cannings and the Peels were there) and, as centrepiece (complete with seating plan) the dinner.

I have drawn the table roughly. The Queen and Prince sat opposite one another. Equerries top and bottom. Down the middle was a plateau of gold, with glass floor, on which were six splendid gold ornaments; and in the middle a large gold box (of pure gold, the rest only silver gilt) presented by an Indian Rajah, worth £5,000 they say. It was sunk with the Great Liverpool Steamer the other day, but fished up again. Round the plateau were sixteen gold candlesticks with four wax lights in each, beautiful to behold. The dishes outside these again. Turtle soup and iced punch and Madeira handed round. Then all sorts of French dishes, wines – still and sparkling. Champagne etc. etc. and so much like a common dinner, but everything was handed round, and grand French names were whispered in your ear by a splendid fellow in a red coat made like a soldier's i.e. buttoned up to the throat, and with gold epaulettes.

Afterwards in the gallery and drawing room the Queen played cards and Henry was left to "do the civil" with the Maids of Honour, to the accompaniment of the band playing Beethoven and Weber.

Doubtless Lorina treasured tiny points of etiquette, unquestionably the *only* way to proceed: no finger glasses on the table ("those that liked, went and washed their paws at the sideboard"); "no gentlemen wore gloves"; frequent, repeated and obligatory "bowing and scraping". In the end, Windsor was not without its slight taint of disillusionment: "Lady Duoro is not so handsome as I have heard her represented." During the next two decades the Liddells were to meet the Queen and Prince Albert regularly and entertain their offspring in Oxford, where Alice was to exchange affectionate glances with Prince Leopold. More than one pair of jaundiced eyes saw Mrs Liddell as angling to catch a royal fish for one of her daughters.

Ina, Alice, Edith and Harry Liddell, photograph by Charles Dodgson.

Ina Liddell, photograph by Charles Dodgson.

Three daughters, the famous "Three Sisters", Ina, Alice and Edith, who were later to enchant Lewis Carroll and excite painters and photographers, were all born at Dean's Yard in Westminster. But the first-born was actually a boy, christened Edward Henry, but thereafter "Harry" to everyone. Lady Smith was suitably enraptured on her first sight of him five days after his birth on September 6th, 1847:

When I first saw him asleep in his cradle, the resemblance to his father was so strong that, diminutive as he was, it was impossible to overlook it: the same forehead, the nose so small and delicate seemed carved in ivory and, when I saw his mouth, the same waving lips and a little snatch or elevation on one side gave his whole countenance such a marked resemblance that were he placed among fifty infants, all dressed alike, I am quite certain that no one who had ever seen Mr H. Liddell could have mistaken the likeness.

"Mr H. Liddell" was not flattered by the cooing comparison; "when the sweet babe's temper was ruffled by hunger", he looked as old as a great-grandfather, "borne down by years and affliction".

The first daughter, Lorina (Ina) was born in May 1849, and a second daughter on May 4th, 1852. She was christened Alice Pleasance (the latter a family name on her mother's side). Lady Smith first refers to "the little unknown, your Alice" in a letter which sets the year of her birth in a historical context, alongside one of the great events of the time, the funeral of the Duke of Wellington; it shows how adept were the Victorians in the ritual of mourning:

Alice, photograph by Charles Dodgson.

Such a day! There has been none before it or since to compare with it in serenity and splendour, and the clear and lovely night on Thursday for those who were returning home. It seemed like a special providence . . . I am told the Dean read the burial service in as fine a manner as could possibly be, and when the coffin was lowered into the vault, the sight of those veterans in arms, Lord Anglesea, Lord Harding, etc, was pitiable. Their gestures and their

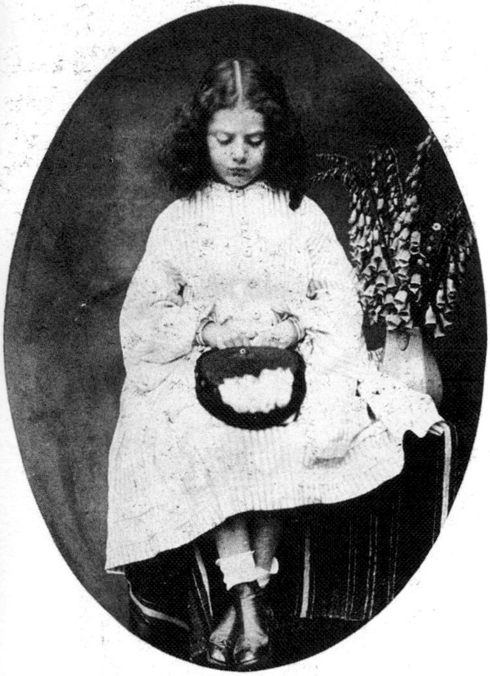

Edith Liddell, photograph by Charles Dodgson.

Opposite:

Letters from Ina and Harry.

agonising looks as they turned away made many spectators scarcely able to refrain from sobbing outright.

Young Harry Liddell watched the pageant of grief.

The third daughter was born in 1854; Lady Smith approved of the choice of names as having respectable literary precedent: "I should indeed like to see your Edith Mary. I used to think Mary one of the most pleasing of names and, if you want to revive your admiration of it, only read Cowper's lines to Mrs Unwin – 'My Mary' – and you will love it again."

In her children's infant years Mrs Liddell passed on to Lady Smith their frequent bon mots: "Ina said the other day – her Papa said: 'Where's the baby?' and she replied, 'In Mama's room.' He said, 'What is she come for?' Ina said, 'To suck Mama's Boosy' – this is only for you." In return and when the children were staying with her, Lady Smith faithfully recorded their precocity. She was solicitious over their education; to her the choice of governess was, if anything, more crucial than the choice of cook. Lady Smith approached euphoria over Mrs Liddell's brother's choice of governess, since she filled his young daughters' minds with "good literature" – Macaulay's essays, Prescott's *Philip II* and English classics. So the Liddell children could not expect Lady Smith to make many concessions to their fledgling minds: "I am no advocate for putting namby-pamby *poetry*, as it is called, into the hands of young children. Can anything delight more than Milton's 'L'Allegro' and 'Il Penseroso', and 'Comus' and 'Lycidas'?"

Mrs Liddell, too, expected her children to grow up quickly. She employed a French Protestant maid at Westminster; she had done wonders for Lady Jervis' children and Mrs Liddell looked for a repeat of the miracle. Before they left Westminster Harry and Ina were well able to record their own doings; in immaculately penned letters they sing of the delights of Dean's Yard.

Across the sunshine, however, fell a shadow. Henry inscribed the stark facts on the fly-leaf of the family Bible: "James Arthur Charles Liddell. Born Dec. 28 1850 at Westminster. Christened in Westminster Abbey, Feb. 24.

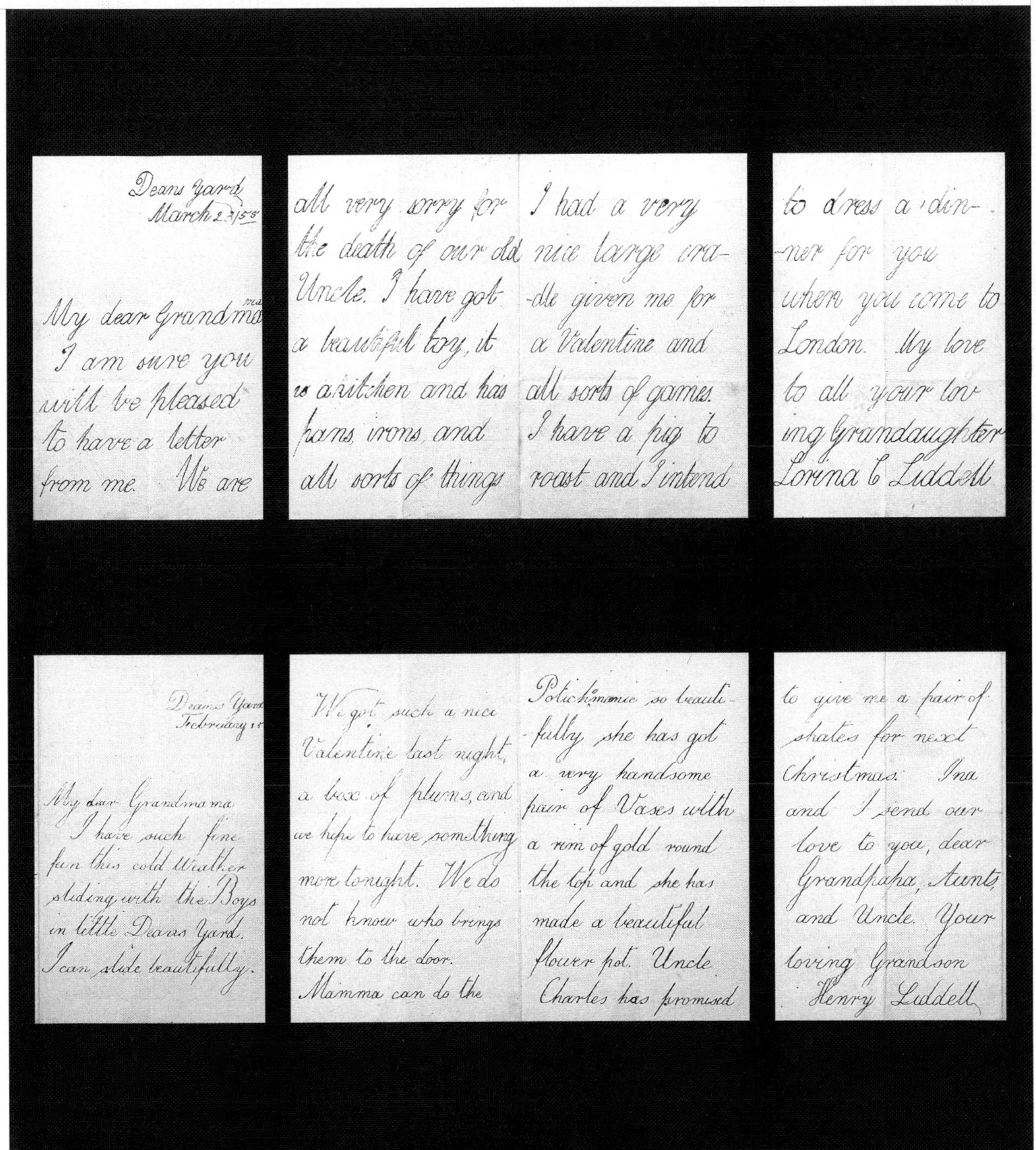

Deans Yard
March 23/55

My dear Grandmama
I am sure you
will be pleased
to have a letter
from me. We are
all very sorry for
the death of our old
Uncle. I have got
a beautiful toy, it
is a kitchen and has
pans, irons, and
all sorts of things
I had a very
nice large cra-
-dle given me for
a Valentine and
all sorts of games.
I have a pig to
roast and I intend
to dress a din-
-ner for you
when you come to
London. My love
to all your lov
ing Grandaughter
Lorina C Liddell

Deans Yard
February 15

My dear Grandmama
I have such fine
fun this cold Weather
sliding with the Boys
in little Deans Yard.
I can slide beautifully.
We got such a nice
Valentine last night,
a box of plums, and
we hope to have something
more tonight. We do
not know who brings
them to the door.
Mamma can do the
Potichomanie so beauti-
-fully, she has got
a very handsome
pair of Vases with
a rim of gold round
the top and she has
made a beautiful
flower pot. Uncle
Charles has promised
to give me a pair of
skates for next
Christmas. Ina
and I send our
love to you, dear
Grandpapa, Aunts
and Uncle. Your
loving Grandson
Henry Liddell

Arthur Liddell.

Died Nov. 27 1853. Buried in Wimbledon churchyard." These vital and fatal dates, with a painted miniature, are the record of a son whose whole life was hardly more than an episode; private letters disclose the agonies suffered. Arthur, born between Lorina and Alice, could for a time be included in Mrs Liddell's picture of her family's robust well-being: "My sweet dears are all extremely well. Harry really gets fat, and Ina broader and more droll, and baby is really a monster and is eleven months old today – he can stand alone and drives a chair all round the room." His promising gestures of independence were soon cut short; and one of Mrs Liddell's regular letters to Lady Smith bore an ominous dark fringe: "Your broad black-edged envelope which I saw on the table as soon as I came into the breakfast room alarmed me and I dreaded to break the seal . . . This is the first severe trial of your life. May it be your last."

The sad facts are these: the family had survived an outbreak of typhoid in 1848, which killed two boys at the school and put Mrs Liddell in danger of her life for ten days. But in 1853, two of the Liddell children caught scarlet fever; for Arthur it proved fatal. The doctors forbad Mrs Liddell to go near the sick boy, but Henry insisted on helping the nurse: "I am sitting by him now, while the nurse goes out to get a little air, and every quick-drawn breath goes to my heart. One does not know how one loves them till a time like this comes." Mrs Liddell endured the pangs at one remove, hearing the progress of the disease in scribbled and tortured notes:

Mr Holt is here, Dearest. We are going to try a little laudanum with the injection. Mr H. just asked if he should cut some of the dry skin off his lips – "No", he said. "Wa' it off." (*Wash* it off.) But it is not proper to deceive you with false hopes. I fear, I fear we must nourish none . . . Dear, dear boy. If ever there was one fit for the society of the angels, it is he – and his poor, pale face and soft, blue eyes seem to me, as I look on them weeping, no more to belong to earth. I dare not leave him . . . God Almighty comfort and bless you, my own love, and save our other darlings.

Hope fluttered and waned by turns, but the inevitable end came quickly, and almost as if no one expected it:

I cannot even yet believe that we shall never see again on this earth his fair face with those gentle bright blue eyes and silken hair. A more healthy strong child never was . . . You will pardon these babblings of fondness. But I watched him alone through that dreadful illness and it relieves me to write so to those who can and will, I know, feel with me.

The grief of bereavement almost broke Henry's health, worn out as he was by the burdens of the job. His school reforms were frustrated, if not by Dean and Chapter, at least by the unhealthy location, squatting beside smart Belgravia "like a beggar at a rich man's gate". He discussed with Prince Albert moving the school into cleaner country air, but in the event the school stood still and the Liddells moved away. On June 2nd, 1855 Dean Thomas Gaisford died at Christ Church in Oxford; Henry Liddell was appointed successor. The family returned to the city that was to immortalise their three-year-old daughter, Alice.

Watercolour by Alice.

3
THE BROAD AND THE HIGH

The Liddells' coming to Oxford was no triumphal, Palm Sunday entry into Jerusalem. Memories of last-minute wranglings at Westminster overshadowed the journey and clouded Mrs Liddell's backward glances to London: "Mr Scott has possession of the dear old Dean's Yard house. I fear I grudge it to him, especially as he has written to ask us to repair cracked windows, rather too bad considering the condition he finds the house in – indeed, he has got a good bargain, though I daresay he doesn't think so." And plans for the new house, the Deanery at Christ Church, were doomed literally to go up in smoke.

The Deanery was an august, stone-built house, original brainchild of Cardinal Wolsey, surveying on one side Tom Quad (the largest in the university and sporting a statue of Mercury lacking a crucial masculine attribute). The Liddells planned new oak panelling for the drawing room and hall, and new stairs (by courtesy of the lexicon profits), as if to demonstrate that reform, like charity, begins at home. All was prepared; then fate intervened, warning Henry Liddell that he could not hope to change even the inanimate face of Oxford in the twinkling of an eye: "Poor Mr Billing, our architect, writes in despair – 'Alas! all the beautiful oak work, prepared and ready for fitting at the Deanery . . . the work of sixty men for five weeks, perished in the disastrous fire at Mr Baker's, and he cannot undertake to replace.' "

Reactionary dons at Christ Church (and there were many), who dreaded the swish of Henry Liddell's new broom, could not have prayed for a better sign from heaven that the Almighty was for the status quo. They had not

Opposite:
Tom Quad, the statue of Mercury and the Deanery, Christ Church.

Charles Dodgson.

Opposite page:
Tinted photograph of Alice by Charles Dodgson.

opened their arms in a welcoming embrace to the Liddells. Whereas the House of Commons had cheered Lord Palmerston's news of Henry Liddell's appointment, sixty miles away in the college itself there rose a murmur of resentment that a liberal helmsman was about to embark who would rock the old boat. A young mathematics tutor, Charles Dodgson by name, wrote glumly in his diary (June 7th, 1855): "The selection does not seem to have given much satisfaction at the college." Already, as a member of the University Commission, Henry Liddell had blown a cold wind through musty corners at Christ Church, which under Thomas Gaisford had cultivated manners as much, if not more than, brains, honing the sons of the rich to a fine edge.

The will and money of the Liddells eventually prevailed over ill luck in the simple matter of new panelling: they clad the Deanery walls in oak, and the family moved in. The children actually travelled from London via a dogleg that took them to Lowestoft, where they were spared the ups and downs of the removal. They stayed with – and enchanted – Lady Smith; she lamented their going to Oxford in a letter to Mrs Liddell. It acts as a testimonial to some remarkable qualities – not least the haunting beauty of three-year-old Alice – which would attract eyes and hearts in Oxford:

I am about to lose a daily pleasure in the departure of your dear children . . . It has given me the sincerest pleasure to observe the improvement in dear Ina's disposition and manners since Christmas; at the same time her voice is become softer and more agreeable and her lovely fair bosom and ivory shoulders give promise of her becoming very handsome – more than these – she is so affectionate that I love her dearly. As for Alice, she looks like one of Raphael's Holy Family strayed out of the picture –

Le crespe chieme, l'angelico riso
The crisped locks of pure refulgent gold,
The lambent lightning of the angelic smile,

quite enchant me when in her daily visits she sits by my side and opens her lovely mouth for a few grapes. So attractive is innocence and beauty that we feel indeed that "of such is the

Mrs Liddell.

Kingdom of Heaven". Dear Henry is a charming boy – and he has given us several speeches on different occasions. In returning thanks to the company for drinking his Papa's and Mama's health, he rose to inform us of the great occupations that the Dean of Christ Church was about, and concluded by saying that he was much obliged to the late Dean for *dying!* . . . You have had so much trouble to get into your new abode that methinks I hear the Dean exclaim:

Give me again my hollow tree,
A crust of bread and liberty.

The children arrived at the Deanery to find that, surprisingly for a man with a proven yen for good plumbing, Papa's zeal for change had not reached up to the bathroom. Cold baths every day were therefore the norm. But the children, observing the hierarchical principle, subjected their pets – cats included – to the same spartan regime.

To show off the new oak splendour of the Deanery the Liddells threw a party, at which "the 'Macbeth' music, with choruses some glees and other music" was performed on the forty-foot gallery. Rumour had it that Henry was to play Macbeth; perhaps the authors of the gossip were scurrilous misogynists who really meant to imply that Mrs Liddell was suited to the role of Lady Macbeth. Later Mrs Liddell's detractors chanted their composite ditty:

I am the Dean, this Mrs Liddell,
She plays the first, I, second fiddle.
She is the Broad,
I am the High,
We are the University.

St Aldates and Tom Tower.

Love them or loathe them, you could not ignore the Liddells in Oxford: they made themselves monarchs of much they surveyed and some at least responded with a subject's obeisance. Some doffed hats as Mrs Liddell's carriage and pair trotted in stately fashion down St Aldates; others gazed respectfully across at Mrs Liddell in the University Church in pews reserved for "the ladies of the Heads of Houses".

Meanwhile, nothing – however clandestine or banal –

The New Meadow Buildings, Christ Church, c. 1865.

escaped Henry Liddell's reforming eye. Thus the verger lost the traditional cache of beer which he secreted under the pews, and also the whip he used to drive the dogs away before the service. Like his famous seventeenth-century predecessor, Dr Fell, who planted the seventy-two elms of Broad Walk, Henry Liddell left a permanent mark in Christ Church meadow: he built a new avenue down to the river, in the place of the narrow path beside Till Mill Stream. (This insanitary waterway runs right under the city, and in the 1920s was discovered, trapped in its depths, a decayed Victorian punt with two skeletons keeping an eternal, gruesome tryst.) Henry Liddell showed that the life of the Dean ranged from the ethereal to the subterranean, that its province was the gut as well as the brain. Sewers were one of his abiding concerns; one German professor, seeking audience with the famous lexicographer, was told that Henry Liddell had "gone down the drain" – and could be found underground beneath Christ Church meadow.

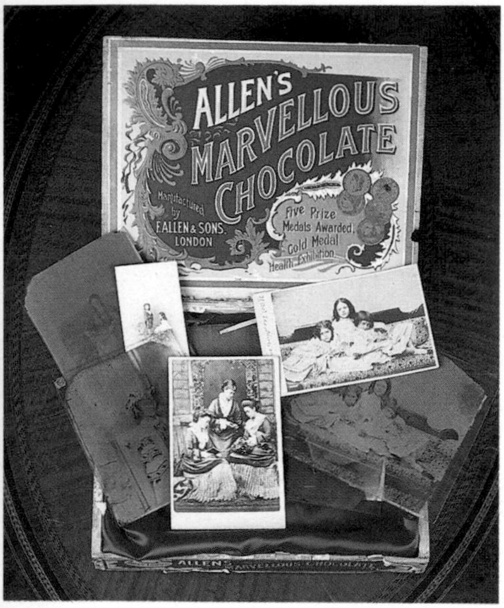

People, however, proved less tractable than blocked drains, and it took a long time to change the image of Christ Church as turning out gentlemen rather than scholars. Its students were traditionally drawn from those who, secure in their future landed inheritance, had not the spur of having to earn a living to incline them to any industry. To them the beagles and buttonholes were matters of greater concern than books. And fate even hindered Henry Liddell when he made examples of some *pour encourager les autres*. In 1869 he ordered a dandy young student to give up his racing stud (he had already entered a colt for the Derby). The young man, Lord Rosebery, refused and was "sent down" (expelled); but he still made it to Prime Minister. Few, however, seriously bewailed the growing habit of hard study at Christ Church; there was a louder grumble when Henry Liddell proposed altering the buildings. Among the most vociferous – indeed, on occasions openly derisive – was the mathematics tutor, Charles Dodgson.

A brittle reminder of Dodgson's place in the lives of the Liddells turned up at Tetbury in the unlikeliest of places. Among the odds and ends in a chest of drawers lay an old wooden chocolate box, with an injunction on its side: "protect the contents from heat and damp". Hungry fingers had long ago devoured the contents, but replaced them with a quite different range of "sweets". Hidden among untidy strands of synthetic straw were a dozen or so small pieces of glass, unevenly covered in a yellow-brown coating. Held up to the light, the top one revealed a pensive profile of young Alice, with black teeth and albino eyes. On the other pieces Alice was joined by her sisters, lolling on chairs and masquerading as orientals, and all with the same spectral look. Negatives, of course; glass photographic negatives meticulously made by Charles Dodgson, half a century before the age of the snapshot and only fifteen years after the invention of photography. Dodgson's carefully nurtured pictures, some pocked and scratched with mishandling, had been casually dumped in a drawer.

Charles Dodgson's posthumous disciples have, if anything, murdered him by their almost literal dissection. Interest in his life has strayed beyond the curious to the obsessive and fanatical. His illnesses are the subject of detailed study (and extensive bibliography): seven expert neurologists have vouchsafed their professional opinions on his two recorded fainting fits of 1886 and 1891. Could one of those transient moments of oblivion have been caused, we are asked, by Dodgson's high collar pressing on the carotid sinus while he was kneeling in chapel before breakfast?

Considering this modern appetite for the most insipid Dodgson titbit, he was ill-served in the memories of famous people who actually knew him. One suspects an element of embarrassment and deliberate neglect. Dean Liddell's biographer never even mentions his name (though he wrote Dodgson's obituary for the *Oxford Magazine*). Nor does Dodgson rate a mention in the "Lives" of other notable acquaintances – Benjamin Jowett, Arthur Stanley and John Ruskin. It is as if there were a conspiracy to make Dodgson an "un-person". Mrs Liddell also insisted that Alice destroy all Dodgson's letters to her. Dodgson's own diaries for the years 1858-62, crucial years in his friendship with Alice, have mysteriously disappeared. To put it at its most melodramatic – was Dodgson a skeleton in the Oxford cupboard, not to be rattled at all costs?

Alice, photograph by Charles Dodgson.

Like other staid dons at Christ Church, Charles Dodgson saw the Liddell children regularly in the precincts of the college. In public, the proverbial rule for the children was to be seen and not heard – and then only to be seen walking (demurely chaperoned by the governess), *never* cavorting or even running. Dodgson, however, saw beyond the image of propriety, the white cotton frocks, white openwork socks and black shoes: he had a privileged view through the Old Library window of the children's games in the Deanery garden. There in the shadows he watched them playing as real children, tantalisingly close, but still a gulf apart, distanced not only by the glass panes, but by age, rank and prudish decorum. Had the children known that Charles Dodgson, far from putting away his childish things, had made a toyshop of his rooms, they might have immediately scorned etiquette to approach him. At various times in his life, they would have found Dodgson sharing his rooms with: music boxes, dolls, wind-up animals (including a walking

Alice, Ina and Edith, photograph by Charles Dodgson.

Charles Dodgson's sitting room at Christ Church.

bear), an American "orguinette" (a kind of musical instrument), "Bob the Bat", a microscope, field glasses, telescope, pocket sundial, magic lantern, mathematical instruments, dumb-bells and mechanical exercisers, aneroid barometer, human skull, gasolier, printing press, "Dr Moffat's Ammoniaphone" (for speech therapy), magic pens, typewriter (with his own modifications), wire puzzles, "Nyctograph" (for taking notes in the dark), and a humane mousetrap.

If the miscellany sounds bizarre, it had at least a precedent at Christ Church, in the rooms of William Buckland, first Professor of Geology. He died the year after the Liddells came to Oxford. His rooms were more than menagerie than study, the animals sating both intellectual and physical appetites. At least two visitors (including John Ruskin) remembered being served with horseflesh, crocodile and mice in batter. Buckland himself claimed to have eaten his way through most of animal creation: he first decided on mole as the nastiest dish, but eventually opted for blue-bottle. At Nuneham he gobbled down the heart of a king of France, preserved (though not for his exclusive delectation). In Naples he attended the annual liquefaction of the blood of St Gennaro, but, falling on his knees to lick up the drops, asserted that they were bats' urine. A bear stalked his room in Oxford, Carolina lizards decimated the flies, monkeys fought with guests over the fruit dish and guinea pigs nibbled at unwary toes. Mrs Liddell must have sighed with relief at Dr Buckland's timely demise, lest he licked his lips and slavered at the sight of her delicious children.

By comparison, Charles Dodgson must have appeared less an ogre than a dotty uncle. But, had Mrs Liddell been able to forsee events, she might have banned this mild eccentric altogether from her children. Had she seen Dodgson a decade later, adept at meeting little girls in trains and on beaches, carrying a black bag of wire puzzles and safety pins to pin up the trailing skirts of paddling nymphs; had she divined Dodgson's passion for kissing little girls (or closing his letters to them with 10,000,000 kisses, or $4\frac{3}{4}$ kisses or a two-millionth part of a kiss); had she seen Dodgson's diary for the March, 25th, 1863, listing the names of 107 cherubs "photographed or to be photographed" (grouped under Christian names, with dates of birth) had she scented Dodgson's later predilection, not for a little girl dressed-up, but for a "natural child", with ruffled untidy hair, revealing drapes or, at best, "*sans habilement*" – Mrs Liddell might well have deprived Dodgson of even his distant view of her daughters; and no one could have been surprised. It would not have been Alice Liddell, if indeed anyone at all, who tumbled headlong down a rabbit-hole.

As it was, within a year of the Liddells arriving in Oxford, Charles Dodgson found the perfect, genteel approach to the family, which held out the promise of intimate contact with the children. And for that he had to thank his uncle, Skeffington Lutwidge. This lovable bachelor brother of his mother's had interests to match his boffin's name. He had always been a favourite with Charles Dodgson, since they shared a curiosity in new-fangled things. As a boy, Charles

Ina and Alice, photograph by Charles Dodgson.

had included puppetry and sleight-of-hand tricks among his hobbies: later he invented puzzles, games (including a new kind of croquet for the Liddell children – though not actually played with flamingoes), and a mnemonic for remembering numbers (he himself knew "pi" to seventy-one decimal places). In 1852 Uncle Skeffington diverted Charles Dodgson with several "new oddities": a lathe, telescope stand, crest stamp, map measurer and refrigerator. Three years later, on a summer holiday at Croft Rectory, Skeffington introduced his new nephew to the "black art" in which Dodgson was to become master: he showed him (unsuccessfully, as it turned out) how to take photographs, at the local church and bridge. Back in Oxford the next year Dodgson wrote to his uncle in London asking him to procure him a "photographic apparatus" to give him "some occupation here other than mere reading and writing".

Certainly taking photographs would usurp more than odd spare moments; there was rather more to it than today. Pressing the shutter – or, in those early days, taking the cap off the lens – was only the midpoint in a long and unreliable process. From the making of the plate to the mounting of the print it was do-it-yourself or not at all; so the photographer literally carried his darkroom with him, looking like a combination of intinerant showman and quack. For his travels Dodgson wrapped every item – lenses, plates, bottles, dishes – separately in paper until at least twice the bulk, and sent the whole lot in advance by train or cab. He developed an annoying habit of descending on friends unannounced with his mountain of equipment. He once made a dramatic entrance into the home of the playwright, Tom Taylor, by rudely waking the whole family at eight thirty in the morning. In a London where "morning" calls were not paid until the afternoon, breakfast was a sacrosanct domestic ritual.

For early photographers the route to a good picture was not only circuitous but pitted and strewn with obstacles: impure chemicals, fluctuating temperatures, dust and the routine tasks of polishing the glass plate, mixing the "collodion", pouring it evenly on the glass, sensitising it in silver nitrate solution, taking the picture (with an exposure

Edith, Ina and Alice, photograph by Charles Dodgson.

of many seconds) *before* the plate dried, developing, fixing, varnishing and printing. Small wonder that Dodgson concluded, "Mystic, awful was the process."

But not as awful as the sitters could be; Dodgson quickly learned their foibles. Within two years of buying a camera he sketched the trials of the photographer in a parody of Longfellow, "Hiawatha Photographing". In sequence, all the members of a family – by turns, arrogant, volatile, fickle and wilful – sit for the camera. First, Father, in patriarchal stance, contemplating the distance, his dignity shored up with photogenic props, but unable to stand still; then Mother, gorgeous, simpering and chattering like a monkey; then ugly Daughter, with pretensions to "passive beauty", but hampered by her squint and twisted smile; and so on, down the scale, to the Youngest Son, rough, red-faced, dusty, fidgety and much abused by his sisters. And in a mighty hurry "thus departed Hiawatha", trundling a barrowload of boxes away to less troublesome subjects.

To Christ Church, perhaps? There with his friend, Reginald Southey, Dodgson started by pointing his camera at objects that scarcely moved and never answered back – the meadow and the buildings. Ironically, in pursuit of such

Reginald Southey, photograph by Charles Dodgson.

The Deanery garden, sketch by Alice.

dull quarry, Dodgson first came face-to-face with young Alice. His diary for the day, April 25th, 1856, Dodgson inscribed "with a white stone" (his equivalent of the usual "red-letter"). Meeting three-year-old Alice rippled the surface of his routine, though Dodgson actually planned something less vibrant – helping Southey take a picture of the cathedral. That attempt to capture something so massive and immutable proved a total failure; but close by, in comparison incorporeal and fleeting in their white cotton dresses, Alice, Ina and Edith played in the Deanery garden. At first Dodgson invited the girls to sit in the foreground of the cathedral picture, trammelling the vision within banal limits. But the girls refused to sit still and the picture proved hopeless. Nonetheless, Dodgson confidently recorded that at the end of, say, an hour they had become "excellent friends". A week later Dodgson's own camera arrived from London. With his fifteen-pound contraption he could make inoffensive overtures to the alluring Liddell children, more alluring certainly than Oxford's stone-faced buildings and dons. Dodgson could flatter the most natural of Mr and Mrs Liddell's vanities, their desire as parents to see cute and novel pictures of their darlings.

Actually, Harry Liddell was the first to turn Dodgson's head: they met "down at the boats" on the Thames and Dodgson concluded from that brief meeting that "he is certainly the handsomest boy I ever saw". Praise indeed from one whose shyness of boys sometimes showed as phobic aversion: "I am fond of children (except boys)." Dodgson was humiliated by the boys at St Aldates school where he tried unsuccessfully for a month to teach part-time: "The difficulty of teaching being, not to get and answer, but to prevent all answering at once." Perhaps they mocked his cockeyed look: one shoulder higher than the other, smile askew, eyes unlevel; perhaps they practised his jerky gait, played on his deafness and mimicked his stammer and trembling upper lip. Retreating into the seclusion of his rooms at Christ Church from those who exercised the normal prerogative of youngsters of being "noisy an inattentive", Dodgson resigned himself to the fact that "boys are not in my line; I think they are a mistake." He answered them back with his pen, parodying G.W. Longford's:

Speak gently; it is better far
To rule by love than fear;
Speak gently; let no harsh word mar
The good we may do here.

In *Alice in Wonderland* that becomes:

Speak roughly to your little boy
And beat him when he sneezes;
He only does it to annoy,
Because he knows it teases.

In *Alice in Wonderland,* too, the infant boy (entrusted by Alice to the Duchess) turns into a pig; in a later book, *Sylvie and Bruno Concluded,* a monster child called "Uggug" ("a hideous fat boy . . . with the expression of a prize pig") turns into a porcupine; and a postscript to a letter to young Maggie Cunningham sets the comic seal on Dodgson's aversion:

My best love to yourself, to your Mother
My kindest regards – to your small,
Fat, impertinent, ignorant brother
My hatred – I think that is all.

Harry Liddell.

Harry Liddell seems to have escaped Dodgson's usual opprobrium. And they stayed friends until Harry became pupil, not just handsome young boy and brother to Alice. Then their failings as a teacher and pupil soured things. In January 1857 Dodgson calmly recorded, with no sense of apprehension that he was about to be bitten for the second time, that Harry would come to him three days a week "to learn sums". The first report was optimistic: "He is quick but knows very little." Less than a week, and there was trouble: Dodgson saw a letter from Grandma Reeve in Lowestoft "in which she expressed great alarm at Harry's learning 'mathematics' with me! She fears the effect of overwork on the brain. As far as I can judge, there is nothing to fear at present on that score . . . " Five days later, and Harry had had enough: "My pupil is beginning to tire of the arithmetic lesson – today I could get him to do nothing." Miss Prickett, governess, was summoned as mediator, and the breach repaired – or, rather, papered over: "Harry did well today: it is doubtful how long the change will last." Fortunately, the project was short-lived.

For the details of Dodgson's "special" friendship with Alice the world clings to feeble records: mainly brief, factual entries in Dodgson's dull diaries, which are rarely readable for intrinsic interest. There are invitations to lunch and dinner at the Deanery, boating and picnic outings with the Liddell children. Personal intimate moments are few in the diaries: they comprise occasional resolutions – "I am getting into the habit of unpunctuality, and must try to make a fresh start in activity"; or the querulous and perennial despair of the teacher: "I am weary and discouraged . . . It is thankless, uphill work, goading unwilling men to learning they have no taste for . . ." But on the days marked with a white stone invariably Dodgson had met the Liddell children and let some sunshine in on the gloom of his drudgery. In the first few years the children shared his affection equally; the event which moved Dodgson to record near-euphoria was a boating picnic with Harry and Ina (not Alice – she was too young) in "high spirits": "Mark this day, annalist, not only with a white stone, but as altogether *Dies Mirabilis*."

In later life Alice was reticent to the point of absolute silence on her friendship with Dodgson. She would not be drawn in public, until in 1932, aged eighty, with the spur of Dodgson's centenary and with her son almost literally guiding the pen, she published fragmentary recollections. She painted a bland and cosy image of her "Carrollian days" seventy years before, in which Dodgson plays the charming and avuncular eccentric, diverting her with toys, bewitching her with extempore stories or trying her patience with a camera. Alice fed a waiting world the diet it craved. After all, the dull and wet afternoon of July 4th, 1862 (the first telling of Alice's adventures) seen through the rose spectacles of old age, had become a "blazing summer

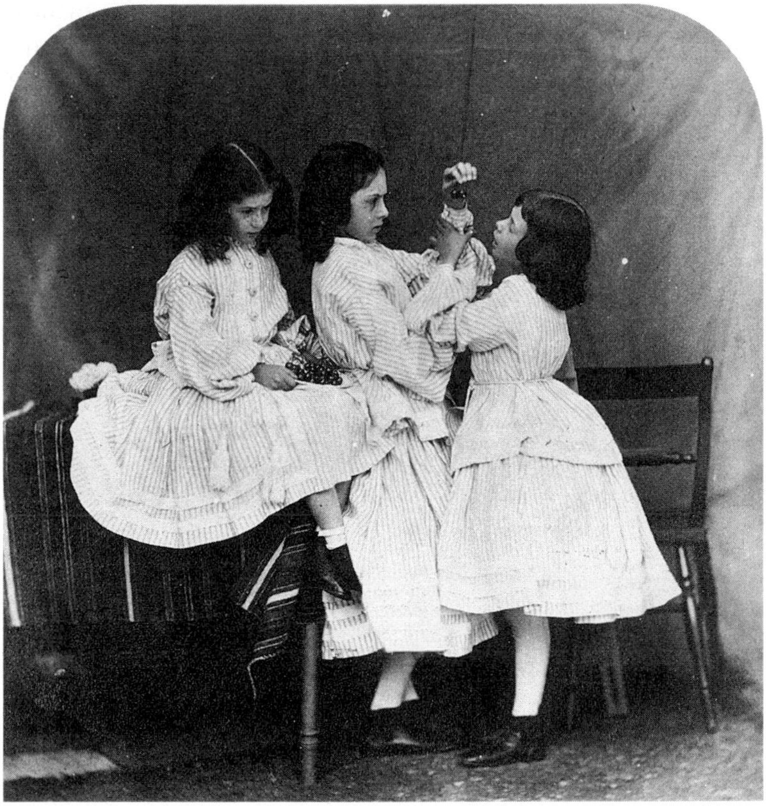

Edith, Ina and Alice, photograph by Charles Dodgson.

afternoon". Dodgson's image too, probably basked in sunlight. But what did she say earlier and in private?

No one knows what Alice really felt as a child for "Mr Dodgson", though some have filled in the gap in a spirit of sentimental Alice-olatry, partly perhaps because they confuse Alice and "Alice", or because Dodgson hymned her as the ideal child friend, or simply because they *hope* it was like that. History is badly served by representing such wish-fulfilment as if it were fact.

In all her surviving letters, diaries and journals Alice only mentions Charles Dodgson once (and that in a letter when she was eighty): "Hilda [her niece] told me that the Bolshies, or some such people *very* particular about children's books, have put *Alice in Wonderland* top of their list. How pleased poor Mr Dodgson would have been!" The adjective "poor" is probably not significant. Alice's records do not contribute to the ardent debate as to whether Charles Dodgson was really "in love" with her – that is, on his own peculiar terms, since it seems likely that he could not love any one in the fullest meaning of the word, anymore than could the maimed statue in the middle of Tom Quad. Although Dodgson referred in his *Pillow Problems* to "unholy thoughts, which torture with their hateful presence the fancy that would fain be pure", in the matter of sexual passion he was retarded and immature. Even by strait-laced Victorian ethics he was a prude: he had plans to bowdlerise Bowdler's edition of Shakespeare, to make the Bard *truly* fit for the eyes of respectable wives and blushing daughters. And when his child girlfriends reached the age of puberty, "that awkward stage of transition", Dodgson almost literally ran away. Once he was alarmed to discover that a girl he had kissed was seventeen; he wrote a letter of apology to her mother, but she was most definitely not amused.

Nonetheless, within these limits, Alice was Dodgson's favourite. He saw the writing of *Alice in Wonderland* as "a task where nothing of reward is hoped for but a little child's whispered thanks, and the airy touch of a little child's pure lips". And his myriad other child friends were "quite another thing". But Mrs Liddell's ambitions alone would have made the hope of alliance a sad fantasy. Anyway, she had the darkly disastrous failed marriage of their friend, John Ruskin, as a sad paradigm of impotence. In fact, at the very time Dodgson was preparing *Alice* for publication, the middle-aged Ruskin's dreams were haunted by another young girl, Rose la Touche, who, at twelve, was the same age as Alice. Ruskin suffered his pangs for six years, returned to Ireland to see Rose, fell further under her spell and carried around with him one of her letters encased in gold. When she came of age, Ruskin proposed to her; but she rejected him and his unorthodox gospel of an earthly paradise of craftsman artists. Ruskin took refuge in Assisi, racked by a brain fever. Two years later Rose tragically died, but she continued to haunt Ruskin. If Dodgson had any hopes of Alice's heart, Mrs Liddell saw to it that he did not act out the tragedy of John Ruskin. Whatever sacrifices Dodgson made on the altar of his love, Mrs Liddell made a burnt offering of all his letters to Alice. Dodgson, who had a thick skin when it came to persisting with those who had had enough of him, sensed that early on Mrs Liddell found his frequent visits to the Deanery "a nuisance".

Welcome visitors at the Deanery in Alice's childhood form a roll of honour in Oxford's past. Their names appear on chits and notes in boxes at Tetbury, items of little account in themselves, like day-to-day exchanges of courtesy and information. But behind the scraps of paper, and doubtless in the shadows of the Deanery still, stand the spirits of those who made the place a focus in Oxford, and a stimulating (if somewhat awesome) world for the Liddell children to grow up in. Pre-eminent among them, and, with Dean Liddell, forming a kind of enlightened triumvirate, stood Benjamin Jowett and Mark Pattison.

Benjamin Jowett, Master of Balliol College.

In one short note at Tetbury, Jowett, Master of Balliol College, invites Alice's sister to a party. The crabbed, minuscule handwriting and puny signature belie the immense stature of the man. Though his body was squat and robust, it was surmounted by an angel's face and a huge brow which proclaimed, "Brains!":

Here come I, my name is Jowett;
There's no knowledge but I know it;
I am the master of this college;
What I don't know isn't knowledge.

Nicknamed the "Jowler", he vowed to "inoculate England" with Balliol men, a ruling elite striding out through the portals of his college. He never lacked confidence – arrogance, some would have said; he is remembered as a master of the crushing snub and author of the intransigent dictum: "Never regret, never explain, never apologise." In classical learning he was second to few; he spent nearly half a century translating Plato. And for years was intimate friend of Florence Nightingale. In her he saw a more ardent and even acrimonious side than the popular "Lady of the Lamp"; asked what she was like, he replied, "violent, very violent" – though he found a phrase in Homer which put it more politely. Asked what he thought of Mrs Liddell, he framed a

Mark Pattison, Rector of Lincoln College.

masterful, double-edged compliment: "I have always admired the way Mrs Liddell has preserved her youth."

Henry Liddell first linked arms with Benjamin Jowett over the famous scandal of the latter's salary. The reactionary dons of Christ Church (with Canon Pusey at their head) refused to increase Jowett's stipend (as Professor of Greek) from a miserly forty pounds per annum, a sum unchanged for three hundred years from the time of its instigator, Henry VIII. Jowett, they said, preached an ungodly religion; they even prosecuted him for heresy in the Vice-Chancellor's court, which, after the suit was dismissed, *The Times* derided as "a rusty engine of intolerance".

Like Henry Liddell, Jowett was indeed a moderate, a "Broad Churchman", if easily mistaken for a radical freethinker in the cloisters of Oxford. But if Jowett stood with his head in the clouds, like Liddell again, he planted his feet firmly on the ground. One of the "new" men of Oxford, he enjoyed the things of this world. He recalled his own "conversion": "I found that Ward was going to be married. After this the Tractarian impulse subsided and while some of us took to German philosophy others turned to lobster suppers." Jowett saw a place for the theatre in the university, encouraging students in an activity which was usually execrated as dangerously pagan. He felt that student actors could evade the devil's clutches provided no men played women's parts and provided they imported no "professional actresses".

Jowett did not like anything that smacked of theatricality in church; as a gesture against the fancy pageantry in St Mary's, the University Church, he refused to wear his scarlet array as Doctor of Divinity when processing with other heads of colleges. Instead, he paced conspicuously in black. And beside him, in sympathy, strode another sable figure – Mark Pattison, Rector of Lincoln College. He, too, frequented the Deanery at Christ Church and struggled, though not without pain, to reconcile demands of soul, mind and body, in a way that struck many as outrageous; he lectured brilliantly on Aristotle and married a ravishing paragon.

Dean Liddell, contemporary cartoon.

Mark Pattison was almost a student contemporary of Henry Liddell's, coming up to Oriel in 1832, a self-conscious, gauche Wensleydale boy, son of a neurotic evangelical father. He never shook off the reticence, even decades later as head of a college, when he invited students for long walks. The tension and awkwardness of these excursions were legendary among his young companions; he opened the conversation with one poor victim with, "The irony of Sophocles is greater than the irony of Euripides." The pair marched on in total silence for several miles, until the rector added the monosyllable, "Quote".

Like Henry Liddell, Pattison came under the spell of High Church reform, hating the ungodly indolence of his college, and appalled by the time squandered in common room on cards, wine and gossip. But the world gradually eroded his vigour and his faith declined to a depressed "don't-know": "My heart is now on the world entirely, not by its own choice, but because it seems to have nothing else left to look to" (Diary, May 1847). The closing picture, forty years on, is in the words of a student caricature:

Cross the quad the Rector goes
With a dew-drop at his nose;
His chilly hands those long black gloves enfold,
Irresistibly, I fear,
Suggesting the idea
Of a dissipated lizard in the cold.

Not, one would think, fit consort to Emilia Frances Strong, later Lady Dilke, whom Pattison married and who, in a choice between Society and Salvation, would put her friends before God. She took Oxford by storm, in a rustle of silk and an alluring cloud of perfume. She dazzled some, and shocked more, with her rolling eyes, her advocacy of fencing for women, her Sunday supper teagowns and – worst of all – her cigarettes. Another Oxford wife carried two visions of Mrs Pattison in her head, one of her draped elegantly out of a window, "as though a French portrait . . . had suddenly slipped into a vacant space in the old college wall", the other of "a lady in a green brocade dress, with a belt and a chatelaine of Russian silver, who was playing croquet".

The Liddells and their circle brought a fresh style of enlightenment to the university. Henry epitomised a new breed: man of God, of books, of politics, of art, of travel, of the dining table – and of home. He and his kind were to the Victorian age what Sir Philip Sidney had been to the Elizabethans – the ideal of (apparently) effortless all-round accomplishment. As the university gradually threw off its celibate shackles, admitting four Fellows at a time to connubial bliss, lesser men than Henry Liddell with more modest resources strove to ape the externals of the full life: their wives in slightly outmoded dress (or assertively avant garde) gave dinner parties in houses frantically furnished à la mode.

Although at the time of his marriage, Henry Liddell had been cast by Lady Smith in the role of saviour to Lorina, the redoubtable nonagenarian kept a wary eye on their milieu, ever ready with precepts and warning against the snares of showy vanity: "I have never heard what occasioned your first introduction to Mr and Mrs H., or whether there is anything beyond their wealth and equipage to make their society valuable. I never heard of their having any other pursuit than that of their carriage and horses, and have sometimes feared they might be reckoned among the fashionable *fast* . . . My love and friendship bid me say 'Beware!' " Another close friend of the Liddells Lady Smith confessed not wholly to understand: "Lady Copley has lent me one of Ruskin's books on leaves – that he is a man of genius no one can doubt – but I met with some things in this volume which made me think him not quite sane – certainly he soars above my plain conceptions." At times John Ruskin baffled and disconcerted the Liddells – and all Oxford, too.

Let us start the story of Ruskin and the Liddells in Oxford with a curious survival at Tetbury – a pile of several dozen slips of pink blotting paper, spattered with doodles of boats, stone walls, trees and faces. Not, one might think, precious heirlooms, but these pink scraps changed hands at a price in Oxford common rooms a century ago. The doodler who thus acquired fame was Henry Liddell; as chairman of the new

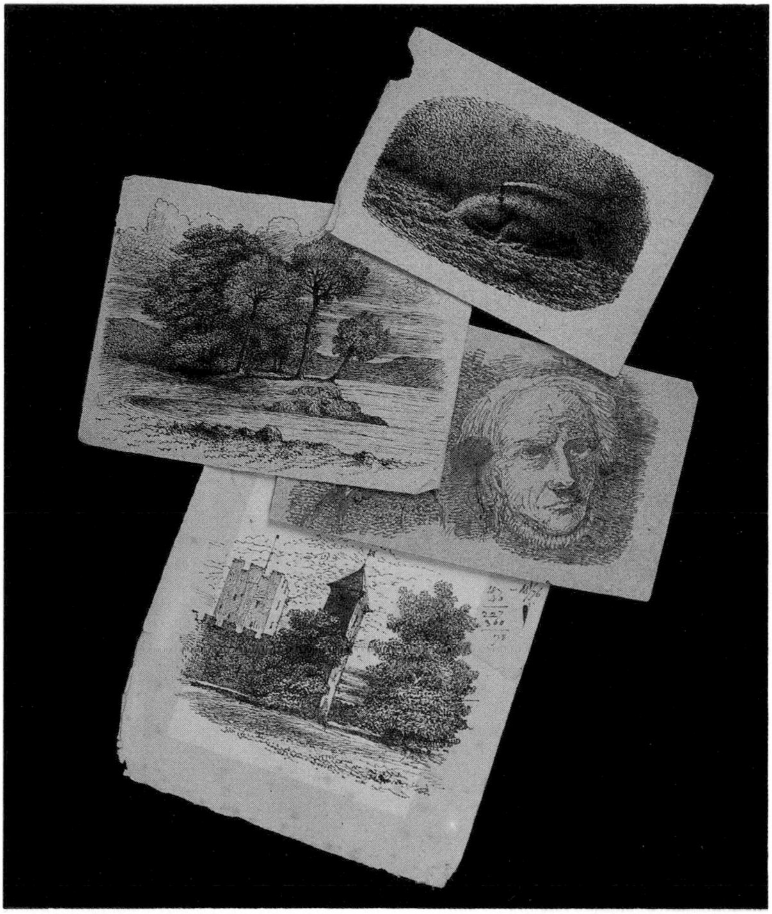

Blotting-paper sketches by Dean Liddell.

governing body of Christ Church, he whiled away the interminable meetings by taking out his gold pen, wiping it carefully on his sleeve and drawing on his blotter. It is a tribute to both his skill and the longueur of the meetings that hundreds of his sketches were carried off and treasured by admirers.

John Ruskin, whose critical word for many was as law, also thought highly of Henry Liddell's drawing; he lamented that Henry had followed the wrong course in life, wasting years in patient drudgery over the lexicon: "I fancy it was his adverse star that made him an Englishman at all – the prosaic and practical element in him having prevailed over the sensitive one." Ruskin thought that Henry would have

The Science Museum, Oxford, designed by John Ruskin.

been better occupied "drawing trees at Madeira", not because (as the phrase might suggest) that would have been a more genteel and indolent career, but because the man who drew well actually furthered the art of *seeing:* "I think, too, that it is impossible to trace the refinements of natural form, unless with pencil in hand – the eye and mind never being keen enough until excited by the effort to imitate." Ruskin would never allow that drawing was merely a fashionable pastime; his sense of the high seriousness of art (which became for him at once a religion and political manifesto) he attributed to Henry Liddell, "who first showed me the difference between classic and common art".

It was not wholly coincidence that Ruskin renewed his links with Oxford in the year the Liddells took over the Deanery. First the university asked him to design its new Science Museum. Ruskin jumped at the chance with a spirit that was characteristically sublime and ridiculous: he would show the world in stone what he meant when he preached the gospel of work – the museum would be a monument to the untrained workman's artistry. To prove the point and to complete his soaring Venetian Gothic design, Ruskin imported a rumbustious family of Irish navvies, the O'Shea's, and let them loose with mallets and chisels, doing their own thing, "conveying truthful statements about natural facts" – that is, carving monkeys, cats, fruit and veg.

With the same misplaced zeal Ruskin "inspired" his workers with communal daily prayers, and with casual deliberateness he left books lying around for their edification. Ruskin actually built one of the columns himself, but it had to be demolished and done again. (Ruskin's Science Museum provided the setting to a spectacular clash between Church and science at a meeting of the British Association for the Advancement of Science in 1860 to discuss Darwin's theory of evolution. "Soapy Sam" Wilberforce, Bishop of Oxford, spoke of the dignity of man, and appealed to the Victorian sense of gallantry to ladies in a feeble joke – surely it could not be on his grand*mother's* side that Darwin claimed descent from an ape? In the audience sat T.H. Huxley, surgeon and zoologist; he whispered to his neighbour, "The Lord hath delivered him into my hands." And rose to demolish the bishop: "I would rather be descended from an ape than from a divine who employs authority to stifle truth." One lady in the audience fainted and was carried away.)

Bishop Samuel Wilberforce, photograph by Charles Dodgson.

The high and pathetic farce of the Irish navvies Ruskin played out again in the "Hinksey Diggings", when with a small group of zealots, he tried to repair the village road at North Hinksey. Ruskin lured students away from college sport to soil their hands and uplift their souls in the venture.

The Hinksey 'Diggers'.

But high minds lost out to low matter, and Ruskin summoned Downes, his gardener, to show them how to lay the stones level.

Perhaps the authorities knew best, then, when they did not consult Ruskin over Rossetti's proposed murals on the new Oxford Union. But Ruskin could have explained the art of painting fresco (that is, on damp plaster). Instead the Pre-Raphaelite pictures quickly faded. Only then and too late was Ruskin called in; he recommended as the only remedy a quick coat of whitewash.

By then, 1870, Ruskin could speak in his official capacity, as the first Slade Professor of Fine Art at Oxford. Henry Liddell had spoken loudly in his favour, though he must have had private qualms about Ruskin's growing Quixotic behaviour. In his letter of thanks to Henry Liddell, Ruskin vowed "scrupulously" not to voice any of his "peculiar opinions", though Henry doubtless wondered just how long good intention would prevail against impulse. He knew from of old just what rhetorical outbursts of rage and protest Ruskin gave way to in his letters:

> . . . the English go on with their amusements while the earth around them becomes a cemetery . . . while the rate of deaths, by violence, of men, women and children east and west of us is to be counted in thousands – ten thousands – sometimes fifty thousands a day. Deaths not unforeseen and accidental – but deliberately accepted as results of an inevitable and providential arrangement, and we go on praying, preaching, dancing, drinking and partridge shooting – without making as much as a wry face . . . You clergymen are the root and first captains of all this crime – you pretend to preach Christianity, and you dare not touch one selfish abuse, one rite of devil or money worship, for your lives. You ought to refuse the Sacraments to every living soul in England. You ought to close your churches, tear your black rags from your backs, and go out to the fields and highways and hedges to curse this nation between God's earth and sky, rather than see things done, and *not* done – which you see done daily and lick your lips in benediction over . . .

Sometimes Ruskin pointed the accusing finger more directly (this one in the eye of the Prime Minister):

I have never had enough talk with you for you to know my blackest prejudices. I hold Mr Gladstone to be one of the most mischievous conduits of loquacity that ever overflowed a nation pestilently incapable of drainage for half a century. The only monument I would erect to him would be – Why waste your time with would-be's.

Unfinished copying exercise by Alice.

The agenda for Ruskin's first series of Oxford lectures, however, seemed innocuous, even arid; but the shrivelled seeds of the titles ("The Relation of Art to Religion", "Methods of Study: the Relations of Organic Form") bloomed in the telling into bizarre and garish flowers. There was no knowing where Ruskin would stray from the path of his lecture or take flight in sudden lunacies: in a lecture on birds he used a passage from the Psalms, suddenly remonstrating against Mendelssohn's "Oh, for the wings etc", reciting, dancing, flapping his MA gown and with a distorted look on his face. He did inspire many in his audiences to their first passionate love affair with Italian art, but he also bewildered them with his antics. In 1872 Mrs Liddell attempted a synopsis of one histrionic performance in a letter to Alice:

It was of the wildest kind. First, the art of rowing and dancing – contrasting bad rowing and catching a crab with the perfection of the "Varsity" boat – and the lovely dancing of the minuet by a pair of lovers. Then the Dance of the Demons he had seen at the Gaiety Theatre – then yesterday – he abused chemistry and the making of nitroglycerine and mitrailleuse – and allowing the poor people of Persia to perish of famine (I could not quite see how we could help the famine) – he compared the niggardly refusal of England to purchase the finest Raphael in the world for £25,000 to forced payment of the American claim in millions – of the difference of wisdom and prudence – and catching a cold in star gazing – two girls, the one wise, the other foolish – which was most to be admired? – the one who caught the cold

Sketch by Alice.

John Ruskin.

in the head or the one who reflected how much care she would give her mother by catching a cold? Now can you make out anything of Art in this extraordinary conglomeration? The Dean says he shall not go again to listen to such nonsense.

Mrs Liddell was more patient than her husband: "I am going to Mr Ruskin's next lecture – wonder if it will be as wonderful and incomprehensible as the last." It was: it included bullfinches, Shakespeare and Holborn Viaduct.

For all his waywardness in public, Ruskin held true to his affection for the Liddells, at least until his enfeebling madness brought even the longest standing friendship within the circle of his rage. Until then he loved the Liddells and envied them their joy in the children: "I am too envious of you when they are at home – to come and see you! – and when they are away – I with beautiful rationality complain how unfortunate I am!" As an indifferent world skittled his ideals, Ruskin saw in the Liddell children reminders of his own happy childhood, rambling on the shores of Como and Lucerne, among "pure, wild, solitary, natural scenery", which led him to the paintings of Turner. He could not but desire the unbruised hopes of the Liddell children – "If only I could hope to be, on *any* day of my life again, what that sweet lady you tell me of today is: counting a birthday in the freshness of youth."

It would be surprising if Ruskin had *not* been vulnerable to Alice's beauty. Young girls haunted his dreams, but, more tragically that Charles Dodgson, he tried, failed and vainly tried again to translate his infatuation into adult love. He taught Alice to draw (as he did Rose La Touche). Years later, he remembered one tantalising moment of thwarted intimacy with Alice, like having an elixir dashed from the lips. One snowy evening, after Mr and Mrs Liddell had set off for dinner at Blenheim and "the eastern coast of Tom Quad was clear", Ruskin settled by the fire in the Deanery for tea with young Alice. But the parents returned, finding the roads blocked with snow, and "There was a sudden sense of some stars having been blown out by the wind." Ruskin returned next door to his own college, Corpus Christi, "disconsolate". Ruskin usually taught Alice in the privacy of the Deanery; he lent her paintings by Turner to copy, assuring her that the task would require no skill beyond that of a child! Alice also enrolled as a pupil in Ruskins Art School and in 1870 won first prize for a sketch. Later Ruskin accepted one of her drawings for framing and permanent exhibition in his school. There Alice eventually and unwittingly added to Ruskin's sense of disillusion: he resented her going to draw skeletons there, and he told the Dean so: ". . . Sending your daughter to draw skeletons in the room, when I had denounced anatomical study – was the very head and font of the opposing power which rendered my best efforts useless." Drawing bones smacked too much of scientific exactitude and that, in some strange way, was a betrayal of his trust. In 1878 Ruskin had submitted to Alice a proof of a chapter from his new book on naming plants: "the value of the system depends, however, you must remember, on its incorporation with the teaching in my new elements of drawing, of which the vital principle is that Man is intended to *Observe* with his Eyes and Mind, not with microscope and knife." (The knife, in fact, cut Ruskin's last tie with Oxford: he resigned in 1886, when the university voted to allow vivisection.)

AN APPEAL TO THE LAW.

NAUGHTY CRITIC, TO USE BAD LANGUAGE! SILLY PAINTER, TO GO TO LAW ABOUT IT!

The Ruskin v. Whistler trial, 'Punch' cartoon.

Ruskin's self-esteem, however, was shattered by his disastrous squabble with the American artist, Whistler. In 1877 Ruskin had seen for the first time one of Whistler's *Nocturnes*, hanging in the Grosvenor Gallery. It was a moody composition of murky blues and bright gold spots, and Ruskin, arbiter of the taste of his age, felt obliged to thunder against such a sloppy travesty of Art: "I have seen and heard much of Cockney impudence before now but never expected to hear a coxcomb ask two hundred guineas for flinging a pot of paint in the public's face." As Ruskin grappled with dead spirits in an attack of his brain fever, Whistler strutted wittily through his libel suit – and won (though the court awarded derisory damages of a farthing). Ruskin saw only one course open – to resign from Oxford, "because the professorship is a farce, if it has no right to condemn as well as to praise. It has long been my feeling that nobody really cared for me on any point of art whatsoever –

if a scamp who should have been sent either to the workhouse or to gaol before now can bother my friends for a year and make me pay half a year's income to lawyers for it."

No persuasion from the Liddells would weaken his resolve: "I am absolutely incapable of talking about anything now: and of thinking, except about my own business . . . Oxford must look to her own business now; I don't peddle and meddle in what I once resign. I must go instantly back home and watch the spring flowers; I've lost a step or two even in this one week, and I can't have many more Springs now to draw them in . . . All my friends must think of me with such kindness as they can and content them that I am yet alive – if that does content them, but what I was, I can be no more."

Ruskin did return briefly to Oxford in 1883: "It is something of a risk for them and for me." But he had mellowed: "I keep to my work and don't try to say clever things instead of helpful ones." The Liddells saw little of him; he had drawn curtains round his self-imposed solitude and refused Mrs Liddell's invitations to the Deanery: "I

John Ruskin at Brantwood, 1881, watercolour by W. G. Collingwood.

Brantwood and Coniston Water.

never dine out, tired or not. There is really nothing that makes me more nervously uncomfortable than the sound of voices becoming indecipherable round a clatter of knives." He turned a cold shoulder for the last time in 1886 and retired to Brantwood in the Lake District, where, with a slackening grasp on his sanity, he drew wild flowers and admired the sunsets, while threatening to "let loose" his lawyer on the university for maltreating the pictures he lent them.

Ruskin's last letters to the Liddells are immensely sad; sometimes his frenzy drove him to write matter in madness: "My Very Dear and Revd Mr Dean, You seem to me at present like the Sacristan of Melrose Mills – not clearly to know whether you are priest or layman – lover – I should say lawyer – or Monk: whether you are on your head or your heels, and whether you are dead Prince Leopold's – false witness – a liar, John Ruskin's compulsorily true one." Such nonsense arrived at the Deanery with an apologetic covering note in pencil from Ruskin's cousin, Joan Severn: "My poor cousin, Mr Ruskin, is still in a very strange state – and has quarrelled with us and gone to the hotel nearby to stay . . . I cannot bear sending you such letters as the enclosed, written when he was ill . . . if he does remember them I hope he will be heartily ashamed." The Liddells never saw him again.

Sketch by Alice.

4
REELING AND WRITHING -WITH EXTRAS

If John Ruskin played the Old Conger Eel, who played the Old Turtle and Crab? The answer is Miss Prickett (though she wouldn't have been flattered by the description). The question refers to Alice's schooling. In *Alice in Wonderland* the lachrymose Mock Turtle, in a tale punctuated by sobs and marine puns, tells of his past schooldays; the Old Conger Eel was, like John Ruskin, the "drawling master", and taught "drawling", "stretching" and "fainting in coils". The Old Turtle and Crab shared between them the "Reeling and Writhing", Arithmetic ("Ambition, Distraction, Uglification and Derision"), "Laughing and Grief".

The real-life Alice had no cause to shed tears over *her* education: a small army of private tutors taught all that was necessary and fashionable. At their head marched Miss Prickett, governess, whose province was the "Reeling and Writhing". She was "Pricks" to the children, though it is a moot point whether that was a term of endearment. Doubtless it depended on how you said it. Unlike some of her scandalous and neurotic counterparts in Victorian fiction, Miss Prickett neither seduced her master nor corrupted his children, but kept the relatively noiseless tenor of her way as sober, black-clad companion to the young Liddells both at Christ Church and away. In general the Victorian governess attracted condescension rather than envy: although it was almost the only work a young lady could do without forfeiting her class it was often a public acknowledgment that her family had hit "hard times" or that her father was poorly paid (such as a vicar). For those who counted a lady's marriageability in pounds, that inevitably carried stigma;

Miss Prickett.

and Miss Prickett may have been sensitive on this point: she described her father as a "gentleman" – a neatly ambiguous word, since he was really a "gentleman's gentleman", a kind of steward at Trinity College.

Isolated uncomfortably between family and servants, the equal of neither, most governesses found their work a poor second best to the desideratum of marriage. In the modestly genteel world of tutoring, working for the Liddells in their glittering circle must have brought kudos; Miss Prickett bathed in the reflected glory for fifteen years. At one stage the students of Christ Church had married her off to Charles Dodgson in their gossip. More than a little piqued, he resolved to scotch the rumour: "I shall avoid taking any notice of the children in future, unless occasion should arise when such an interpretation is impossible." We don't know how flattered Miss Prickett felt by the students' choice of her paramour. But in 1871, at the age of thirty-eight (when she must have felt the spectre of "old maid" almost enveloping her), Miss Prickett married Charles Foster, widower, wine merchant and owner of Oxford's fashionable Mitre hotel. As proprietress, she could visit Alice years later as a lady of some substance; when she died she left over £9,000. Looking back in 1932, Alice recalled Miss Prickett as *not* "the highly educated governess of today"; but she superintended the basics with enough discipline to allow Alice to pen for her grandparents at the age of eight or nine an immaculate letter rich in details of her enviable life.

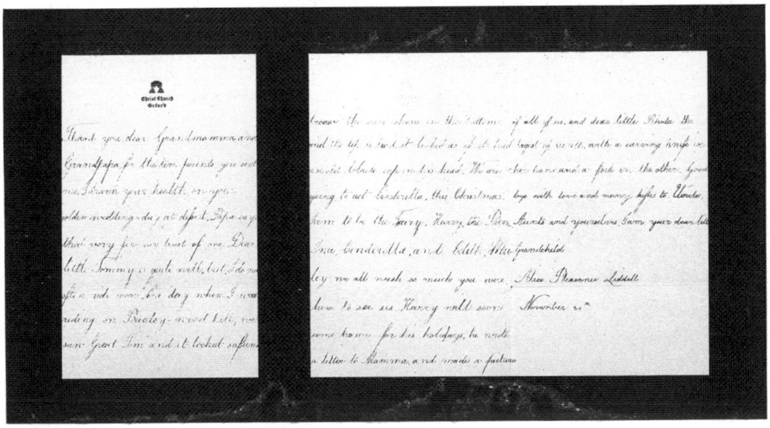

Christ Church
Oxford

thank you dear Grandmamma and
Grandpapa for the ... presents you sent
me. I drank your health on your
golden wedding-day at dessert, Papa says
that very few can boast of one. Dear
little Tommy is quite well, but I do not
often ride now. One day when I was
riding on Bagley-wood hill, we
saw Great Tom and it looked ...

because the sun shone on the bottom of all of us, and dear little Rhoda the
and the top is twisted it looked as if it had ... of us all, with a carving knife in
... black cap on his head. We are ... hand and a fork in the other. Good
going to act Cinderella this Christmas. bye with love and many kisses to Uncle,
... to be the Fairy, Harry the ... Aunts and yourselves. From your dear little
Ina, Cinderella, and Edith ... Grandchild
ley; we all wish so much you were Alice Pleasance Liddell
here to see us. Harry will soon November ...
come home for his holidays, he wrote
a letter to Mamma, and made a picture

Arthur Rackham · 07

"With extras?" asked the Mock Turtle of Alice's fictional self in their talk about her lessons. "Yes," said Alice, "we learned French and music." For these more hazardous pursuits in real life (and including German and Italian) Miss Prickett gave way to other masters and mistresses. Alice mastered French adeptly enough to boast (before she was ten) of "a doll with wax legs and arms that Papa and Mamma gave me for my French prize".

The tearful Mock Turtle recalled his dancing as a game, not a lesson, but the nonsensical Lobster Quadrille, with its advancing and retiring, changing lobster partners, throwing them out to sea, swimming out to recover them, turning somersaults and returning (all in the *first* figure) was a caper complex enough to be considered advanced study. The real-life quadrille was a fashionable square dance in five figures *de rigueur*, for the Liddell children. In Lowestoft a dancing master literally took them in hand; Grandma Reeve reported on their progress:

Grandma Reeve.

> Your darlings took such a nice dancing lesson yesterday. Ina's progress, N. says, is astonishing. There was a country dance, she said, "Oh pray let me try, Gran, to dance it"; so I asked N. and she managed it as well as the rest. But you would have smiled to have seen Mrs Jodrell's two eldest girls quarrelling for Harry. Mr N. went to his rescue and said he was quite astonished at the young ladies. Harry said, "I would like to dance with both if I could, but they will pull me to pieces." "Ah," said N. "Gentlemen always choose their partners – which will you have, sir?" "Why, the prettiest, to be sure." I thought all the room would never have ceased laughing! N. is so pleased with them, I hope five or six lessons more will make them dance a quadrille and polka.

Although Charles Dodgson might join the children singing popular songs, like "Star of the Evening", or the Negro minstrel song, "Sally Come Up", when they danced he stood an inept spectator. He explained his distaste for dancing in a letter to Gaynor Simpson (a girlfriend who earned his mock-offence by misspelling him as "Dodson"): "I never

Opposite
The Mock Turtle, illustration by Arthur Rackham.

Hubert Parry.

dance, unless I am allowed to do it in my own peculiar way. There is no use trying to describe it: it has to been seen to be believed. The last house I tried it in, the floor fell through . . . Did you ever see a rhinoceros and hippopotamus . . . trying to dance a minuet together?"

Music was somewhat more than an "extra"; it was, after all, one of the few pursuits in which genteel young ladies could excel without being thought less feminine. The Liddells brought good music with them from London and demonstrated to the university that the full life should be lived to the sound of fine music. Before the Liddells arrived the university worshipped the Muse of Music less fervently than some of her sisters, as if she were not quite respectable, a flirt or a courtesan rather than a modest consort. The city boasted to have, in the Holywell music rooms, the earliest concert venue in Europe built expressly for music, but few young gentlemen would risk being seen tinkling the ivories in the place for fear of a reputation for effeminacy. Henry Liddell may have struck discords in his attempts at college reform, but he had a well-tuned ear, to the immediate chagrin of one of the cathedral choirmen, whose alto singing was so excruciating that he was relegated to bass (presumably as less obtrusive). But the Liddells performed as well as criticised – or, in Mrs Liddell's case, harped as well as carped. She also taught her daughters to sing. The *Oxford Journal* of March 21st, 1868, reported "a grand concert of sacred music to a most distinguished company, numbering between four and five hundred", given by Mr and Mrs Liddell in the dining hall at Christ Church. It was an occasion where to be seen was as important as to listen – one half of the newspaper report lists the ranks of local worthies, of professors, sirs, aldermen, marquises, earls, mayors and sheriffs, presidents, provosts, principals, masters, doctors, and honourables – all "en grande toilette" – who thronged the hall. At the door to receive them stood Mr and Mrs Liddell, "surrounded by their four daughters, the two youngest of whom held pretty little baskets filled with programmes". Lorina sang Mendelssohn ("charming"); Mrs Liddell ("the leading spirit") accompanied on the harp ("ably played"); while Alice sat in the orchestra – though whether she played, turned pages or simply looked harmonious, the paper omits to say.

Almost certainly in the audience was Hubert Parry, recently arrived at Exeter College, and already a Bachelor of Music (while still a schoolboy at Eton). His praises are usually sung jointly with Charles Stanford's, as twin pillars of a late-Victorian musical renaissance. In concerts at the Deanery and elsewhere Ina, Alice and Edith charmed Parry's ear sufficiently for him to write three trios for female voices specially dedicated to them. Earlier by several years, another young musical talent frequented the Deanery – John Stainer, student at Christ Church from 1860; at twenty-one organist to the university; later Sir John Stainer, organist of St Pauls, Oxford Professor and great composer of church music.

The Liddells' melodies also echoed through polite drawing rooms and salons well away from Oxford. All the children performed in public; in their world to sing and/or to play was an accomplishment as automatic as an Elizabethan courtier composing sonnets. Ad hoc musical fun formed part of the routine of the aristocratic house-party. In the 1880s the Liddells and the relations were to get up the "Oakley Park Troupe", raising money in light-hearted concerts. On the back of one programme is a list of the names and professed talents; three participants, lacking expertise, but determined not to be left out, identified themselves merely as the "claque" (i.e. hired applause).

The Deanery also rang to less formal music – the chirping, mewing and whinnying of the children's petcompared to Dr Buckland's menagerie of crocodiles and bears which had roamed his rooms and alarmed guests on the other side of college, the Liddells chose conventional playthings. Ina and Harry were presented with two tabby kittens, called Villikens and Dinah after the tragic hero and heroine of the popular Victorian ballad. As if he knew the melodramatic catastrophe of the song, Villikens died after eating poison, but Dinah lived on to be doted on by Alice and earn immortality in a better-known, fictional role. There were canaries at the Deanery, too, but never a white rabbit. Lions stood sentinel on the corner posts of the banisters – carved

The Deanery garden.

lions borrowed from the Ravensworth crest and which frightened the children. One other four-legged occupant lived out in the stable – an old pony, Tommy. He was adopted late on in life, a present to Harry from the man who piloted through Parliament the Great Western Railway. After the hard life of a pit pony, Tommy retired to Oxford, where all the Liddell children learned to ride on him, under the eye of the improbably but spectacularly named coachman, Bultitude. As the children grew too heavy Tommy earned a genuine retirement.

The new pony proved an unhappy choice for Alice. On Boxing Day 1862, while out on the Abingdon road, the pony crossed his legs and fell, breaking Alice's thigh. Dean Liddell rushed off for help and Alice lay by the side of the road until passing Samaritans loaned their wagonette and carried her back to Oxford on a feather bed borrowed from a nearby farm. For six weeks Alice was laid up in bed; and seventy years later still felt it worthy of comment that "during all these weeks Mr Dodgson never came to see me".

Anonymous cartoon.

Above right:
Violet Liddell

Above left:
Rhoda Liddell.

As the children augmented the family with animals, Mr and Mrs Liddell, in a fertile flurry, begat a second generation of children. They wrote a chapter which repeated the joys and sorrows of the first. Another daughter, Rhoda Caroline Anne, was born in 1859; and another daughter, the youngest, Violet Constance, in 1864. In Lady Smith's eyes, she confirmed the inexhaustible richness of the Liddell genes: "She seems the crowning rose in your wreath of beauty – a perfect sample of infantine liveliness." Like all the children, however, Vio was not allowed to dally over her infancy; even the Dean proudly records her precocious command of words: "Today we went up to the wood beyond Bagley . . . to gather primroses, and Miss Vio had a basket for the little ones, of which she offered me a share; when I declined, she said the little ones would 'appreciate' it. Her brother made faces and she reproved him and told him not to make such 'grimaces'."

Frederick Francis ('Eric') Liddell.

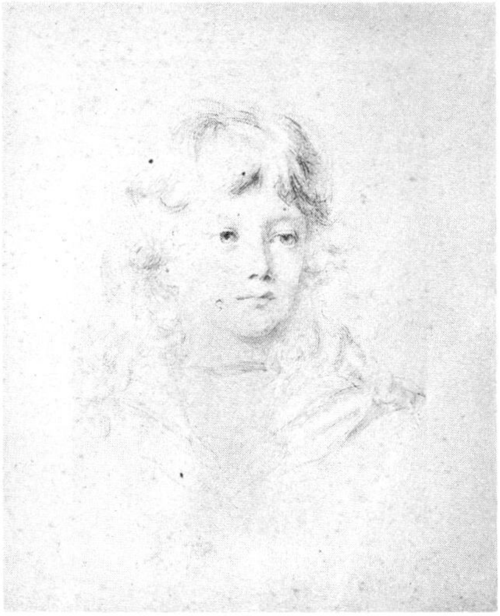

Lionel Liddell, drawing by W. E. Miller

Two more brothers evened out the balance of the sexes: Frederick Francis (born 1865) and Lionel Charles (born 1868), who both flourished later in public life – the latter as Consul at Lyons and Copenhagen; the former, after a scholarship at Eton and a first-class degree at Christ Church, as Sir F.F. Liddell, KCB (1916), Fellow of All Souls, barrister, Counsel to Parliament and to the Speaker of the House of Commons.

Alice was already sixteen when her youngest brother, Lionel, was born, old enough to take an almost maternal interest in his, Violet's and Frederick's ("Eric's") development. As she finished her education with foreign travel, they extended their childish horizons in games and tableaux at the Deanery, which revived memories of Alice's own childhood there:

This morning a box of chocolates came by post for Lionel; he said I suppose they's come cos I'se so good. Last night the young ones did some impromptu tableaux arranged by Rhoda – Eric was an Egyptian prince and she had dressed him out of nothing to capital effect, Lionel a courtier sitting cross-legged with a turban and the green velvet cover out of the schoolroom as a cloak, Violet as a disconsolate mother praying for her son, in white turban and red pinafore – they were all such capital figures and amused the Dean very much, which, as he had a toothache, was very thankful, for that and three glasses of wine cured him.

The next day Eric and Lionel, as the Princes in the Tower, were "murdered" in their temporary bed on the floor, while Violet wept over them, "an angel in a bath-sheet, looking quite lovely".

In 1862 the whole country still wept over a dead prince; the tragic death of the Queen's husband threw an obstinate shadow over the remaining forty years of her long reign. Lady Smith defined the sad event as "one of the greatest calamities, in my belief, that ever fell upon this country . . . I doubt if any human being passed away so honoured and so mourned." Lady Smith had a friend close to the tragedy, in Sir James Clarke, the royal physician, who vouchsafed her his own opinion: "I never expected the prince to live to a great age and he did not think so himself and was always despondent when he was ill – not from any fear of death, but it was his nature. He was the very worst subject for typhoid fever. The death of the king of Portugal depressed him; he had overworked his brain for years and his nervous system was completely exhausted." The Liddells paid a small tribute to the great man, by naming after him a son born in 1863. The gesture took on a more public and symbolic meaning, when the christening was delayed until the visit of the Prince of Wales and Princess Beatrice to Oxford in June 1863, when the prince had agreed to stand godfather to the infant, Albert Edward Arthur.

As the Liddells prepared rooms fit for a prince, Charles Dodgson looked forward to adding royal lions to his photographic collection. He stalked big game to shoot with his camera with the persistence of an avid hunter. He survived rebuffs with resilience and chased even the most elusive of butterflies. One prized trophy was the head of the Poet Laureate, Alfred Tennyson, whom he first pinned down in the Lake District. Dodgson sent in his card, having added under his name in pencil, "Artist of 'Agnes Grace' and 'Little Red Riding Hood' " – a reference to two photographs of a young niece of Tennyson's who had also inspired a sonnet from Palgrave (of *Golden Treasury* fame). In a subtle campaign Dodgson photographed Tennyson's sons, Hallam and Lionel ("the most beautiful boys of their age I ever saw"), and then the parents. Eighteen months later, and under the cloak of pretended etiquette, Dodgson invaded Tennyson's privacy at Freshwater in the Isle of Wight: "Being there I had the inalienable right of a free-born Briton to make a morning call." He found the poet off-duty, mowing the lawn, "in a wideawake and spectacles"; but Tennyson did not recognise him. Dodgson showed Mrs Tennyson and the children his album of pictures and had cause to regret his habit of appending lame verses to each photograph. Lionel Tennyson misread aloud the crass subscript to his father's picture ("The Poet in a Golden Clime was born etc."), starting, "The Pope . . . ". "What's this about the Pope?" asked Tennyson, startled into attention; but no one

Sketch by Alice.

Lionel, Eric and Violet Liddell.

The Royal visit to Christ Church, 1863.

enlightened him and so spared Dodgson embarrassment. They forgot the incident and, it seems, Dodgson, too: Hallam Tennyson did not mention him in his three-volume life of his father.

Dodgson's attempts to focus on the faces of the royal family had been equally assiduous and his reception even more mixed. While the Prince of Wales was a student at Christ Church, Dodgson angled for a sitting, undeterred by the initial brush-off: "His Royal Highness is tired of having his photograph taken." Face to face with the prince at the Deanery, Dodgson worried at the heels of the subject of cameras, but ended up with only a royal autograph. Several months later, Dodgson found the Prince of Wales' brother-in-law, Prince Frederick of Denmark, more amenable to being photographed: "He conversed pleasantly and sensibly and he is evidently a much brighter specimen of royalty than his brother-in-law." Note the word – "specimen"! A month before the royal visit to Oxford Dodgson ensured that the Queen's eyes fell on some of his pictures; she admired them and deferred characteristically to the judgment of her dead consort: "They are such as the Prince would have appreciated very highly." The testimonial came to Dodgson only secondhand; but he repaired the gap by composing several letters from the Queen to himself.

Despite the royal acclaim for his efforts, the nearest Dodgson came to photographing the happy couple in Oxford was a picture of the royal bedstead, with Alice and her sisters on the window-seat behind. On the great day itself, he set up his telescope in Thomas Bayne's rooms (breaking a window to accommodate it) and admired from afar the prince and the princess as they presented prizes in Great Quad. In the afternoon there was a bazaar at St John's, where the Liddell children offered white kittens for sale. Since Alice was too shy to offer hers to the princess, Dodgson (who on this occasion had overcome his natural distaste for bazaars) pleaded on her behalf. The princess told him she had already bought a kitten from Ina; Dodgson took the reply as a rebuff – "the only reply *she* is ever likely to make to *me*". The day closed with a grand banquet in Christ Church hall.

The planned christening of young Albert Arthur Liddell had not figured in the day's programme. The choice of his names – one a tribute to a dead prince, the other to a long-dead brother at Westminster – proved doubly ominous. Three weeks before the planned visit, the baby took ill and the Dean was summoned hurriedly from morning chapel for a foreboding christening. The other children walked in silence round Christ Church meadow, hoping for a miracle but fearing the worst. Albert died two days later, on May 28th:

Eric and Violet Liddell.

Our little child "fell asleep" this morning at a little past nine – so tranquilly that it was impossible to say when this life ended. Poor Ina showed most outward signs of grief. God knows that, with the happy children we have, we aught not to augur ill; and yet to depart so peacefully, so painlessly, so entirely without touch of sin or sorrow . . . The scene I have just gone through revives in the most painful way the death by recollection of a fair-haired boy we lost some ten years since. Will you be so kind as to let the prince know of the frustration of his kind offices?

Oxford, sketch by Alice.

Among the children on whom the Liddells still pinned their hopes for the future, Rhoda was old enough in the year of the

Alice, the last photograph by Charles Dodgson.

royal visit not to be left swaddled in her cot. She attended the bazaar in the arms of Dodgson and was carried on expeditions to the river. Alice took an elder sister's amused interest, in a letter to her mother (convalescing in Lowestoft) and in which she naively records a request from Charles Dodgson that would have caused Mrs Liddell a relapse or brought her scurrying protectively back to the nest: "We are very glad to hear that you are better again. I have been illuminating some people's names into my crest book and I think they look very pretty . . . Has dear little Rhoda said any funny things lately? Mr Dodgson wrote and asked me (for fun) if I would send him a piece of hair (he did not mean to send it) so I send him really a piece and he wrote and told me I was stupid. Goodbye."

For Charles Dodgson it was indeed the beginning of a long and gradual goodbye. Already in October 1862, he had sensed he was out of favour with Mrs Liddell "ever since Lord Newry's business" – though what the offending business was and what conspiratorial or neglectful part Dodgson played in it still remains a mystery. At Easter 1863, Dodgson was aware that Ina had reached, for him, a dangerous age – "so tall as to look odd without an escort", though her height is a rather euphemistic criterion. A year later, in May 1864, Mrs Liddell put the younger daughters out of Dodgson's reach by refusing them any more outings with him on the river – "rather superfluous caution", recorded Dodgson with chagrin. Already, however, a regular gallery of new young misses paraded in front of his camera and satisfied his passion for innocent kisses. The next year (actually the year of the publication of *Alice in Wonderland*), Alice, too, then aged twelve, suffered the sea-change in Dodgson's eyes: "Alice seems changed a good deal and hardly for the better – probably going through that awkward stage of transition." Awkward for whom?

Alice's growing up was for Dodgson a reluctant awakening from a dream. He could never envisage his child friends as adults, and assured one of them, Gertrude Chataway, "You will always be a child to me, even when your hair is grey." But Alice did grow up and Dodgson lamented his sense of separation from her in the sad preface to *Alice Through the Looking-Glass:*

I have not seen thy sunny face,
Nor heard thy silver laughter;
No thought of me shall find a place
In thy young life's hereafter.

About this time Dodgson photographed Alice for the last time, and then only in the presence of her mother. Alice's face was neither sunny nor laughing, but glum and very faraway. For his new book Dodgson had anyway wooed a surrogate heroine – a young cousin, whom he met at his Uncle Skeffington's in London. Her name, Alice Raikes, guaranteed her attention: "So you are another Alice. I am very fond of Alice's." Dodgson set her a puzzle, standing with an orange in front of a mirror, and she started her solution with, "Supposing I was on the *other* side of the glass . . . " Which is exactly what Dodgson did.

Julia Margaret Cameron, c. 1850, portrait by G. F. Watts.

Above:
Alice, photograph by Julia Margaret Cameron.

Opposite:
Alice, Edith and Ina, photograph by Julia Margaret Cameron.

Meanwhile the haunting beauty of Alice excited other suitors with cameras, among them Julia Margaret Cameron, who ardently devoted the last fifteen years of her life to what she called the "divine art" of photography. In the 1860s and 1870s she assembled a moody gallery of portraits of the famous; brooding, impressionistic, sometimes ill-composed, but penetrating beyond blurred externals to the heart beneath. At Freshwater, Tennyson's home in the Isle of Wight, she pictured Alice as a rather unearthly Pre-Raphaelite heroine, like some golden damozel of a drug-induced fantasy, and (surely out of character) as one of Lear's vicious "pelican" daughters. One letter, which somehow eventually found its way to Tetbury, praises these images of Alice as quite electrifying:

M. Cameron came to us yesterday for a couple of days and brought with her divers photographs of the Miss Liddells, daughters of the Dean of Christ Church, who have been occupying Alfred Tennyson's home at Freshwater Bay for some weeks. I have hardly seen any photographs of hers which are more beautiful in themselves or seem to represent more beauty in the person photographed than three or four of her photographs of Miss Alice Liddell. I wonder whether you know her and have seen the beauty in her which I see in the photograph.

The writer, an idol of Miss Cameron's, was Sir Henry Taylor, in the first year of his retirement in Bournemouth, after forty-eight years labour as a clerk in the Colonial Office, but feted more as poet and playwright, and honoured by the university at Oxford with the degree of D.C.L.

Charles Dodgson visited Julia Margaret Cameron's house for an evening while on holiday in August 1864, a few months after she had taken her first picture. She annoyed him by declaring her own efforts to be "triumphs of art"; he found some of them "very picturesque" but others "merely hideous". It was not a meeting warmed by mutual magnanimity. Like their animal counterparts, these two lions of Victorian photography, circled each other, jealous of their territories: he patiently sought neatness, accuracy and

Given to Mr. F. C. Spray

Harry Liddell.

My dearest Alice & Edith – I feel myself so honoured by your kind wish to possess my portrait that I know not how to express the gratification it gives me, for I am afraid

Letter to Alice and Edith from Lady Smith, aged 99.

design; she intensely courted passion and soul. So they stood on opposite sides of an abyss, throwing pebbles at each other: "She wished she could have had some of *my* subjects to do out of focus – and *I* expressed an analogous wish with regard to some of *her* subjects."

However flattered were the Dean and Mrs Liddell by the eligibility and fame of their children, it brought with it dangers, marking them out as prey to those with less honourable motives. Harry, it seems, narrowly eluded the web of some spider in 1871. Lady Smith alludes to the enigmatic scandal in terms that make it fit episode for the more sensational kind of romantic novel:

> Deeply was I grieved to hear that you had to bear a very unexpected disappointment. The best alleviation in such a case is to think of what you have escaped that might have been worse, and here you do possess a relief – I refer to the base, the treacherous conduct of Mr Walker. Thanks to heaven and dear Edward's discernment that he escaped the trap this artful and pretended friend set for an unguarded youth. I think I am not uncharitable when I suspect that a worse blot than the lady's seniority made her unprincipled father attempt to ruin your son's happiness. (Five years later Harry found his happiness in the arms of Minnie Cory, heiress to a family fortune made in mining. Unlike his younger brothers, Harry lacked the Liddell academic genes, but consoled himself with the life of an affluent squire.)

In the same letter Lady Smith bewailed the current destruction of Paris by Prussian guns; not many people's memories could, like hers, compare it with the tumult of the French Revolution eighty years before. But all the vicissitudes of old age only seemed to show that Lady Smith was well-nigh indestructible: "she got up to put some coal on the fire, caught her foot in the rug and fell, just missing the fender – Grace could not pull her up, but she soon got herself up and said, 'Never mind, my dear, I do not fall as heavy as you, and to show you I am not hurt, I will put some coals on. Wonderful at ninety-nine!' " The accident prompted Alice to beg a tangible image of Lady Smith to add to her memories of her. The reply is a touching tribute to her unfailing humanity:

> I feel myself so honoured by your kind wish to possess my portrait that I do not know how to express the gratification it gives me, for I am assured it proceeds from love of me. I never had indulged the expectation of so much affection as you bestow on me; it is balm to my mind and I love you all with unfailing affection and have often wished to show it by some tangible token of regard and have as often been restrained, for what could I send? Not books, for to send books to Oxford would be to verify the old adage of sending coals to Newcastle; not money, for where its want is never felt, it seems the meanest of gifts; not jewels, for I have none to give. I seem to have nothing left but my love – and a small card representing me seventy-four years ago.

On her hundredth birthday, May 11th, 1873, the Queen sent Lady Smith a present, which left her, for once, at a loss for words – not as to how to reply (full of "profoundest, reverence, loyalty and affection") but as to how to address the envelope!

Lady Smith died in 1877, aged one hundred and three years and nine months, proud of her longevity and the sense of perspective it lent her judgment. But among all the shifts against which she had railed, one event made her think she had lived just too long. She took to the grave memories of the greatest tragedy that befell the Liddell family – the death of Alice's sister, Edith, at the age of twenty-two. The Liddells knew no sorrow to equal it; they never spoke of it afterwards and could not bear to be reminded. The morning light which filters through the St Catherine window at the east end of Christ Church cathedral still illuminates their loss; it picks out a Latin inscription: *Ave dulcissima, dilectissima Ave.* ("Hail, our sweetest; our dearest, Hail"). It alludes, too, to a tragic irony in the timing of her death: *Vix quinque dies deponsa* ("scarcely five days engaged").

The sombre facts of Edith's death and of the young man who won and lost her in a week emerge from another bundle of letters at Tetbury between Dean Liddell and another

The window of St Michael's Chapel, Christ Church Cathedral, part of which (the image of St Catherine) was dedicated to Edith Liddell by Burne-Jones

Arthur Stanley, photograph by Charles Dodgson.

Aubrey Harcourt.

lifelong friend, one of the greatest of Victorian churchmen – Arthur Stanley. In these letters mitres and academic gowns fly about as if they were workaday garb. Liddell and Stanley were united by the spirit of tolerance in a world where people usually forged their bonds partly by damning those outside the circle. Henry Liddell preached at Arthur Stanley's ordination in Oxford and warned him off religious fracas: "Few have entered into controversy without repenting of it." Stanley made a motto of the words and lived by their precept. He made tongues to cluck years later as Dean of Westminster by inviting all the scholars working on the Revised Version of the Bible to Communion at the Abbey – including a Unitarian. For many that amounted to penning a wolf or a goat with the sheep.

Alice referred to Arthur Stanley as the "little Dean", to distinguish him from her father, but that was no reflection on his stature. In some ways he learned to live with feet of clay – he was tone-deaf, colour-blind and had little sense of taste or smell; he was baffled by all numbers and buttons (which he usually married to the wrong buttonholes). But that made him the more endearing. Schooled at Rugby under the great Dr Arnold, Stanley (who was the original of "Arthur" in *Tom Brown's Schooldays*) hero-worshipped his headmaster. The *Life of Arnold* established Stanley as a man of letters as a young man in his twenties at University College, Oxford.

News of Edith Liddell's death reached Stanley at Westminster in June 1876 from Henry Liddell:

You have no doubt heard of the great sorrow that has overtaken us – as sudden and unexpected as death by lightning. My dear, dear Edith became engaged to Aubrey Harcourt of Nuneham on Tuesday the 13th last; on Sunday the 18th she was taken ill and on Monday last, the 26th, she died. To us the loss of so good and sweet a child is – I can find no word; but to him, poor fellow, it is indeed heart-breaking. "Two years of patient waiting," he said, "and four days of happiness." It is a real tragedy of common life. Her death was caused by the purely accidental lodgement of some hard substance, such as an orange pip or a cherry stone, in a

Edith Liddell.

particular part of the intestine, which produced peritonitis and slew her. There was no remedy. Paget saw her and said that nothing had been left undone which could have been done, but alas! that was next to nothing. The only consolation save that through God's mercy we have our other dear children is – that it was better for her to die thus in the midst of her health and sweetness of life, than to linger on a hopeless invalid – which was the alternative. God make us fit to join her pure spirit.

There is sad irony in the timing of Aubrey and Edith's engagement to coincide with Oxford's Commemoration Week. Aubrey and the other Liddells went through the outward motions of pageantry – the procession of boats on the Isis, the University Ball amid sumptuous surroundings of gilt ornaments, rich drapes and flowers – while Edith lay in miserable discomfort, then in increasing pain which the doctor (and soon the family) knew could only be relieved by death. Instead of wedding bouquets there were wreaths – roses, camelias and lilies that smothered the coffin, tragically the first to lie in the family vault at Christ Church.

Stanley felt the Liddells' loss the more keenly, since his own wife had died only weeks before. She was Lady Augusta Bruce, daughter of the 7th Earl of Elgin, Resident Lady of the Bedchamber to the Queen, and whom he married in 1863 – a marriage the Queen, somewhat selfishly, described as "my greatest sorrow and trial since the death of Albert – I thought *she* would *never* leave *me*". Dean Stanley had lived with persistent reminders of bereavement at Westminster; the Queen called on him to perform a private memorial service on the anniversary of Albert's death. She wrote in her journal, "The room was full of flowers, and the sun shining in so brilliantly . . . I said it seemed like a birthday and Dr Stanley said, 'It is a birthday, in a new world.'" In 1876 Stanley's own wife died after cruel suffering, during which her husband lived only from day to day and prayed for a release. Only weeks later came the news of Edith Liddell's death; the Queen, too, heard the news, from her son, Leopold, in Oxford and wrote to Stanley: "I am sure your kind and most sympathising heart will feel most deeply . . . It is horrible – happening at this very moment of their greatest joy is quite overwhelming. Leopold, who had only just told me of the engagement which caused them so much happiness, is greatly distressed, as he is much attached to the Dean and his family, who have been so very kind to him."

For the Liddells the death of Edith was a wound whose smart would only be lessened by time. Their immediate concern was to remove themselves from daily reminders in Oxford. They retired for a time to the calm of Sir Thomas Acland's house at Holnicote. It was not the first time they had concurred with the seventeenth-century Anthony Wood's complaint that "Oxford is no good air."

Sketch by Alice.

5 VAULTING AMBITION

"There have been so many deplorable events in Switzerland this summer that I will consider this comparative slight one as a *warning* to avoid vaulting ambition." Thus, without actually saying "serve him right", Lady Smith received the news in 1865 that Henry Liddell had broken his ankle climbing a mountain in the Alps. He paid for his "folly" with pain and discomfort; he was carried off the mountain at night and transported to Paris, where a surgeon (in full evening dress) set the bone. Lady Smith, although just in her sprightly nineties, now only travelled vicariously, inspired or alarmed by the derring-do of others – including the Liddells. She could not approve the English craze for assaulting high peaks, reducing their Gothic awesomeness and whittling them down to toys in the playground of Europe. But she knew that Liddells roved with a distinct taste for the intrepid: Mrs Liddell reported their exploits, such as Henry's ascent of Scafell Pike – "a tremendous scramble – I could not have attempted it – Henry said in many parts it was like climbing a ladder – I met them at the bottom of the pass – Henry had cut his shoes to pieces, and there being no shoemaker within ten miles he was obliged to buy the landlord's boots of the farmhouse where they slept. Could you have seen the shape and size of them and the funny figure Henry looked, you would have been amused . . ." Lady Smith might just have permitted herself a smile. For thirty years she mentally (and at times apprehensively) tracked the Liddells across continents and oceans, up mountains and into museums. The evidence – letters, journals and sketchbooks – prove collectively that

The St Bernard Pass, photograph from a family album.

The Liddells on holiday – sketch by Alice.

the Liddells took their talents with them on holiday and were as vigorous away as at home.

One journal in the Dean's hand suggests that hazard stalked the family even when they looked for repose. A year after they struck root in Oxford, Henry Acland, the family doctor, ordered the Dean to Madeira for the winter; he was worn out by work and Oxford's dank air, subject of perennial complaint. What Acland intended was a siesta well south in the Gulf Stream. Congestion of the lung a week before departure almost confined the Dean to a wintry Oxford bed; as things turned out, that would have been more tranquil.

They (the Dean and Mrs Liddell and the Aclands) sailed on the maiden voyage of HMS *Satellite* (by kind permission of the Admiralty), though the captain was "somewhat staggered" by being asked on active service to make room for a lady's maid. His passengers were real strangers to the open sea; they hardly knew more than that the temperature of the water was warmer off Brighton than off Northumberland (and in spartan spirit they yearned for the colder North-East). On board the alien nautical terms confused them: "The officer of the watch came in as we were sitting round the captain's fire and reported: 'Just made the Lizard, sir.' 'Made what?' exclaimed Mrs Liddell with a tone of great surprise and some alarm. It did seem an odd way of beginning Creation afresh."

The captain boasted that his ship was "the finest in

service", with the same air as others later advertised the *Titanic* as unsinkable. The history of the officers, had the Liddells known it in advance, might have given them qualms. Captain Prevost had explored the isthmus of Panama in 1852, where four of his companions were shot by Indians; Mr Reid, the Master, lay off Balaclava in the *Vesuvius* during the infamous gale of 1854; Mr Piers, Chief Surgeon, spent four winters trapped on board the *Investigator* in the ice off Baring Island, rescued just eleven days before the deadline they had given themselves for attempting a suicidal escape on foot across the ice. As this trio of officers swapped stories of hair's-breadth escapes, the Liddells must have pondered the possibility of peril on the sea ahead.

It struck in the form of a gale in the Bay of Biscay which blew up on Christmas Eve. Even the officers, for all their charmed lives, were ill and declared it "no joke". The Liddells could not even rise from their bunks, where they lay, "like dogs, very ill". The sea quickly found the bad workmanship in the new ship: the porthole covers were not watertight, and the Dean had the "full benefit of a showerbath every half-minute, and the floor of the cabin was deluged". Meanwhile, the maid sought refuge on the floor (awash), wrapped in sodden blankets.

Dean Liddell.

Sudden panic diverted thoughts from the fast approach of Christmas Day: "at about a quarter before nine at night I heard a loud musical twang over my head. As the log words have it, we had 'carried away the starboard wheel rope' . . . In effect, all I knew about it at the time was that the master, with a bearded quartermaster and barefooted carpenter climbed over my sofa and entered a dark cavern behind." The ship was steered only by ropes, with no tiller in the event of one snapping. There was no festivity on Christmas Day: the storm raged unabated; six inches of water sloshed around on the lower deck; there was no fire to cook meals. Then the ship lost its cutter. Before it blew itself out two days later, the storm claimed a victim. Ordinary Seaman William Brewer fell off the boom while loosing the jib. The ship hove to, and a boat was lowered to search, but to no avail.

Penmorfa.

The Dean ends his journal with a thankful arrival at Maderia, as if, after the journey, the holiday was an uneventful lull. According to Acland, they feasted on the sight and taste of turtle, bananas and green peas. He left for home before the Liddells, with an eight-foot crate which the sailors said housed a corpse and cursed the homeward journey. Although the ship ran aground, the contents of the crate – a huge tunny fish – survived for exhibition in Oxford's University Museum. To the Liddells the air of Madeira smelled sweet, sweet enough to outweigh the horrors of the passage and entice them back the following year, this time with the children. Again, the journey was treacherous: thick fog delayed the ship's departure; then it ran aground on a mud bank in the Thames; once afloat, the ship rolled badly, the ladies' cabin flooded, and the passengers needed a holiday to recuperate from the bruising. For the children it was all adventure, with moments of magic as they were charmed en route by a "black trader" with stories and promises of parrots.

The Liddells indulged their penchant for remoteness closer home than Maderia: "I did not expect to see such savage scenery in so sweet a solitude . . . Do you see any of the old Bards among the rocks?" – Lady Smith again; this time in wide-eyed response to a picture of the unspoilt coast of North Wales sent her by Mrs Liddell. The family were to give birth to a stranger "creature" among the rocks than old Bards.

The story of this flirtation with "savage scenery" opens on a piece of paper on which Alice (aged eighty) scribbled fragmentary memories of her "Carrollian days". She recalled that Henry Acland lent her parents a house at Bude in North Devon for holidays; but Mrs Liddell so disliked the air that they migrated north to Wales. On tour, they saw in an architect's window an advertisement for a house (as yet unbuilt) which they thought "would suit them and was not expensive". If that conjures up an image of a cosy cottage in the country, the impression is misleading: over the next three years there arose at Llandudno, on the barren rocks at the foot of the Great Orme (round which no road yet ran), a

Penmorfa, photograph by Charles Dodgson?

rara avis in stone, a misplaced Gothic pile which would give any conservationist nightmares. Looking due south over the sands of the Conway estuary, surrounded by virgin rock and backed by precipitous cliffs, perched Penmorfa – transplanted, one might think, from among the plush villas of North Oxford, no more Welsh than Welsh rarebit, and as incongruous as a dinner jacket at Stonehenge. The Liddells did sue the architect, not for want of propriety, but for overcharging – and won. They loved Penmorfa, and spent nine summers there, until the spreading resort of Llandudno encroached and threatened to engulf them.

The Liddells on the Conway sands.

One fascination of Penmorfa – given that it was ever built – lies in the procession of famous pilgrims to the seaside shrine. Matthew Arnold, in North Wales for the Eisteddfod, dined at Penmorfa and admired the setting sun. William Gladstone stayed, and suffered an attack of mortal weakness unbecoming in an aspiring Prime Minister; among the tussocks of coarse grass on the Orme he suddenly took fright and had to be led down, eyes closed, and with the rest of the party between him and the sea, offering him the minimal consolation of knowing that, if he went, they would all die together.

In the summer of 1864 a young man arrived at Penmorfa for a stay of eight weeks. He was a son of the famous painter, George Richmond, and destined himself later to succeed John Ruskin as Slade Professor of Art at Oxford, to be knighted and earn the honour of KCB. He bore in his Christian names – William Blake – the burden of his father's early idolatry of the artist/poet. (Meeting Blake for the first time on London fields, George Richmond felt he had "walked with Isaiah"; he later closed the "prophet's" eyes at his death.) In christening one of his sons "William Blake", George perhaps pre-empted his choice of career, but he also passed on a family talent with the brush that went back three generations. The fruit of William Blake Richmond's two-month stay at Penmorfa was a picture of Ina, Alice and Edith – the famous "Three Sisters".

Sir William Blake Richmond.

For eight to ten hours a day the sisters sat for Richmond, while in the next room the Dean patiently worked at the lexicon, sneezing punctually at noon; he was in all things regular. Richmond's professional eye approved the family's egregious good looks: "Mrs Liddell was remarkably beautiful, of a Spanish type, although I am not aware if she has Spanish blood"; the Dean "was as handsome a specimen of aristocratic manhood as could be seen in a lifetime." But in his manner there was coolness and distance: "In most people the Dean inspired awe . . . he disliked shyness in others, although he was the shyest of men himself . . . [his family] feared him not a whit, although at times he would reprimand them with asperity, if they were inaccurate or made what he considered silly statements."

Richmond's picture of the three sisters betrayed his admiration of Ruskin and the Pre-Raphaelites; the master, Ruskin, found it "supremely beautiful", except for one

'The Three Sisters' by William Richmond.

detail: "Why the devil did you paint the damsel's shoes instead of her feet?" Ruskin put his critical finger on a contradiction in the canvas: for all the wild rocks in the background, it is a formal studio portrait, with the wild back-cloth added later. Later, in April 1865, the picture hung in the British Institution, where Charles Dodgson saw it. His response has a touch of the chagrined rival about it: "Ina looking a little too severe and melancholy – much, I am sure, she would have looked sitting to a stranger; Alice, very lovely, but not *quite* natural; Edith is the best likeness of the three." (There was no love lost between Dodgson and Ruskin: the latter had already estimated Dodgson's skill with the pencil as too trifling to be worth pursuing; Ruskin liked naturalistic detail, whereas Dodgson's talent was for grotesquerie and cartoon. In return Dodgson refused to be impressed by his first meeting with Ruskin, finding him at breakfast in the common room at Christ Church with "a general feebleness of expression, with no commanding air, or any external signs of deep thought, as one would have expected."

In the same year as the "Three Sisters" William Richmond painted a portrait of young Rhoda with a basket of fruit, and in 1867 paid a half-intended tribute to Velasquez in a portrait of Violet in distinctive Spanish style. The hackneyed charm of the child-and-dog image belies the reality: the dog constantly barked and dribbled – Richmond "detested" it.

Richmond remembered Dodgson at Penmorfa, though whether he actually set foot in the house has since assumed the status of great mystery. Alice owned an album of photographs, apparently all by Charles Dodgson, and including two of Penmorfa; but she denied any memories of him outside Oxford. In the 1930s Llandudno resolved the enigma in its own favour, though at the risk of being seen with egg on its corporate face – but that episode properly belongs later.

In April 1872 the Liddells severed their links with Penmorfa. Mrs Liddell wrote glumly to Alice: "Mr Taylor has written to offer £2,000 for Penmorfa – we have taken time to consider. Poor Penmorfa! Well, we all had some

Rhoda Liddell, portrait by William Richmond.

Violet Liddell, portrait by William Richmond.

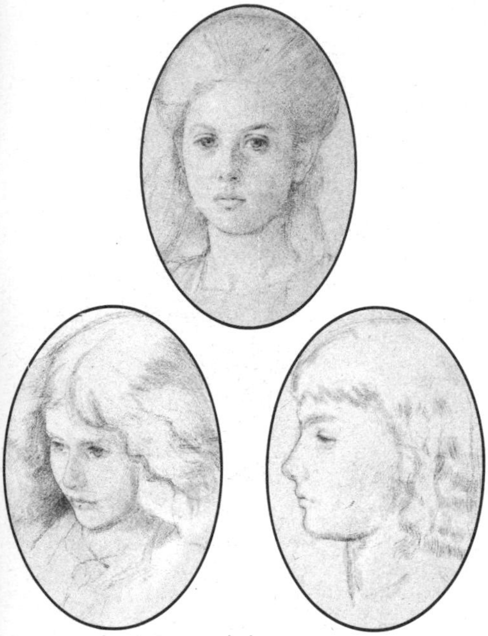

'The Three Sisters' sketches by William Richmond.

happy days there:" Her mother's lament reached Alice on holiday in much sunnier climes.

Another journal, a sketchbook and a batch of letters prove that before she was twenty Alice (with Ina and Edith) achieved what the great Dr Samuel Johnson proclaimed "the grand object of all travelling" – seeing the shores of the Mediterranean. It was no Thomas Cook nine-day wonder: more a Grand Tour from February to April 1872 through France and around the coast of Italy. To the Liddell nucleus of the party was hitched a battery of attendants – guardians, chaperones, go-betweens, couriers, a doctor (whom Alice found a "tiresome prig"), and "Murray" – not Mr Murray in person, but his distinctive red guide-books which, in the words of *The Times*, swung open the gates of the continent to "the veriest Cockney, the greenest schoolboy and the meekest country clergyman".

En route by steamer to Boulogne the party had a moist introduction to the accuracy of *Murray* – "In rough weather passengers are likely to be wetted." And they found *Murray* no more sanguine about the next stage of the journey, by coach to Paris, either by *cabriolet* ("heavy, lumbering and jolting . . . necessarily clumsily built to withstand the terrible crossroads in France"), or by *patache* ("a rustic cab, verging on the covered cart . . . he who rides in a patache must be prepared to be jolted to pieces"). According to Alice, Paris beckoned them with a "red sunset", but their guardian spread dark clouds over the journey with a typically English lamentation over all inferior Gallic things: "the lighting in the streets, the gas seeming only half turned on, and the shops dark, a good many shut up altogether and the streets lonely and deserted". Nor did the hotel lighten the gloom; but *Murray* had forewarned them: "Many of the most important essentials to personal comfort are utterly disregarded and evince a state of backwardness hardly to be expected in a civilised country . . . Fail not to take soap with you, a thing never to be found in foreign bedrooms."

The next day shed light on one more reason for woe – the havoc and ruin wreaked twelve months before by the "Insurrection of the Commune", when citizens released

Above left:
Alice and Edith.

Above right:
Edith, Alice and Ina.

30,000 criminals from prison and armed them for a reign of terror ending with the burning of the city. Sightseeing for Alice and her sisters was more of a tour of ruins and sites of atrocity, from Notre Dame (where the last three successive archbishops had been murdered) to Mont Valerian ("looking terrible with houses pierced through and through by shells"). But amid the blackened walls and fallen arches smart Paris still strove to be "gay": in the Bois fine ladies, dressed à la mode, "waddled – very few of them could walk . . . most of the ladies have an immense amount of fur about their dresses." At a lower level Alice and her sisters, reassured by *Murray,* ventured in the five-acre market of

France, sketch from a family sketchbook.

Les Halles Centrales, three pretty English misses daintily tripping through dark corners of Parisian working-class discontent: "The flowers were lovely but the smell of the fish was too horrible, and we held up our handkerchiefs to keep it out, using some eau de cologne to help; this made the fish people rather irate and I heard them calling out, 'Ah, ils sentent de l'eau de cologne! Ils trouvent le sent mauvais!' "

The real shrine in Paris, however, was the Louvre, where they "worshipped" several times: "What need I say more? We enjoyed it more than anything." For once the guide-book was found wanting, and Alice turned to the ultimate authority, her father, to explain why in his paintings of the Virgin Mary Murillo included a crescent moon. Almost by return, the Dean had the answer – a biblical reference to "a woman clothed with the sun, having the moon under her feet and with a crown of stars".

Later, from Avignon Alice casually enquired about fourteenth-century popes seated there, and the Dean sent back three-and-a-half pages of close historical detail. He expected his daughters to see beyond pretty vistas and hear more than the frou-frou of modish silks and satins. Equally, Alice had learned French not merely as a social grace; an English girl speaking it abroad was rare enough to attract notice: "an old Frenchman sat next me yesterday at dinner, a fine old man with white long hair and dark great eyebrows . . . the only thing he found not quite *commode* was that only one *demoiselle* in the hotel spoke French." And from "Marseille", feeling quite the native, "I hope you will remark the way in which I spell the name of the town we are in, the real thing, if you please, and no 's' added by us English."

Well schooled in the history of the French Revolution, Alice seems to have visited the radical sins of the earlier fathers of Marseilles on the later sons of the town: "I never saw such horrid-looking people as they are here: most of the men look real ruffians, I think, and the women horrid; no wonder it is a red republican place." Even the bookseller's did not provide the usual English haven – no Macaulay's *Essays* (Alice's choice of holiday reading!); she resigned herself to "making do" with Jane Austen. Monaco, with its

Elba, watercolour by Alice.

licensed gambling, the "ring of anxious, horrid-looking faces", appalled the sisters more. Warned off by *Murray*, they could not resist a visit, but regretted it: "Ina seems to have been made almost ill by the agitation of God's creatures debasing themselves so much."

They fled from this iniquity to Italy, on board the private steam yacht, *Kathleen*, their floating home for the next four weeks. That style was the prerogative of the few, who, even on holiday, could afford to employ a crew of up to a dozen and hire a schooner at, say, £450 per month, in days when thirty shillings was a good working wage. The *Kathleen*'s first port of call was Genoa, the Liddell sisters' first sight of the new "Italy", unified and self-governing. Genoa somewhat tempered the ideal – beautiful, but dirty, smelly, disordered, noisy and decayed. (The Dean and Mrs Liddell had seen Italy in 1859 under Austrian rule, accompanied everywhere by soldiers with cocked pistols, and finding Venice more an army state than a dream: "in the great piazza there was nothing but an Austrian band playing to Austrian soliders and a few strangers.")

Palermo, watercolour by Alice.

For Alice, Ina and Edith Venice would be the touchstone – either a haunt for the imagination or an everyday place with slums, stinking waterways and mosquitoes. Like others, Alice sensed the pathos – what Byron half a century before called the "dying glory" of a time when "Venice sat in state, throned on her hundred isles". The gondolier, especially, was the weathercock of the plight of Venice. Byron saw him as a dumb adjunct to the crumbling palaces – "silent rows the songless gondolier"; Dean Liddell's memories are equally gloomy: "I do not think the gondoliers sang when we were in Venice; I suppose under Austrian rule they were mute." Though freed from the foreign yoke, the gondoliers did not serenade Alice, Ina and Edith, as the trio, clad in sealskins and white coats, "glided down amidst the beautiful palaces". Alarmed that his daughters might drift idly past the splendour, the Dean sent them a stern injunction – "ask the names and remember them".

(Though the silent gondoliers failed to confirm the idea that Italy rang to the sound of music, the sisters heard *Aida* – two months after its premiere to celebrate the opening of the Suez Canal – at La Scala, Milan, and the famous Madame Patti in concert at San Carlo, Naples. They listened with informed and practised ears, not merely awed by the occasion. For Alice, Miss Patti's style was too much embroidered, with "cadenzas, trills and turns and all the various little things" that took the heart from the music.)

Rome, the Tiber, 1871, from a family album.

South to Rome and Naples – where the three sisters trod ground the Dean had never seen, though he might have been anxious had he known in advance that the ground included the summit of Mount Vesuvius, still active and, after the eruption of 1868, higher than ever. The small town of Rosina made its living out of this foolhardiness of travellers wanting to stand on the very brink of the "hell of boiling fire". There were guides galore (most of them answering to the name Giovanni Cozzolino – whom *Murray* recommended), sedan chairs with bearers, and a horde of peasants enticing climbers with baskets of bread, eggs, wine and fruit.

Vesuvius and Naples, watercolour by Alice.

Previous English visitors had recorded burning more than their fingers in the ascent. In 1844, climbing an ice-covered Vesuvius by moonlight, Charles Dickens rolled down from the very lip of the crater with three companions, "blackened and singed and scorched and hot and giddy; and each with his dress alight in half a dozen places". The Liddell sisters were borne progressively closer to the summit by carriage, pony, chair and finally feet; they stood by the crater hot-footed, listening to the "loud reports", amid stifling clouds of sulphur, and "showers of stones and lumps of red hot stuff and puffs of smoke". They scree-ran down through knee-deep cinders. Three days later Ina still felt "knocked up"; the Dean helped revive her with the fact that "the late Duke of Buckingham, a large man, had twenty-eight men to carry him up Vesuvius". A month after the sisters' ascent, Vesuvius erupted again, killing sightseers, damaging towns, flinging huge stones 2,000 feet into the air and darkening the sky. The Liddells were still close enough to reflect that they might well have seen Naples and died.

After Vesuvius, nothing quite so raced the pulses, but visits to Capri, Sorrento and Pompeii helped to make Naples the focal point for reminiscence. Alice recorded their delight sensitively with pen, pencil and brush:

Capri and Ischia, watercolours by Alice.

Sorrento stands at the top of very high steep rocky cliffs and high-peaked mountains at the back covered with a most luxuriant vegetation; further on we came to another high cliff going down sheer into deep clear water, every shade,

Capri, south side, watercolour by Alice.

colour and shadow reflected in its depths of brilliant blue – the sun behind, that is facing us, causing slanting lights catching bits of the bright green and the lovely shades a kind of violet purple, and all the sharp shapes of the hills covered with olive trees, figs, orange and lemon trees – all looking so soft and velvety as the sun caught them . . . I cannot tell or hardly feel myself how perfect it is . . .

Alice usually belittled her own skill: "I drew Mrs Penn and Ina in their hammocks; the chief beauty in this sketch is the extraordinary likeness of Mrs Penn's hat . . . It is most disheartening trying to colour about this part of the world – it is so vivid and beautiful."

At Pompeii the sisters were relieved to disprove *Murray's* disparaging assertion that of the thirty official guides "some are intelligent, but these are the exceptions". They marvelled at the 1,800-year-old shops complete with signs and marble counters; they reflected (ruefully, in the light of their recent experience of continental hotels) that the ancient Pompeians had soap; but they left with one odd question unanswered, to tax the Dean with later – "Could you sit down in a chariot?"

Sketch by Alice.

Towards the end of April the Mediterranean season expired as the fashionable migrated north. When the *Kathleen* returned to Nice, the Liddells found themselves laggards in the general exodus: "Yesterday we were the only people at table d'hôte . . . the Grand Monde took their departure about a fortnight ago." There was a distinct feeling of sitting in the theatre with the play over and the audience gone home; so the remaining days were flat and occupied solely with shopping. Alice apologised for this descent into triviality. Back in London, heads full of sunny images, they met the Dean to see more tangible pictures – at the Royal Academy private view. Then to Oxford on a significant day for Alice: "Saturday, May 4th, twenty years old – home again!"

Sketch by Alice.

"March 21st. Today it is snowing! Happy you to be basking in the Southern Italian sunshine." At home in Oxford the weather and events had conspired to make the Dean and Mrs Liddell gloomy and envious, even within forty-eight hours of their girls' departure: "The house is awfully dull and quiet – Papa and I are quite tired of each other already, and he has removed his place to the side instead of the bottom of the table." Only weeks later the Dean buried his father:

The funeral was on Thursday, when you were, I hope, happily engaged at Rome, seeing new and beautiful things and little dreaming of our sad occupation. The morning was fine; only at eleven o'clock, as we went to the church, it clouded over and a sharp shower fell as we stood and saw his dear remains placed in the grave – over your poor old grandmama, whom you can be said never to have known, so changed was she from what she once was. As we returned, the sun broke out, and there was a beautiful rainbow over Battledown with the dear, old house in the middle of it. It was to me a beautiful and very touching sight – a symbol of bright hope and future promise at the moment when we had parted with the poor mortal remains of one whom I can truly call my oldest and dearest friend.

Dordrecht, watercolour by Dean Liddell.

The bereavement, wintry weather and rheumatism eventually drove the Dean and Mrs Liddell from Oxford on a less Grand Tour of their own – first to Buxton (a disaster), then to Aix-la-Chapelle, which simply proved how much

Mrs Liddell, anonymous sketch.

happier their daughters were in the Mediterranean, free from the medical regimen of "taking the waters". "This place is quite empty and not a little dull. We have a splendid hotel making up two hundred beds, nearly to ourselves . . . Before breakfast we go out and drink two or three glasses of hot water, smelling strongly of rotten eggs, but not tasting as bad. Your Mama drinks a couple of glasses, *why*, I do not know, and she makes Hathaway (her maid) do the same." The snow, too, had drifted over from England behind them: "The room was colder than a cave in an iceberg. I went to bed in a flannel shirt, socks, gown and an eiderdown bed over all, and then I shivered." The Dean and Mrs Liddell were relieved to scurry back to England, though the misery which dogged their trip hounded them to the very shore at Boulogne: "Instead of a roomful (at table d'hôte), we had only eight or nine somewhat vulgar Englishmen and one Englishwoman, fat and forty but not fair . . . We have been down to the end of the pier, seen the boat come in from England, full of pale, cold, miserable-looking wretches – two wedding pairs, woefully, woebegone."

As spreading Llandudno swallowed up Penmorfa, Mrs Liddell set her heart on the remoter wildernesses of Scotland, with a preference for Skye. The Dean shivered at the prospect, and it took him six years even to warm to the idea. He could back his coolness with distinguished authority: Skye's most famous tourist, Dr Johnson, arriving a century before, overweight, hypochondriacal and enduring boundless inconvenience, dismissed the island in a devastating catalogue of epigrams: in general – "conveniences are not missed where they are never enjoyed"; on conversation – "the inquirer . . . by a kind of intellectual retrogradation, knows less as he hears more"; on gardens – "few vows are made to Flora in the Hebrides"; and on Talisker – "the place beyond all that I have seen from which the gay and the jovial seem utterly excluded, and where the hermit might expect to grow old in meditation, without the possibility of disturbance or interruption." Queen Victoria and Prince Albert had, in effect, concurred, venturing only once up the west coast of Scotland, but

Skye, watercolours by Alice.

retreating before bad weather and opting instead for Balmoral.

An entertaining diary at Tetbury shows that by 1878 Mrs Liddell's opinion had prevailed over faint-hearted royalty and the dogmatic Dr Johnson; and to Skye the Liddells went, as guests of the Macleods of Dunvegan Castle, reputedly the oldest inhabited castle in Britain, updated with pseudo-baronial accretions in the 1840s, and boasting Flora Macdonald's stays among its trophies. Even Dr Johnson had conceded that the Macleods, unlike their bellicose forebears who wiped out the Macdonalds, had acquired mainland sophistication and "all the modes of English economy". The Dean could therefore take heart that, however bleak the environs, the castle would be a haven. During their stay three or four of the family took turns in keeping the holiday diary, while Alice added pen drawings as an amusing complement to the narrative.

DISCOVERED AT BREAKFAST BY AN OXFORDSHIRE FRIEND (INVERNESS)

WITH OUR PARCELS WE MAKE A START FROM INVERNESS.

Forty-eight hours travelling from King's Cross, via Inverness and the Strome Ferry, brought the Liddells (with two maids) to Portree on Skye, where they disembarked, only to fare worse than Dr Johnson, who at least secured "a very good dinner, port and punch" at the Royal Hotel. The Liddells found no porters to heave the luggage up the precipitous path, nor rooms or (at first) even food at the hotel: the townsfolk were all busily and exclusively occupied in the important ceremony of the Highland games.

The solution – a quick dinner of cold chicken ("probably stolen from the ball supper"), a telegraph to Dunvegan Inn (twenty-four miles distant), and then on into the darkness by horse and cart on a journey which the innkeeper

NO PORTERS !!

PORTREE HOTEL
HIGHLAND GAMES. THE DOOR OF THE HOTEL. DISTRIBUTING THE PRIZES.

Where are the cloaks?

Ye bankes & braes.

optimistically estimated at four hours. But he forgot the "banks and braes" and their effect on the poor horses. One beast fell soon after starting, and the Liddells had to walk most of the hills; they stumbled into Dunvegan Inn at 2.15 a.m., six hours later.

The next morning they climbed the steps of the castle, their real destination, and joined a house party of two pairs of English lords and ladies and numerous Macleods, including "His Reverence", the Head of the Clan. As Dr Johnson had found, the family boasted "all the arts of southern elegance"; for the Liddells that meant dressing for dinner, whist and a score of *HMS Pinafore,* with which Alice and others "drove the rest of the company crazy".

Trying on H.M.S. Pinafore in the drawing room.

Practise ye offe "H.M.S. Pinafore" in ye Fairie Towere

Two days and a steady downpour of rain later, a "red letter day" – an expedition to Macleod's Maidens – not the clansman's harem, but three spectacular rock pillars at the entrance to Loch Bracadale (and named after the wife and daughters of a fourteenth-century chief who were said to have been shipwrecked and drowned there).

On Sunday some of the party dutifully attended the local "kirk". "The service was in English, but there was a Gaelic christening, prayer and hymn. The music of the hymn was of the queerest kind: the clerk first chanted a line, and then sang it, while the female part of the congregation warbled away at their own sweet wills. At the end came a somewhat comical announcement of 'Whether there will be a service in

this church or not next Sabbath I dunnot know but due notice will be given!' "

A gentle Sunday afternoon sail on the loch turned into a drenching and exhausting labour, because the Liddell crew knew little of boats and could not distinguish between "peak halyards" and "main stays".

At the third attempt – twice thwarted by rain – the party made the trip to Quiraing (a remarkable flat-topped rock with precipitous sides). It was a long day by carriage, steam launch and on foot. On the way Mr Rory Macleod, talking heatedly, suffered from spontaneous combustion as a box of fuses ignited in his pocket. The party also saw for the first time the "real" Skye of poor and insecure tenant crofters:

"We found an old woman, chickens, cats and dogs (generally a cow is included in the livestock) living in one small room, with one small window about a foot square, and the fire in the middle with the smoke finding its way out as best it could amongst the peat and straw composing the roof." (An insurrection of crofters at Braes the next year brought fifty Glasgow policemen over by ferry to fight a pitched battle of sticks and stones. Warships were despatched, and marines even landed at Uig; Gladstone set up a "royal commission of Skye".) On the descent from Quiraing, the brief good weather broke, the steam launch could hardly make way against rain, wind and tide, and Mrs Liddell suffered "agonies of fright" before being landed very wet and very cold but safe back on the rocks of Grishornish.

Scottish watercolour by Dean Liddell.

The next day the family bid farewell to Dunvegan and drove back to Portree (Rory Macleod accompanying them on foot the twenty-four miles at a steady trot). One last excursion, up Glen Sligachan to Cornisk, started in brilliant sunshine but ended after only six miles with thick mist and blinding sheets of rain which turned the track into a watercourse. Back at the hotel came a ritual "comforting" of tea, blankets, footbaths and borrowed clothes.

For three days the family sat imprisoned at Portree by "equinoctial gales! and deluge! ditto, ditto, very much ditto!" before escaping by ferry past Armadale, seat of the Macdonalds, to the dreaded Ardnamurchan Point ("where the Atlantic waves roll grandly in, and one can really say there is nothing between us and America"). While the maids "quickly succumbed", Mrs Liddell "sat bravely on the bridge and defied the power of wind and waves". Thence to the mainland at Oban, and on to Ina at her new home at Pitlour: "Tableau: affectionate greetings and meetings. Dinner. Bed. The End."

Dunvegan Castle, watercolour by Alice.

6
THE VELVET LIFE

May 8th, 1862: "Dear Mama, I have got on very badly my watch is an hour to late made a good hit, your son RGH." Thus in an unpunctuated catalogue of minor disasters in punctuality and triumphs in cricket, began the career at Eton of nine-year-old Reginald Gervis Hargreaves. His doting mother, Anna Maria, had delivered him to the school one week earlier, his trunk bulging with every defence against the world and the devil: "16 shirts, 4 nightshirts, 6 prs drawers, 24 prs socks, 5 prs boots, slippers, 18 pocket handkerchiefs, 3 blanket ties, cap, 6 prs trousers, 4 waistcoats, 5 jackets, railway wrapper, blanket, button hook, hat brush, clothes brush, umbrella, 2 hair brushes, 2 hats, 2 cricketing shirts, dressing-gown, great coat, jersey, deal box, Bible and prayerbook." For all that, he forgot his toothbrush and comb. Nevertheless, he survived; and eighteen years later Reginald married Alice Liddell. It was a marriage that lasted forty-six years.

If Alice had had her way, Reginald's first letter from Eton would have been consigned to destruction along with hundreds of others. At the age of eighty, six years after Reginald's death, Alice disposed of her memories to her son: "I am sending you the rest of the Liddell/Hargreaves correspondence to deal with; probably all to go into the fire." What stayed his hand? Perhaps his eye fell on a cry from the dead, wrapped around a bundle of letters: "I ask my children to read my letters before burning them – they will speak for me."

The plaintive voice is that of Anna Maria Hargreaves, Reginald's solicitous mother. She was in all things nothing if

Reginald Hargreaves.

not earnest and passionate; letters for her were much more than idle communication: in hers she bared her soul, and her heart bled ink. But for her plea for posthumous notice, the immediate story of the family into which Alice Liddell married would consist mainly of scattered smudges in offical registers. Instead, hundreds of unsorted letters and diaries with a beautiful sketchbook survive at Tetbury, fragments of a story both sumptuous and tragic.

Anna Maria's life hung by the thread of her utter devotion to Jonathan Hargreaves, her husband, one of six sons of a family made rich by calico printing in Lancashire. Before their marriage she suffered like any heroine of a three-volume romance, learning Jonathan's love letters by heart and reciting them in his absence. Each day without him seemed an age, and the rooms "vacant and wanting". For weeks Anna Maria kept a lovesick journal, writing by candlelight at midnight on her knees: "How can I tell you what I do, day after day – it is the same tale over and over again, for, let me do what I will, the thought of you is like some sweet low melody, which I love to listen to, but which is unperceived by others." Hers was a passion that would bring as much pain as bliss; Anna Maria had early intimations of tragedy: "I have been crying bitterly . . . I have decided that I could not give you up – if there really is any chance of sorrow, I will share it with you." Had she known the truth, that would have only doubled Anna Maria's love, knowing that happiness had to be counted by the day.

For ten years after their marriage Anna Maria and Jonathan counted their blessings, and in 1856 felt secure enough in the future to buy Cuffnells, a Georgian country mansion in a hundred-and-fifty acre estate at Lyndhurst in the New Forest. Within twenty-five years Alice was to be mistress of the house.

Cuffnells stood grandly enough to attract the attention of those who did for houses what *Burke's Peerage* does for people. Brayley's and Britten's *Beauties of England and Wales* (volume six!) sites Cuffnells on the elite map, as the former property of Sir George Rose, statesman and friend of George III (himself a frequent visitor). Via Sir Edward

Cuffnells.

Sketches by Jonathan.

Anna Maria Hargreaves.

Jonathan Hargreaves.

Poore it passed to the Hargreaves family, and for seven years they lived a mid-Victorian idyll in a spacious setting where to be anything less than stately would have been puny: drawing room 42 feet by 24 feet, dining room 36 feet by 24 feet, library 24 feet square, orangery 100 feet by 20 feet. The best bedroom boasted gold fittings, a gilded four-poster and, inevitably, a plaque announcing that a monarch had slept there. There were eleven other principal bedrooms, four bathrooms, four maids' bedrooms, three rooms for men servants, six W.C.s. Below-stairs: housekeeper's room, servants's hall, kitchen (large), scullery, larders and pantry. Outside stood three loose boxes, coach-house, harness room, groom's room and fully equipped laundry. Two drives, each five hundred yards long, swept away from the house to the roadside lodges.

To the south Cuffnells commanded views over the Solent and Isle of Wight, while in a corner of the estate the family created a prospect that ran from the orient and tropics to the arctic. This acre they called the "Wilderness", a name which belied their careful cultivation of rare trees and shrubs. The family planted a private Eden, which lent Reginald's geography textbooks at Eton a spell denied to others. Reading of "the Victoria Regis, the palm, the baobab, the banyan, teak, mahogany, rosewood, Nicaragua-wood, and a climber on the River Magdalena with flowers four feet in circumference" made Reginald sick for home, while his friends merely conned the catalogue by rote in fear of a flogging.

According to Anna Maria's diaries, the Hargreaves also stamped their extravagant style on the interior of Cuffnells: two imported Italian artists spent seven months on the drawing-room friezes alone. Although she never expected them to be scoured by strangers, the diaries press no family skeletons between their pages; they offer glimpses of the velvet life within the four-score walls – a life propped up by staggering expense (£994 in 1863 for general housekeeping *alone*). On one shopping expedition to London Anna Maria amassed (among many other parcels): ivory brushes, crinolines for her daughters, Fanny and Emma, a cage for Fanny's bird, a gold pen, French books, white satin opera

Sketch by Anna Maria.

cloak, jet earrings and a velvet jacket from Marshall and Snelgrove. The house, too, consumed as ravenously as its occupants, yearly devouring thirty-five tons of coal and seven tons of coke.

Meals at Cuffnells, in an age which dined well as an article of faith in the progress of civilisation, often crossed the fine divide between healthy appetite and gluttony, though the blend of flavours might taste odd on modern palates. "Tea – twists, buns, ham, shrimps, mutton cutlets, potted meat, strawberries, marmalade; early dinner – fish, quarter of lamb, couple boiled chickens, pickled pork, salmon, tapioca pudding, little rice puddings, corn flour mould, gooseberry cream pancakes." Anna Maria entertained so lavishly that at times she seemed to be offering sustenance to all-comers. In July 1861 she reported a "feast" of buns, tea and fruit for over two hundred schoolchildren; their numbers were swelled by the teachers and "our neighbours" (eighty-four of them!) Anna fed the multitude in strict observance of social order: the children gorged buns on the grass; their teachers – with a table set apart on the terrace – munched bread and butter and soda cakes; the neighbours – served at a table which ran the length of the dining room – nibbled ham, roast beef, tongue and veal, and sipped wine. Anna Maria's hospitality knew no bounds: "I had nine dressed dolls for the

Sketch by Anna Maria.

Anna Maria, Fanny and Emma Hargreaves.

Sketch by Anna Maria.

girls to run for and eighteen gay handkerchiefs for the boys to swarm for and twelve bottles of bonbons to scramble for – and a bat and ball for the best cricket player." She does not say what hurt accrued to limbs and pride in the battle for prizes, nor how a hundred boys scrimmaged at cricket in the park on a single afternoon.

Anna Maria dispensed tears as readily as charity. She lived on sensitive heights that made her vulnerable, naive, occasionally tiresome, but unfailingly compassionate – for example, towards a poor neighbour, Betty Fythian:

I went to her old cottage in the forest – we found the door locked and a little cart carrying away some of their goods . . . and a woman told us they were taken to the poorhouse on Monday. Poor things, my heart ached for them to have left all the old familiar things and the tufts of spring flowers in the garden and their free life under the great trees, to be lost among the other paupers in a whitewashed poorhouse. So I begged a bouquet of primroses and wallflowers out of their garden and drove to the poorhouse

Regi, Emma and Fanny.

after lunch and took them flowers and a little tea. I found them both in bed with their arms around each other – as if their only comfort was to be close together and to indulge their sorrow in peace. Poor Betty burst into tears and threw her arms around me and kissed me as if I had been her mother . . . It was a pitiful sight but I intend to go often and see her and bring her here.

The urbane and hospitable face which Cuffnells turned to the world masked the drudgery of some ten servants. In Anna Maria's diaries they usually live on their knees: "Ellen pours a little beer or porter on the oak floors and then scours . . . in waxing she first dusts the floor, then brushes and afterwards polishes with a piece of cloth." Full wages were only topped up after a year's satisfactory toil. One servant, at least, did not last the course: "She is to come this day fortnight if her character is satisfactory – to have £9 9s a year but I am to make it £10 if I keep her the year." Anna Maria later added in angry rubric: "her character NOT satisfactory".

A house party at Cuffnells.

The Gervises at Hinton.

The Hargreaves children – Reginald, Emma and Fanny – lived a cosseted routine of drives, expeditions, teaparties with croquet, lessons in music, drawing and dancing, and outings to Hinton for boating with their cousins, the Gervises. With so little adversity, it was easy to be "good", though the infant Reginald reassured his mother in terms both unctuous and precocious. "Regi said to me, 'Mama, when I am as old as you are, shall you be as old as granny?' I said, 'Yes, shall you love me if I am?' 'Oh yes,' he answered with deep feeling, 'I shan't care if you *are* changed.' And then taking my hand very fondly and looking in my face, he added, 'I shall be a thousand times gooder to you when I'm a big man than I am now.' "

Reginald.

Although Cuffnells was home, the Hargreaves owned an earlier family seat, an outpost in the North, Oak Hill, near Accrington. There were still prospects sylvan enough for Anna Maria to reach for her paintbrush, but she found the North stark and grim: "Went with Barbara to Haworth, the dreary home of Charlotte Bronte . . . I made a little sketch . . . saw the register of the marriage which she had signed with shaking hand. Mrs Gaskell's is a very good and not too overdrawn description of this stony, drear, upland village; I have seen many of the same general character in

Lancashire, but none so utterly hopelessly bare and devoid of every adjunct which give a grace and charm to life."

The grace and charm of life at Cuffnells distracted the family from chronic fears over Jonathan's health. There were alarming symptoms of decline in 1859 and Anna Maria consulted a doctor in Malvern; he prescribed a harsh regimen of three different baths every day and an insipid diet of lean meat, bread and butter and cold tea. (This was the infamous Dr Gully, whose aversion to drug therapy and hot drinks led to his setting up a fashionable hydropathic practice; he numbered Darwin, Tennyson and Carlyle among his patients. Later, Dr Gully was ruined by the sensational scandal over his love affair with Florence Ricardo and the poisoning of her husband by antimony.) Despite Dr Gully's cranky intervention, Jonathan recovered, and for three more years metaphorically the sun shone. In the winter of 1862 the family sought the sunshine abroad, but the journey was to end under a tragic cloud.

Accrington, watercolour by Anna Maria.

Crossing the Channel, they shared the boat – the West Indian Packet – with a crowd of Creole ladies escaping from New Orleans, where they had abandoned their property, "glad to save life and honour". They warned Anna Maria of the drunken brutality of the ship's captain, but the family reached France unscathed and travelled south to Cannes, where Fanny and Emma had music lessons and they all promenaded under the orange trees with their scented blossoms. Jonathan ate well, slept well and his breathing eased. Anna Maria shared her relief with her sister, Mary, at home: "Such a flood of light, bright, sweet, warm air must do everyone good."

Exhilarated, they moved on towards Rome, via Leghorn, where Anna Maria bought souvenirs on a typically grand scale – four alabaster ornaments, two marble pillars and several bronzes. In Rome after Christmas they felt like pilgrims at the shrine. For a month they engaged "a handsome pair of black horses and two carriages (one open, one closed), with a civil intelligent coachman". The journey ended at Rome in a sense that none had foreseen. For two weeks Anna Maria's diary was blank; then she pencilled a hurried tribute to Jonathan which could only be

Two Italian pictures from Anna Maria's scrapbook.

Wurzburg, watercolour by Emma Hargreaves.

posthumous: "never spoke against anyone or remarked upon their defects – never at any time, even with me alone spoke of women without virtue . . . as far as earthly virtue can be – actual perfection".

The events of that silent fortnight in Rome emerge from Anna Maria's letters: "January 15th. I have great anxiety over Jonathan, who is unwell – he was attacked a week ago with incessant coughing which lasted a day and a night without intermission – so that you may imagine how extremely reduced he is." The doctor diagnosed bronchitis and prescribed mustard plaster. Anna Maria took heart – "Jonathan is now sleeping as I write (noon) and more tranquilly – I trust it may please God that the worst is now over." But on January 25th Anna asked her sister to send two pounds of tea, all Jonathan could allow past his lips. He could not even lie down in his bed of Indian corn leaves; so they propped him up with cushions in the faded grandeur of the sitting room, with its painted ceiling, hangings of rich cherry and gold damask, and massive centre table of marble on gilt legs. There Jonathan died the next day.

Anna Maria was inconsolable. Although the family doctor painted the grimmer alternative of a "longer decline with all the inevitable sufferings of extreme exhaustion", Jonathan's sudden death threw a long shadow over the rest of her own short life. She never wrote of her husband without standing him on a pedestal of superlatives: best, purest, most unselfish, liberal, modest, guiltless. Eleven months passed before she received any neighbours at Cuffnells, and a year and a half before she allowed herself a public smile: "I gave a croquet party – the first gaiety at Cuffnells since my best beloved, my precious, pure husband died."

Brighter images punctured the gloom at Cuffnells in Anna Maria's letters to Reginald at Eton. "I am having the grass mown in the Wilderness and it looks charming – the young trees look so much taller without the high grass around them." "I have been round the Wilderness and the rhododendrons are a blaze of colour . . . It is quite like an enchanted grove. . . and then I loiter under the refreshing deep shade of the great birches with the wood sorrel and ivy making such an exquisite carpet for the stately feet to rest on . . . Fanny and Emma are playing croquet in front of the library window . . . The water hens are strolling around on the lawn." Fanny and Emma rode their ponies, Hall Barn and Gypsy, took music lessons and embroidered. They also kept tame chaffinches, one of which, called Tiny, was "so tame that this morning Emma let him fly about her dressing room and it came to her and pecked some crumbs from her lips".

Reginald and the Bishop of Lichfield.

Anna Maria had always observed and felt with the sensibility of a fine artist. Now she read sermons in stones, and saw haunting reminders all around her: "Yesterday we went to the castle (the one you can see from both Wolhayes and Sandhills and belongs to Lady Stuart). It made me think of Italy – the out-of-repair dilapidated look and the collection of furniture indoors and the groups of ilexes in the grounds completed the illusion, for the ilex so nearly resembles the olive – and the fountain and the stone balustrade – all neglected and yet gay with tangled flowers – carried my thoughts back to the Mediterranean. The gorgeous colouring and the dark shadows were, however, wanting. Do you remember the Appian road with the aqueducts leaping across the campagna? And the glorious sky and the distant snow-capped mountains? How beautiful it was!"

The spirit of Jonathan breathed from the most mundane of things, and Anna Maria focused on Reginald at Eton a love frustrated in the death of his father. Her love could scarcely brook physical separation, and at the end of each term Anna Maria yearned for her son with the longing of a separated lover: "It is music to think of really seeing you next week – to put my hands on your shoulders and look into your face." With Jonathan's mortal weakness to haunt her, Anna Maria begged Reginald for news of the slightest sniffle or sore throat. In 1863 Reginald caught measles (having escaped scarlet fever); Anna Maria whisked him back to Cuffnells: "he wore a respirator – had medicated cotton wool all over his back and chest – his great coat – Fanny's fur coat – his cap – and his little plaid over it."

The health of Reginald's soul obsessed Anna Maria even more; hardly a letter to him closed without a homily that he should strive to be a soldier in Christ. She paraded in front of

The family at Fleetwood, watercolour by Anna Maria.

him a gallery of heroes to emulate, chief among them by a head his dead father: "I will tomorrow copy out a short psalm which seems to me such an exact portrait of your dead Papa's character." Stonewall Jackson also marched in the ranks of worthies; and in 1864 Reginald reported awestruck, on the visit to Eton of another – at least in popular esteem – great, good, modest hero: "Yesterday I saw Garibaldi just as I came out of mathematics he was driving a carriage and his beard and hair are reddish." Three days later: "On Monday he went away from Eton . . . there was a tremendous crowd but I managed to get within two feet of him . . . he has grey not red hair." (A few months later, appeared "Garibaldi" biscuits; Reginald found them "awfully jolly".) Anna Maria directed Reginald's gaze to qualities less accidental than the colour of Garibaldi's hair: "I am so glad you saw Garibaldi . . . He is a great man – so simple and pure from personal ambition – that you may be pleased in years to come that you saw his noble head as a boy at school."

Reginald's letters from Eton were for his mother "the

Emma and Fanny at Swanage, watercolour by Anna Maria.

greatest treat I get – they drop like sunbeams into my heart". But what more dispassionate beams of light do they throw on Alice's future husband? For whatever reason, Reginald never mentioned his father in a single letter; and he usually ignored his mother's injunctions, apart from the occasional misspelt boast of his piety: "Today I said the nineteenth plasm." Reginald did acquiesce readily in *one* of his mother's wishes – to put his health before work. His letters were dictionaries of symptoms – partly of others (such as his friend, Chandos Pole, who was committed to the sanatorium – "he has hiccups bad, the truth"). But the chief patient was himself: he suffered an unending series of coughs, colds, boils, blisters, minor injuries and teeth falling out; they conveniently meant "staying out" – that is, not going in for lessons. Two other recurrent themes indicate his real interests – cricket and food hampers.

Reginald's time at Eton fell within one of its most momentous decades in its history. For those who believed in portents, symbolic acts of God – an earthquake and several

George Meyrick.

floods – suggested that the corrupt old order was about to be swept away. The moths of reform had fretted at the ancient fabric and left it looking threadbare. Tales of the legendary John Keate still spiced the air; he arrived as headmaster in 1809 to shake up an idle and debauched staff, one an opium-eater, who often appeared incoherent before his classes, two more who spent dissipated weekends in London and might or might not have been fit for school on Monday. Keate assailed the boys with the birch, impelled by a simple principle: never believe a boy is telling the truth if there is the slightest possibility of his lying. In 1810 he publicly beat eighty boys at one go, while being showered with rotten eggs by the onlookers. Half a century later in Reginald's letters boys and staff still fought: "Last week a master told a boy to do Horace, to which he replied, 'How will you have it, sir – roast or boiled?' And another boy, when his tutor said, 'You are an ass,' said, 'Then there are two of us.' "

Reginald was an *oppidan* – he boarded out in one of a number of houses run by redoubtable "dames". That spared him the privations of the school's poorer relations, the seventy scholars, who worked little, ate less, played much and slept hardly in Long Chamber. *Oppidans,* by comparison, dined off the fatted calf, garnished in Reginald's case by frequent hampers from Fortnum and Mason: potted meats and pies, ham, tongue, strawberry jam, Yorkshire pie, rabbit cake, "jujube" and *sucre de pomme* – probably all at one sitting. Breakfast provided the opportunity to impress friends and outdo rivals. "George came to breakfast this morning. I regaled him with grilled turkey, chutney and marmalade." George was a cousin and younger than Reginald; for that he paid the inevitable penalty: "I have been up to George's room this afternoon. I always eat some of his things when I go there to prevent his having enough to get ill on."

The *oppidans* brought a flash of the debonair to the greyness of lessons. Reginald filled his letters with redolent details: "Piggy Colville has been to Sweden aboard his father's yacht"; "there is a new boy called ffarington, who spells his name with two little ff's"; "On Friday I went to Lords and divided my time between the carriages of Lady

Manners and the Walkers." The *oppidans* paraded themselves, precocious masters of fashion, dressing well so as not to be shown up by their peers. The teachers copied their wardrobe, afraid to be shown up by the boys. (E.C. Hawtrey, headmaster from 1834 to 1853, cut a dash more as gentleman than as scholar: it was reputed that he "stood up in £700".) When a boy wanted (or needed) new clothes, he applied to his tutor for an "order", which was then handed to his tailor. "Need" was broadly defined, otherwise Reginald would have been hard-pressed to reason his needs. At the age of eleven he demanded real onyx buttons for his waistcoat (at twelve shillings a set); silver buttons he dismissed as "second-best". A year later he felt the uncomfortable frowns of more chic colleagues: "I want to get a silk umbrella because everyone here has them and I should feel ashamed to go about with an alpaca." In the Remove he sported a sealskin waistcoat and crowned the effect with floral swank: "I have made a contract with a woman to have two flowers for my buttonhole every week to the end of the half for 2s 6d."

Watercolour by Anna Maria.

The keystone of Reginald's curriculum at Eton was, still, as it had always been, the study of classics; though, if keystone implies solidity, it might be more appropriate to say that classics still shored up the flimsy structure of lessons. Reginald had no pretensions in this field: "I am getting on badly with my Latin and worse with my Greek . . . I hope I shall not get swished." He could consider himself fortunate: until ten years before, every boy had to draw a map of part of the ancient world every week and learn the names of obscure modern hamlets on classical sites. While they were allowed to remain blissfully unaware of the whereabouts of Moscow or Boston, boys were flogged for not knowing Ramadan Oglu.

Reginald's first tutor, Jack Hawtrey (one of a famous family that bred a Provost of Eton and a popular comedian), reported on his "manliness and good sense", and so fed Anna Maria the food she craved; Reginald only yearned to escape

> Out of the clutches of birch and block;
> Out of the clutches of Hic, Hac, Hoc.

Eton versus Harrow at Lords.

But he moved on to a tutor, Rouse, who punished him more often and "swished" him for "being on intimate terms with a big boy up in the school". Anna Maria leapt to Reginald's defence: "flogging is no disgrace if unjustly ordered and would not make me a hair's-breadth less proud of my precious boy."

Precious sons of anxious mamas who turn mothering into smothering often fall victims to ragging; and Eton had made an institution of bullying and violence. One boy recalled being ridden over insurmountable obstacles by another boy wearing spurs; the poet Shelley complained he was persecuted, but maltreated his own fags, harnessing two of them to a large brass cannon to drag into college; Lord Shaftesbury's brother was beaten to death in a fist fight that

Eton, the Fourth of June, from a watercolour possibly by the college drawing master, William Evans.

went sixty rounds and lasted two hours. Reginald escaped the bullies, untaunted and unbruised, protected by a genial fagmaster. But he witnessed "Poor Popham", a shy and confused small boy, mercilessly ragged for living under the thumb of a domineering mother. She insisted that he should wear black kid gloves all day.

Adolescent barbarity at Eton found licensed outlet in the new cult of sport. There, if anywhere, lay Reginald's prowess; he won his future battles not at the desk but on the playing fields. The great event each school year for him was the monosyllabic "Lords" – the annual cricket match against Harrow (first played at Lords in 1858). By comparison with these two golden days, all other occasions in the Eton calendar for Reginald paled into dull ritual; only once did he

Sketch by Reginald.

refer to the glorious "Fourth of June", and that disparagingly: "as usual it poured all day". Shouting for Eton against Harrow at cricket in the 1860s, however, was to side with the underdog. For three years in succession Harrow swept Eton for six. Everyone hoped 1867 would be different, with Eton's hopes pinned on the famous hitter, "Bun Jam", C.I. Thornton, terror of the coconut-shy holders at the Windsor Fair. But the match was a draw. Eton lost yet again in 1868, with "Bun Jam" as captain, and despite his hitting a ball clean over the pavilion. Only in 1869, Reginald's last-but-one year, did Eton destroy the old enemy. It was C.J. Ottaway's match: his century gave Eton a single-innings victory. Even the Provost of Eton, a cleric, went delirious, dancing round the ground like a bare-headed bacchanal.

To the compendium of useful knowledge gleaned from the classics in eight years at Eton, Reginald added the freaks of Reading Fair – "a child five years old which weighed eight stone" and "a blue horse with no hair on at all". Although on the evidence of his letters, English punctuation was for Reginald always a dangerous mystery, he knew quite as much as any young gentleman destined for life in a country house could be expected to know. Besides, he dressed impeccably and could shoot straight. With such weapons, Reginald could not be denied entry to the university at Oxford. His time served at Eton, he cast off its trappings: "My boots are now things of the past. I have got a very good pair of shoes from Hay for 12s 6d." Two quaint leaving ceremonies he was spared by recent changes. He did not have to appear before the provost in full evening dress (with knee breeches and silk stockings) to have his gown "ripped" in farewell. Nor was he expected to "tip" the headmaster by leaving a present on his desk; instead Reginald paid a new "capitation tax", which at once removed the embarrassment and the point of the earlier practice.

Sketch by Emma.

Debts settled and boots discarded, Reginald spent a few months relaxing and improving his aim, before his promotion to Christ Church College, Oxford. There he was to see, meet and fall in love with the daughter of the Dean, Miss Alice.

7
THY YOUNG LIFE'S HEREAFTER

Of all the letters Alice received in her life and thought worth preserving, one especially must have brought a lump to her throat and evoked wet-eyed memories of her girlhood in Oxford. It arrived, postmarked Capetown, in 1898, when Alice was forty-six, married for nearly two decades, with three growing sons, and far enough away from her "Carrollian" days for them to belong to a quite different clime. The letter is scrawled in the hand of one suffering pain or beyond caring about appearances; it is signed "Winchilsea" – that is, the Twelfth Earl of Winchilsea, Murray Edward Gordon Finch-Hatton, once Fellow of Hertford College, Oxford, MP for South Lincolnshire and noted agriculturalist. (His brother, Harold, who spent part of his life in Queensland, claimed to be the only white man who could throw the boomerang "like a black"; he married the sister of Edith Liddell's tragic fiancé, Aubrey Harcourt.) On the point of death in South Africa, Winchilsea took up his pen to write off the burden of a long-treasured affection: "Before this reaches you I shall be no more – I have been very ill and feel that it is coming – so I write if I may to wish you a cordial and affectionate farewell. Your husband will, I know, not mind my saying now that I was very fond of you in the old days at the Deanery where you were all so pretty and attractive, but you most of all to me. It was a time in one's life never to be forgotten – nothing was quite like the old Oxford days . . ."

Who else stood in the throng with Lord Winchilsea, among the young bucks of Christ Church, yearning for the soft touch and yielding looks of the daughters of the Dean?

Alice.

Ina, photograph by Charles Dodgson.

Starved of romantic adventure during term, in a university which dismissed women as brainless, if decorative chattels, the beaux of Oxford must have suffered like the princely heroes of medieval romances, who fell in love with distant, though irresistible maidens in gardens of roses. As rival suitors elbowed their way to a waltz or quadrille with Ina, Alice, Edith, Rhoda and Violet at college balls, or enticed them to supper with gallant *billets-doux*, one student, John Howe Jenkins, stood aloof from the crush and viewed the urbane dalliance through cynical eyes.

The main object of his scorn was Mrs Liddell and her (as Jenkins saw them) preposterous aspirations for her fillies in the marriage stakes. Jenkins sharpened up his pen to punctuate Mrs Liddell's inflated hopes in a scurrilous masque *Cakeless*, written in 1874. Jenkins was expelled for this labour of love, and his masque suppressed – though not totally obliterated: a copy survives in the British Library.

The plot of Jenkins' notorious opus centres on a joint wedding for three of the daughters of Apollo and Diana – classical masks for the Dean and Mrs Liddell. A chorus of drunken satyrs assess the state of the marriage bourse:

Apollo was a worthy peer
His daughters cost him many a frown,
Diana held them all too dear,
But Fife he brought the market down.

The unfortunate Fife who thus allegedly devalued the property, as surely as undesirables moving in up the street, was Willie Skene, of Hallyards and Pitlour, Fife, Fellow of All Souls College, and newly wedded to the eldest daughter, Ina, in February 1874.

There is a sentimental convention in fairy tales whereby beautiful princesses, sated with sumptuous offers of marriage from handsome princes commanding fortunes of gold and jewels, eventually fall in love with the plain pauper who offers only his heart. Those who hope that Ina's alliance to Willie is a tale of that ilk are destined to be disappointed. Willie Skene was no tattered indigent, however lowly Mrs Liddell assessed his eligibility. Two clues turned up at Tetbury to show that Ina embraced no bankrupt: first, a picture by Alice of Willie's house at Pitlour – more manor-house than humble cottage; and second, part of a letter, written many years later to Alice, in which Mrs Liddell reckons another suitor's worth in a manner as grand as Oscar Wilde's Lady Bracknell. In fact, Willie Skene was heir to ten or so large estates; and Ina brought him a marriage settlement of £8,000.

Pitlour House, watercolour by Alice.

Ina and Willie walked their red-carpeted way to the altar at Christ Church cathedral in February 1874. The sun on the morning frost, the flowers strewn at the bride's feet, the lace trimmings of her dress and its natural orange blossom – all struck the enraptured gaze of a local reporter, who saw the ladies as "finishing touches upon nature's lovely picture", and declared the whole panorama fit grist for the poetic mill.

If she thought Willie Skene poor on forty of fifty times a working man's wage, how high did Mrs Liddell aspire? Charles Dodgson thought she aimed at the highest seat in the land, the throne of England itself. In a satirical pamphlet *The Vision of The Three T's,* he referred to ". . . the Goldfish, which is a species highly thought of, not only by men, but by divers birds, as for instance the Kingfisher". The last word is a jibe at Mrs Liddell. Those who knew of Charles Dodgson's lickspittle antics with his own camera in front of royalty might have been tempted to remark that it took a kingfisher to know another one. And there may have been personal spite in Charles Dodgson's charge, if he was tasting the gall of a rejected suitor. The author of *Cakeless* thought so: in his masque the anti-hero is the pathetic figure of Kraftsohn (identified in the margin as Dodgson), who stands by furiously "biting his nails" in agonies of jealousy, before protesting to the match and trying to halt the ceremony. He suffers mortification and ragging; he is chased, imprisoned and ducked in the pond.

Christ Church Cathedral, after Dean Liddell's alterations.

If Mrs Liddell did really dream of a royal match, two English princes came at least physically within the embrace of her maternal bosom. The Prince of Wales came to Christ Church for two years' royal polish; the Dean found him "the nicest little fellow possible, so simple, naive, ingenuous and modest and moreover with extremely good wits; possessing

The Prince of Wales, c. 1860.

Prince Leopold, contemporary Oxford cartoon.

also the royal faculty of never forgetting a face." Even if Mrs Liddell concurred and thought this testimonial made him a fit paragon, she would surely have conceded that there was more than a touch of vainglorious presumption in casting the future king in the role of son-in-law, especially since her eldest daughter was only ten at the prince's arrival. The Liddells broke the ice of frigid protocol round the prince more than most; Alice even coyly remembered scuttling out of a room half-dressed as the butler announced His Royal Highness on a surprise visit to the Deanery. Generally, however, at Christ Church such a singular divinity hedged the heir to the throne as to keep a prescribed and measured distance between himself and others. He had private lectures from the Regius Professor of Modern History – attended otherwise by only the prince's tutor, equerry and four or five hand-picked undergraduates "to make an audience and afford the prince a sense of companionship". The professor, poor man, sat pilloried at one end of the room, flicking over the pages of a general history of England, talking extempore as names caught his eye. The small, elite audience sat at the other end. The air between must have been at best tense; and the arrangement favoured a discursive acquaintance rather than scholarly erudition on the part of the prince.

A younger brother, Prince Leopold, came to Christ Church in 1872. He and Alice were within a year of the same age, and inevitably during his stay in Oxford Leopold regularly accompanied the Liddells, sharing their love of the arts. There is, at Tetbury, a scrap of paper, part of Alice's pencilled notes for her recollections at eighty. It seems to be part of a longer story of her friendship with Leopold, and recalls an episode on a boating trip with the prince to Iffley, where Alice accidentally gave the prince a black eye with her oar. Leopold wondered what he would say to the Queen, who, thought Alice, would not have approved of such informal messing about in boats with young ladies. Anyway, Alice concluded, "I was never ordered to be beheaded." Oddly, neither this nor any other story of Leopold reached publication, perhaps because Alice, like others, felt it disloyal to recount that she saw Homer nodding. (There was something of a stir, for example, in 1895 when an early movie pioneer, Birt Acres, gatecrashed a Cardiff exhibition and filmed the Prince of Wales indulging in mortal weakness – scratching his head. To divert hostile attention, Acres felt obliged to explain away the gesture euphemistically as "an elementary placing of the hand to the ear, probably to brush away an intrusive fly".)

Alice's reticence on her friendship with Leopold may also have been mute and belated mourning for his tragically early death. Four years after Alice's marriage and two years after his own (to Princess Helena – the Dean and Mrs Liddell were included among the three hundred invitations), Leopold died at Cannes "from a breaking of blood vessel in the head" (words from the Queen's journal). To his mother it was more than the loss of a son: he was named after her uncle, Leopold, King of the Belgians – "It is a name which is the dearest to me after Albert, and one which recalls the almost only happy days of my sad childhood." She would have warmed to Alice's gesture in naming one of her sons, Leopold, and insisting that the name should be heard: "I have determined, unless you [her husband] object, to have Rex called 'Master Leopold' by the household. I believe it would be a good plan. 'Rex' is a mere nickname, after all. Think of this and approve." Prince Leopold had consented to be godfather to his namesake, and called his own daughter Alice.

There is a claim that a full-blooded romance "blossomed" between Alice and Leopold, that the subject of an impossible marriage between them "constantly recurred", that Leopold avoided Alice's wedding (unable to see her marrying another), and that for the rest of her life Alice carried the scars of a blighted love – but all that is a fancifully royal castle in the air, tottering on invisible foundations. The only direct communication surviving at Tetbury is a letter from Leopold, written on the eve of Alice's wedding, betraying no bruised hopes: "Dear Alice Liddell [even the surname!] . . . I send you the last photograph that was taken of myself, at Montreal. With it I send my warmest and most heart-felt wishes for your future happiness. I shall think much of you and your family tomorrow; for you know

Prince Leopold, signed photograph for Alice.

Reginald Hargreaves.

how I have felt and sympathised with you and yours, in your joys and your sorrows. Your dear sister, Edith, will also be much in my thoughts tomorrow." The letter, the signed photograph and the handsome brooch as a present are the gestures of a magnanimous family friend, whose affection, of course, embraced Alice.

In his masque, *Cakeless*, Jenkins dresses Alice in a see-through name, Ecilia; she enters with her two sisters to announce to mother her thoroughbred catch. But Jenkins' aim is askew: he calls Ecilia's happy man, Yerbua, surely Aubrey Harcourt, who two years later so tragically won and lost Edith. Perhaps Aubrey found Alice and Edith equally alluring and courted them both. If they returned his affection, there was a scenario for wrangling and rivalry.

Alice's real husband-to-be is spared exposure in *Cakeless*. But Reginald Hargreaves already stood in the wings and cast glazed eyes towards one, or two, of the heroines. By 1874, as a student at Christ Church, he had cut a gentlemanly dash at balls, dinners and in the right clubs, such as the St Aldates. Who knows when he and Alice first exchanged feeling glances; but a rapid acceleration in Reginald's pulse can be inferred from some petty lumber at Tetbury, mundane possessions endowed with romantic charisma and treasured for no better (or worse) reason than that they evoked the early days of Reginald's love, when the pounding heart ruled. There are three small, folded cards – dance programmes in which, in those days of formal etiquette, a gentleman would "book" his partners for the evening. Within these prosaic limits, Reginald's love bloomed. At a New Year ball at Chippenham he coolly booked two waltzes with "Miss E. Liddell" and "Miss A. Liddell". If the tunes carried innuendo, Edith took the bouquet with "*Amoretten Tanze*".

Whatever seeds were planted here took root, and six months later, at the summer ball at Christ Church, Reginald "booked" Alice and Edith again, now with trembling hand, on terms intimate enough for them to be recorded as "AL" and "EL", and with sufficient rapture to follow up the initials with strings of exclamation marks. In this solemn matter of punctuation marks (and in affairs of the heart who has not hung on such trivia?) Alice rated eighteen to Edith's fifteen. A year later, 1876, Aubrey Harcourt and fate had resolved Reginald's dilemma as to which sister to set his heart on. That year he was Hon. Sec. of the summer ball; he danced four times with Alice ("AL"), three times with "Miss Phipps" and once with other assorted "misses". Alice eclipsed Miss Phipps not only in the number of dances but also in sentiment: for her Reginald reserved the most romantic moments – waltzes such as "Sweethearts" and "*Le Premier Baiser*".

St Aldates Club, 1875.
(Reginald second from right).

Four years passed between these early flutterings and the marriage (by special licence of the archbishop) in Westminster Abbey, four dark years overshadowed by Edith's death, and on which records at Tetbury throw no light, but in which Reginald waited in agony, with Alice in no mood to think of marriage, so profoundly moved was she by the death of her sister. Then, on July 13th, 1880, Reginald proposed, was accepted and ended his "long miseries of uncertainty". Suddenly, like a bright flash of warm sunlight, came a flurry of letters – all culled now from boxes at Tetbury – which, better than any narrative, catch the exultation of the moment.

Alice to Ina, July 16th, 1880:

Your dear letters do amuse me so. I show little bits to Regi, but you write such embarrassing things in them, I can't show them all. He was "awfully" pleased with your dear little note to him: but, my darling, if the unfortunate man believes all he is told about me, I quite pity him! The congratulatory letters are very nice but how can I show all the pretty things people are so good to say they think of me . . . Katie was so pleased about it: she is a darling and even with tears in her eyes was so glad for me. She said a pretty thing, which, even at a chance of your thinking me "zum" vain, I shall tell you. "As I am a woman I am very glad," she said, "but if I was a man I should hang myself!" Dear Katie, I am so glad I saw her to tell her myself . . . As for the "ten minutes", we said something that virtually settled it, of course, coming away from the opera, but that was really much about the same as your letter in answer to

Cowes, 1877, unfinished watercolour
by Alice.

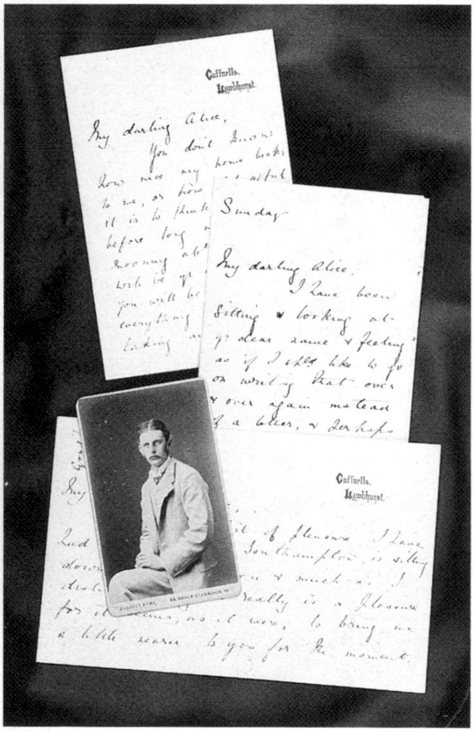

Willie's was! No fear; no one will ever beat you and Willie in your speedy arrangements. What a good old grandmother I was to you then, ma'am! I do miss not being able to tell you and talk to you, so don't mind my letters full of myself, thoughts, doings and Master RH.

Love also lent speed to Reginald's pen, the more remarkable in one who, in Alice's words, did not share *her* family's "craving for epistles".

My Darling Alice,
  I have been sitting and looking at your dear name and feeling as if I should like to go on writing that over and over again instead of a letter, and perhaps if I did so it would express what I feel better than any other words could do. What can I write, what can I say that is not summed up in those three little words, "I love you"? – you are the ocean to the river of my thoughts, for they all end in you, ah how dull it is only to be able to think of you, compared with seeing your sweet face; tomorrow never seemed so far off before,
Your Devoted Regi.

My Darling Alice,
  I watched you as long as I could comfortably with getting my breakfast on the train; what a pace you seemed to be going! I thought of the lines in Molloy's song:

My love has gone a-sailing
A-sailing o'er the sea;
Oh ship, sail fast,
Oh ship, sail sure,
And bring my love to me.

– ah, how happy it makes me to feel that you, my darling, think of me and pray for me as I do for you. I wonder where I shall meet you when I get back? Will you look as glad then, dear, as you did last Wednesday. May I not answer, "Yes"?

My Darling Alice,
  How I long to get your letter. I watched you for a long time at Bishopstoke before the train came past where you were standing and felt half-inclined, or rather longed to get

out the wrong side of my carriage and come across to the Botley train. How often I think of your last dear words to me before Bishopstoke. Do you think of me as often as I do of you, I wonder. It will take up most of your time if you do.

My Own Sweet Love,
The first bit of pleasure I have had since leaving Southampton is sitting down to write to you and, much as I dislike writing, it really is a pleasure, for it seems, as it were, to bring me a little nearer to you for the moment as I know the paper my hand is on will be in yours tomorrow morning . . . All the world here seem to know when and where we are to be married. I wonder if you looked out at the Abbey as you went by and thought how we shall each, and I oh so gladly, within its walls vow to love and honour the other till death us do part; what a solemn yet what a happy moment that will be! – for I shall have made sure of a happiness such as I have dreamt of and prayed for but such as God alone can give or take away from us.

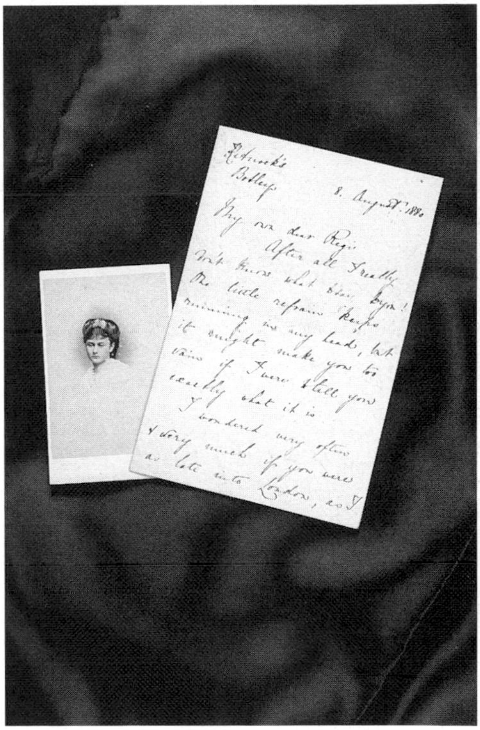

Cuffnells had been closed up since the death of Reginald's mother in 1872, but now the shutters were swung open and the dust sheets swept off:

Dearest Alice,
You don't know how nice my home looks to me, or how delightful it is to think that before long, instead of mooning about alone, it will be your home, too, and you will be looking at everything with me and taking an interest in the place I am so fond of. I think you would like it independently of me if you could see it this evening with the soft light of the sunset on it. How glad I am that it is not as ugly as the ring I gave you, or perhaps you might object to coming here at all.

A week before the wedding the new mistress saw Cuffnells for the first time:

Dearest Regi,
After all, I really don't know what to say to you! One little refrain keeps running in my head, but it might make you too

vain if I were to tell you what it is . . . I did not say very much to you yesterday, I think, but can you guess a little bit how enchanted I was? I hope it will be a real fairyland to us both as long as we are both permitted to enjoy it, dear; "Wonderland" come true to "Alice", at last! I thought you were not going to see me as your train went out of the station. Would not that have been terrible? But you did, and I felt a little glad.

Only one Liddell was not caught up in Alice's joy, but looked on the communal delirium with a cool adolescent gaze. That was young brother Eric, currently immersed in the works of Thucydides, Sophocles, Horace, Livy and Voltaire at Eton. From them he imbibed a somewhat cynical notion of wedded life, and penned some lines from Horace's *Epistles* which he hoped "would about express Regi's sentiments":

— Lectus genialis in aula est
Nil ait ipse prius, melius nil coelibe vita;
Si non est, jurat bene solis esse maritis.

– the gist of which is that bachelorhood is like most other blessings: you don't know how lucky you are till you've lost it!

Watercolour by Alice.

Eight weeks from proposal to marriage gave little enough time to plan a pageant splendid enough to sate Mrs Liddell. Letters and diaries of the interim are punctuated by a sense of thrilled panic. Things were done on a grand scale: the search for modish bunting for dresses took Alice, Rhoda, Violet and "the boys" across the Channel to Cherbourg. Storms at sea then imprisoned them in France; the boys regretted that they couldn't use Alice's wedding as a pretext to make safaris further afield to Timbuctoo; while Alice, pining in Cherbourg harbour in a storm which prevented even the crew going ashore to "forage for breakfast", went hungry – both for food and for sight of her Reginald. Then came the querulously feminine "I've got nothing to wear", in a letter to Reginald, from London: "It is very difficult to get anything – all the dress-makers are away on holiday, and if you wanted me with a great many gowns, you would certainly have to wait longer than September 14th. I suppose I can have a wedding gown made, however, – with a struggle."

In the event, Reginald only had to postpone the onset of his bliss for twenty-four hours, until three o'clock on September 15th. Dean Stanley was delighted to be called on to perform the ceremony. Alice and Rhoda stayed with him at Westminster Deanery on the Tuesday evening; while the rest followed to London early on the Wednesday. In one respect the occasion lacked the full gloss: although the organ trumpeted under the hands of Dr Stainer, the choir-stalls were empty, the choristers on holiday. Alice was actually relieved at this minor loss of pomp: "*I* am rather glad at this but the others, I am afraid, are sorry; however, it cannot be helped. After the wedding we go to the Jerusalem Chamber, a dear, old room, lined with cedar and with tapestry, and in which Henry V was born. It leads out of the Abbey through a few passages, I think, so there is no getting in and out of carriages." Reginald bought the bridesmaids each a little spray, with diamonds in the leaves and with pearls as flowers.

One of the most delightfully intimate tributes to the first enchantment of Alice and Reginald is a letter from Alice to Emma (Reginald's sister), thanking her and her husband for

Caen, 1877, watercolour by Dean Liddell.

the loan of Sedgwick Park, Horsham, for a secluded, three-week honeymoon: "I think Sedgwick will be a long time before it shelters two more foolishly happy creatures than Reginald and me." In lovely summer weather, they drove to the nearby monastery, Alice acting as "charioteer", and found it "exceeding hideous"; mushrooms studded the park, and they picked them by the hatful; "Regi quite forgot and told Austin to give 'Miss Liddell' the potatoes – he tries to practise the new name, but has hardly got used to it yet." Regi also shot (only) one partridge, but wounded another and bagged two waterhens – which in those more callous times was a gesture of machismo, a sophisticated, if ritualitic version of "bringing home the bacon".

Even John Howe Jenkins could not accuse Reginald of being "Cakeless" or devaluing the marriageable property at the Deanery. But Alice's was the last daughter's wedding over which Mrs Liddell could weep tears of huge joy. If she cried later for Rhoda and Violet, they were tears of genuine unhappiness. In *Cakeless* Rhoda (Rosa) and Violet (Psyche) boast of noble consorts; but the author's aim is as blind as Cupid's: in real life neither Rhoda nor Violet trapped any one at all – prince or pauper, though not for want of heartache and trying. They both gave their hearts away more than once, so that Alice saw her father's retirement in 1891 as something of a blessing: "Much better for Rhoda and Violet to be away from Oxford, I think, they make too much of these youths." In the end they had to resign themselves to being unwilling spinsters, and wear the mantle of old maid in a world where that was seen as the uniform of failure.

Brief glimpses of Rhoda's lonely search emerge from Alice's letters to her husband. Like Alice, Rhoda mixed in notable company, though Alice reserved judgment on some aspects of their eligibility: "At the Pembers they had several good games [of tennis] . . . Rhoda played with Lionel Tennyson, the laureate's second son, who is not bad-looking without his hat; *with* it he is a fright and makes such hideous faces when he is playing, especially when serving, that he frightens his opponents." Anyway, at that time, in 1883, it seemed that Rhoda had found her beau, though with an ominous air of desperate relief: "Rhoda is delighted at the

Rhoda Liddell.

idea of being given, 'at last'." That proved not to be the end of her quest and in Alice's eyes she squandered her feelings over another: "Only Rhoda distresses me: I feel she lives quite outside the family. I can't but think that it is true what old Hathaway (Mama's maid) used to say years ago, 'Miss Rhoda is not like the others, she comes from the Islands.' Poor dear, I heartily wish Mr Grant had never come up to the House." Three months later "Kitty" Grant left Christ Church for London, but Rhoda pined on: "I suggested Eric saying something should the 'Kitty' craze come on again – but I don't think he will interfere." Rhoda found no one, and lived only with memories and might-have-beens; she became Alice's companion in old age and survived her by fifteen years, last but one to die of the ten Liddell children, in 1949.

In *Cakeless* Violet Liddell is disguised as Psyche, and there is unintended irony in the choice of name. In the classical myth Psyche was a mortal princess of remarkable beauty, who lost her lover; but the gods eventually took pity and restored her to immortal wedded bliss with her nonpareil – the God of Love himself. No happy denouement, however, for Violet in real life: her story stops at the solitude. Three letters from Mrs Liddell to Alice piece together Violet's passionate but abortive bid for marriage:

Valentine to Violet.

I am troubled about the youth – hearing he is very *rowdy* – and Mr Morier, who Rhoda and Violet met at Leacox, did not restrain his language about him – so Lionel tells me today – he says he is not the least good form and is very unhappy of Violet's thinking about him. It appears he is Mr Laycock's great friend, and Mr L. has constant parties where they mostly get drunk and young Davison is not averse! All this makes me very unhappy because I feel he has stolen Violet's heart without her knowing what she is about . . . as I said, I know nothing about him. His only care is for horses. I don't see happiness in store in any way. Lionel said he thought it was the greatest cheek to make up to Violet – he and Eric are both furious about it . . . I can only think of what you and Violet will decide and if she will have the courage to show him she does not care for him – if only she had not

Violet Liddell.

encouraged him and flattered him by dancing with him as she had done, it would be much easier . . .

I had a long talk with Mr Davison who has behaved most honourably and like a gentleman in the matter – I have promised that you shall not prejudice Violet against him – but to talk it all over calmly together – that you will allow although he is only twenty-one that he is old for his age and that he bears an excellent character and is deeply attached to Violet. He is, I fear, delicate, he says he has not been strong since he grew so rapidly. In the young man himself there can be no objection *except* age and want of occupation, his fortune is not *under* £4,000 a year and not over £5,000 and with valuable building land near Sevenoaks and in Durham – means are quite sufficient – but then comes this point: *is he the man* to make our dear Vio happy? – I think from what he said he feels how superior her powers are to his and though the *love* may be great, it surely needs something *more* to secure a life of happiness. I fear he will have to look to Violet for counsel and not she to him. I am sure you and Regi will talk the whole matter over in all its bearings with her, whether he should go quite away without further speaking . . . Vio must also consider the whole thing and only she can decide . . . if she decides not wishing to see him again he has determined to leave Oxford at once . . . she knows, I hope, how entirely and solely we have *her* future happiness in view – of course she really knows nothing of him and we know absolutely nothing. I have never spoken to him till this morning and your father did not know him by sight even. His aunt, Miss Wood, is a very nice person, but of his other relations we know nothing, who they are, what they are.

It does in one way alter the case materially – that is, Ina and Willie on that income are very poor at Pitlour and Willie has no expensive hunting tastes like this young man – and we all know how easy it is beforehand to think to give up anything and everything and how little satisfactory this is in the end – if the young man was twenty-eight or thirty even it would be different, also if he had any literary tastes or occupations – but he does not and it is no use disguising this fact – he looked but a mere boy too when he was talking to me – that though I felt so sorry for him I could not but feel there would come disenchantment to my dear Vio and then what would my dear V. have to fall back on? I am greatly vexed with Mrs S-B. I don't think she behaved fairly . . . I cannot trust her after this – she is eager to get Vio – she has, I am quite sure, urged him to this step. I can only hope my dear Vio will listen to you . . . I do feel he is *not* the husband for her.

Alice, Reginald and a solicitous Mrs Liddell all prevailed over Violet's consuming passion, and Mr Davison disappeared from Oxford and Violet's life. Whatever pangs she felt at the time, in retrospect Violet thanked God for a merciful escape from the fatal flaw of impressionability: "I *do* thank God always, always that he helped me to choose the right, it makes it so much easier, and I also thank Him for the dear sister and brother who were just everything to me in that bad time."

Who was the mysterious "Mr Davison," who caused all the heartache? Mrs Liddell says nothing about blue blood in his veins to suggest he might be listed in *Burke's Peerage;* but there is a propitious clue in her reference to his fortune and building land in Durham and Kent. This suggests a gentility just below the true nobility, and those on this rung of the ladder have their own directory, *Burke's Landed Gentry.* This dictionary of country squirarchy is worth a browse for its magnificent names. Between the covers of the three

Watercolour by Alice.

Lady Smith, aged 103.

volumes life proves recurrently more outrageous than fiction (not excluding P.G. Wodehouse). By comparison with the De Sales La Terriere of Dunalastair, the Bastards of Kitley and Cazanoves of Cottesbrooke, the Davisons, in name, are as prosaic as Joneses. Two Davison families are listed. The "Davisons of Thorngrove" have the wrong geographical link; but the others have two seats – at Carlton (in Durham) and Underriver (in Kent), which perfectly match Mrs Liddell's letter. She needed have no qualms over the parentage ("we know nothing, who they are, what they are"): the Rt. Hon. J.R. Davison, QC, was Judge Advocate General in 1871, and MP for Durham 1868-71. He had two sons: Arthur Pearson (b.1866) and John Robert (b.1869); they were both educated at Harrow, whence John Robert went up to Christ Church. He would have been twenty-one in 1890; Violet Liddell was then twenty-six.

In effect, Violet Liddell was a creature of a different generation from Alice's; she was accordingly the victim of social change, stretched on the rack of a world in which women fought to be recognised as people but were still treated as delicate, unworldly objects. The battle was already engaged in the Oxford to which Violet returned from Alice's wedding. Assertive ladies were probing the cracks in the university's male panoply, while the die-hard misogynists fought hard to keep women in their (supposedly) divinely ordained place. Thus Dean Burgon in a sermon at New College in 1884: "Inferior to us God made you (women) and inferior to the end of time you will remain." He was preaching to the unconverted male, but some at least actually rubbed shoulders with living exceptions to the principle. Notable blue-stockings strode down the High, dutifully chaperoned, to lectures, where their matronly escorts provided an accompaniment of clicking knitting needles.

Twenty years before, the redoubtable Eleanor Smith, outspoken sister of a professor at Balliol, attended lectures with her dogs. In the campaign to provide education for ladies at Oxford, she had the sympathy of Mark Pattison – and, of course, his wife. Although in 1871 Ruskin forbad "bonnets" at his Slade lectures, saying that the subjects would be too obscure for the "female mind", his later lectures on Italian art inspired many ladies to a love of painting. The year before Alice's marriage, the first two ladies' colleges were founded, Somerville and Lady Margaret Hall, the latter under the firm hand of Miss Wordsworth, granddaughter of the poet William's brother. Some, like Mrs Pattison, worried that in the quest for learning ladies might neglect the art of dress. She set a flamboyant example, and the new generation of female cognoscenti copied the aesthetes of London, in their peacock-blue serge dresses with crewel-worked sunflowers, trailing evening gowns of ruby velveteen, wide lace collars and long strings of amber beads, which in Miss Wordsworth's view were the *sine qua non:* "every lady of true culture had an amber necklace." As Alice left Oxford to become the wife of a country gentleman, the university opened its doors to such remarkable women as Gertrude Bell – historian, archaeologist, traveller and writer, mapmaker in Arabia, instrumental in the establishment of Iraq, and friend and advisor to King Feisal in Mesopotamia.

For the last time we hear the venerable voice of Lady Smith on the new breed of women. For all that she was herself weaned early to a love of books, the change she most lamented in the modern world was the formal education of women: "That foolish person, Miss Becker, had better have held her tongue. I am no advocate of university education for girls. The world, however, seems turned topsy-turvy." The death in 1871 of Henry Mansel, Dean of St Pauls, represented for Lady Smith the passing of an old order: "He has left a disturbed and agitated world . . . that which I notice as the worst sign of the times, is the change in the fashionable life of the education, habits and the pursuits of women . . . When ladies talk of horse-racing, betting, steeple chases and cricket, they make very poor companions for *Gentlemen*, and lose all their charm as women.

Ye virgins fond to be admired,
With mighty rage of conquest fired
And universal sway,
Who heave the uncovered bosom high

And roll the fond inviting eye
On all the circle gay!

You miss the fine and secret art
To win the castle of the heart
For which you all contend,
The coxcomb tribe may crowd your train,
But you will never, never gain
A lover or a friend.

If this your passion, this your praise,
To shine, to dazzle and to blaze,
You may be called divine;
But not a youth beneath the sky
Will say in secret with a sigh,
'O were such maiden mine'."

Violet Liddell.

Not surprisingly in the circle in which she moved, Violet Liddell caught the spirit of independence. Though a "virgin fond to be admired", if she was to win "the castle of the heart", it would not be by feeble capitulation or sacrifice on the altar of male dominance. She was brought up among stimulating and intelligent company, and she would not forfeit that to an enervating etiquette whereby the ladies retired while the gentlemen exchanged anecdotes and prejudice over the port and madeira. Violet wanted to be ranked on equal terms with her brothers; she competed with them on the squash courts and in political discussion; and she chafed against custom: "We have got a kick-up here on the 21st – the Brassey's to dinner and a selection of fossils to meet them. *I* am going out, as my special bugbear is among the acceptees. It is almost tiresome old term again and I shall have to leave off appearing in my oldest frock and walking out alone and playing squash in the courts. Bother the lordly undergraduate!"

Returning to Oxford as wife and mother, Alice sensed the changed climate and was called on to play an unaccustomed role: "I chaperoned Violet and Xie Kitchen, and I felt very like old Pricks must have done in the old days when she used to play 'Dragon' for us!" Suddenly, at thirty, Aice was made

The seven surviving Liddell children as adults.

to feel old: "How manners are changed since we were young!" On Violet's seventeenth birthday, in 1881, Alice was abroad, but it was a kind of watershed for her: "It seems so funny to think of sweet girl Violet seventeen . . . for some reason or another seventeen is made such a milestone in a girl's life. I wonder if it will be a snowy birthday, as the March 9th was in 1864, and you in consequence were nearly named 'Snowdrop'." Reginald added a postscript: "And now a word of advice. Please beware of the youthful frivolity of dancing. It only makes you hot and thirsty, especially if you take a new partner in the middle of a dance, as I hear is the custom." One can hear Violet's blood boiling at this combination of sentiment and fuddy-duddy precept. "Sweet girl" and "Snowdrop" indeed! She can't have liked "Violet" much either; to be saddled with a name that connotes shy, modest and fragile beauty, when you only play the lady upon compulsion!

Unhappy in love, Violet was also frustrated in her bid for public acclaim. That thwarted struggle is bordered by a frame on the walls at Tetbury; it contains an oil painting of Alice by Violet, done in 1886. Alice modestly disowned the

Watercolour by Alice.

likeness: "Vio did a great deal of the picture this morning and I do wish I could believe I am like it – the picture is a lovely creature. I suppose I shall have to say what poor Lady Cavendish used to say about her picture by Willie Richmond, 'Well, it's what I hope to be like in another world.' " Not that Alice thought Violet usually erred on the side of hagiography: "Whatever else our private artist may fail in, she always is successful as far as likeness goes."

"Private artist" probably stung Violet: she sought more than family patronage. She painted not in the cosy, genteel spirit in which better-class young ladies dabbed at obligatory watercolours of flowers and leaves; Violet plied her brush in the bold hope that she would be taken seriously. She may have felt galled when the master, John Ruskin, heaped praise on Alice: "Violet and I paddled out in mackintosh and umbrellas and went to the Ruskin school where I delivered over my drawing to his tender care . . . he seemed quite pleased . . . He even said he wished he could teach his pupils to draw trees as I do! What do you think of that? – and think of the hours I have spent struggling and struggling."

A sketching party at Oxford, anonymous cartoon.

Violet struggled, too, and sought the good opinion of the arbiters of public taste who frequented the Deanery: two Slade professors (Richmond and Herkomer), and G.F.

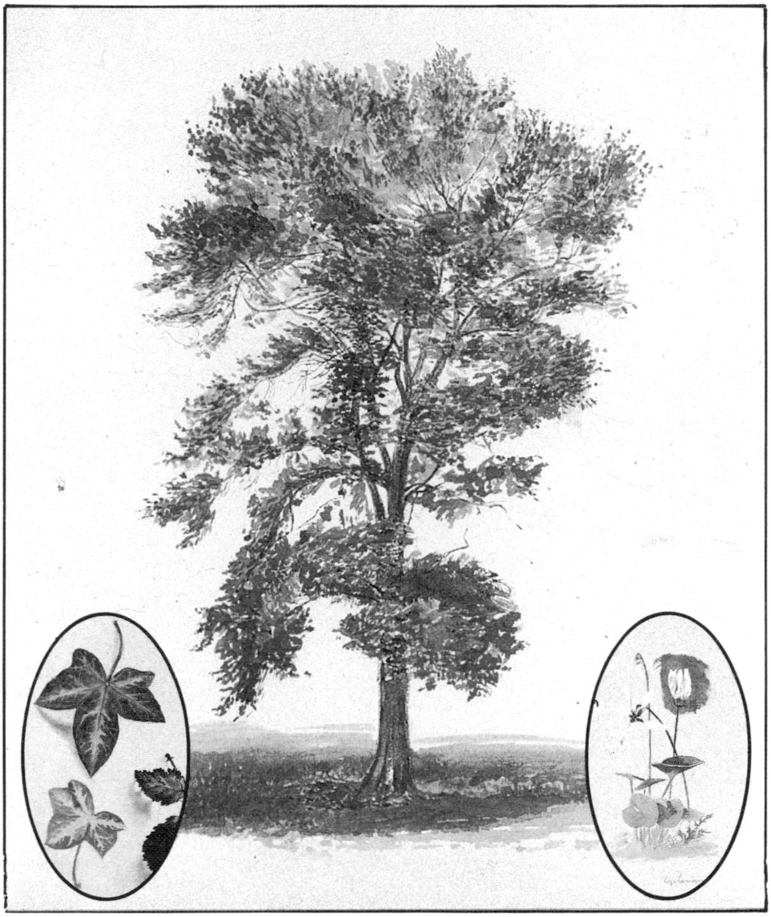

Sketches by Alice.

Watts, one of the most revered of Victorian artists, who had just refused a baronetcy from Gladstone and was a friend of her mother. They variously encouraged and snubbed her:

Mr Macdonald [tutor at Ruskin's art school] came to lunch, and Mr Herkomer, today. The former was delighted with Alice's sketches and has given her one or two hints which will be of use, I expect. Mr Herkomer hardly deigned to glance at my pictures. I had no idea he was so dogmatic and intolerant; but he evidently thinks nothing can be right but his own broad style. He is so unlike Mr Richmond who, even when he wants to cut you up, gives you words of encouragement, and anyhow a painting of which Mr

Portrait of Alice, 1866, by Violet.

Richmond and Mr Watts spoke of as they did of my "Alice" must be worth just looking at. You will see your "Birdie" is rather hurt in her feelings but indeed all he said was, "Oh, she'll know better how to paint next time", which is no doubt true.

In 1888 she thought she had shown them all by having a picture "accepted" for the Royal Academy summer exhibition. But her delight turned sour when she learned that "acceptance" was only a preliminary to "selection" and that her picture failed the second hurdle.

Before she died, Violet did make her mark, though unremembered either as wife or artist. She was immortalised by an MBE for public good works.

8
THE CASTLE OF THE HEART

Even in a frenzy of patriotism most of us could not sing beyond the first verse of the National Anthem; if we could, if we had all the words, we would still be puzzled by a stanza loyally inscribed on a piece of paper at Tetbury:

Lands far across the sea,
Empires that are to be,
All homage bring;
One in united might,
For God and King to fight,
God save the King.

The author was Reginald Hargreaves, thirty years after his marriage to Alice; he won second prize in a nationwide competition for adding this fourth cheer for the Empire. Fired by the spirit of his time, he saw foreigners as lower appendages, limbs of an expanding British dominion gradually staining pink the atlas of the world. Reginald had harboured his conviction for a long time; nothing else quite so confirmed him in the faith that other flags hung limp in the shadow of the briskly fluttering Union Jack than a holiday in Spain with Alice three months after their marriage. For Reginald it was the sting in the tail of an otherwise perfect long honeymoon.

It was, indeed, surprising that they went to Spain at all; it can only have been in a spirit of heady adventure. In these days, when a thousand identical hotel façades front the costas, enticing the English with the promise of other English tourists, exclusively English beer and nothing more

Reginald Hargreaves.

IN consequence of R's refusing to take
An Umbrella Abroad, This is the manner
in wh we had to walk abt Malaga on a wet day.
WET DAY.

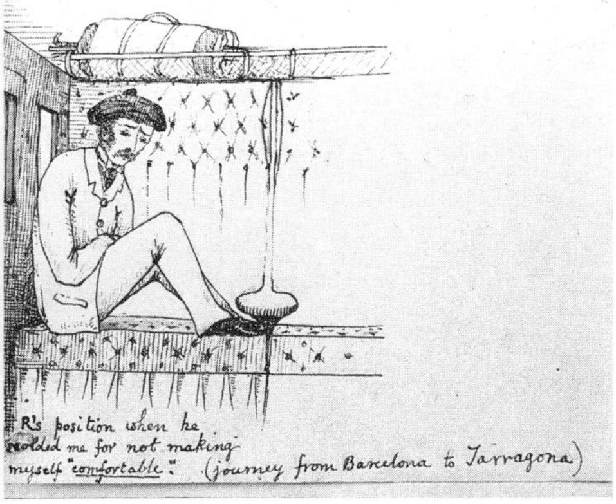

R's position when he
scolded me for not making
myself "comfortable." (journey from Barcelona to Tarragona)

un-English than paella and chips or sunshine, it's hard to envisage the alien and unpredictable peninsula that awaited the occasional Victorian tourist. But Reginald and Alice travelled forewarned, their eyes fully opened by Murray's *Guide to Spain.* It was a land that combined poverty with political instability; in 1872 (which saw the despatch of four presidents) some of the poorer rustics saw more rulers than hot meals. On one thing Alice and Reginald could rely – the Spaniard's love of his cigar: "the poor man's friend, it calms the mind, soothes the temper and makes men patient under trouble, hunger, heat and despotism"; "the spell wherewith to charm the natives – the traveller who grudges or neglects it is neither a philanthropist nor a philosopher".

So in Murray's *Guide to Spain* rhapsodised Richard Ford, once of Trinity College, Oxford, where he described Canon Pusey's influence in the city as a sin rivalled only the by the "tremendous habit of smoking cigars". Ford spent more than a decade in Spain, in the 1830s and 1840s, much of it on horseback, for want of wheeled transport. He poured the distillation of his harsh experiences into the text of a guide-book that must have deterred more visitors than it encouraged: "The Peninsula inns, with few exceptions have long been divided into the bad, the worse and the worst, and the latter are still the most numerous." Not the place, Ford concluded, for the hackneyed English tourist accustomed to carrying round with him his "tea, towels, carpets, comforts and civilisation"; in Spain he would see, and smell, the natives' "want of ablution", even though the air was now sweeter than heretofore in this land of Castile soap, and "warm baths were not unheard of in the larger towns". Ford also damned the kitchens and their unvarying brown sauce, as orthodox as the country's religion. He wondered which were the more deadly – the robbers, the Castilian sun or the doctors: "The doctors give the patient up almost at once, although they continue to meet and take fees, until death relieves him of his complicated sufferings . . . they shrug their shoulders, invoke saints and descant learnedly on the impossibility of treating complaints under the bright sun and warm air of Catholic Spain." Although a later editor expunged many of Ford's "passages of acrimonious controversy", Alice and Reginald were still warned off: "Let us advise the mere idler or man of pleasure to go rather to Paris, Vienna, St Petersburg, Florence or Rome, than to Madrid or Spain, for Iberia is not a land of fleshly comforts . . . God there sends the meat and the Evil One cooks; there are more altars than kitchens."

THE SUNNY SOUTH.
(GRANADA)

Undeterred, Alice and Reginald sailed from Southampton, accompanied (so says the passport) by that universal hallmark of civilised travel – a "lady's maid". And that despite a stern warning from Ford:

English servants, whom no wise person would take on to the Continent, are nowhere more useless, or greater incumbrances, than in this tealess, beerless, beefless land; they give more trouble, require more food and attention, and are ten times more discontented than their masters, who have poetry in their souls, and with whom an aesthetic love of travel for its own sake more than counterbalances the want of gross material comforts, about which only their pudding-headed, four-full-meals-a-day attendants are thinking.

R's coiffure at
the end of five weeks.

Alice's maid, Black, to judge by the letters and journals, endured her discomfort in silence, or at least, complained *sotto voce*. If Alice and Reginald assumed Spain now civilised enough to accommodate a lady's maid, they would also have ignored Ford's advice to include in their luggage an achromatic telescope, full-sized revolver and breech-loading fowling piece.

Alice left England with the sanguine air of the seasoned traveller, indignant on the Channel ("smooth to tameness") that the stewardess included her in the "general distribution of basins". As always, she travelled with her enlightened Liddell curiosity, and her pen, brush and paint to record the picturesque and comic moments. She loved Spain, but felt in the end that its beauty eluded her, as at Granada's Court of Myrtles, where they sat on a dazzling white marble pavement and fed the goldfish in the green, sunny water. She did, however, capture what Spain meant to her in a long

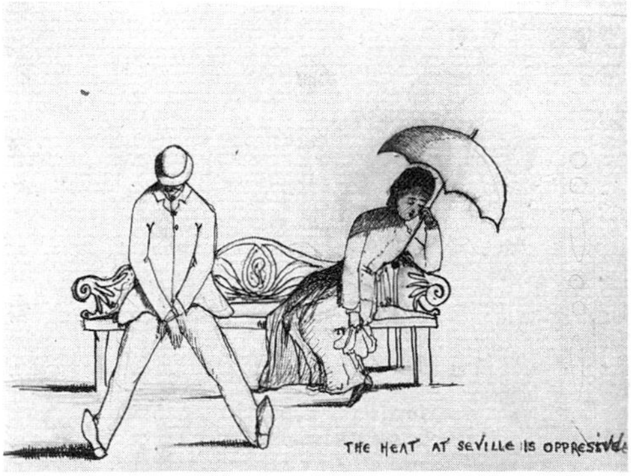
THE HEAT AT SEVILLE IS OPPRESSIV

Watercolour by Alice.

letter home, retelling a two-day safari by mule from Tarragona to Montserrat:

I feel as if there was so much to tell you that I hardly know where to begin – a confusion of sunniness, jolting roads, mules, bells, Spanish saddles and glorious scenery all jostling each other in my brain! . . . [The mule trek started at Collbato, where Alice and Reginald explored the famous caves and sipped wine that tasted like rotten pears] . . . Montserrat is so wonderful, it rises about 3,800 feet above the sea and stands alone in rugged and rocky grandeur. I had to mount a Spanish saddle and my mule persisted on walking on the very outside edge of a path, very steep and stony, and perfectly sheer above and below. I confess my poor heart leapt to my mouth several times during that ride and though the view was so glorious, occasionally I could not look at it for giddiness. All this time we had the most magnificent day imaginable, the sky intensely blue and the air so clear there was no haze to be seen even in the furthest distance, and the sun glowing with such heat . . . The higher we got, the more beautiful it was. We could see quite over the vineyards and hills below and beyond, and over to the sea, and the river winding along in and out of the hills like a silver thread in the red earth glowing in the warm sunshine . . . Some of the convent

Montserrat, watercolour by Alice.

schoolboys must needs come running and racing down the hill after us, and my mule, so frightened by the flight of black-robed urchins, came cantering on, so entirely upsetting the nerves of one of the small boys that he pitched headlong into a bush of ilex, and nothing was seen of him but two feet sticking out soles upwards . . . Our room at the convent was a tiny apartment with tiled floor, three chairs, two beds and a washstand with a pretty pitcher for water . . . [They left Collbato next day by carriage] . . . The carriage was drawn by five mules, only the "wheelers" having reins; our driver, a dreadful old man, who smelt of garlic and smoked a cigar, managed the reinless mules by throwing stones at them, which he kept in a basket by his feet. We only once saw him miss his mark . . .

Reginald also kept a journal in Spain but he saw a quite different country. In his curt jottings, boredom and scorn vied with xenophobia. He found the tomb of the Scipios "a shameless take-in", the streets of Malaga "dusty and smelly" and its cathedral "hideous"; in front of the paintings of Murillo he alarmed Alice "by saying that if they belonged to me I should sell to the first good bidder"; he sucked sugar cane and voted it "nasty"; and he turned up his nose at pimento – "a very nasty vegetable, which one at first imagines to be slices of tomato". Reginald had no stomach either for the carnival at Seville: "One of the principal amusements seemed to be throwing a handful of chopped paper into any lady's face . . . in the evening there were fireworks of the most feeble description." In these deserts of strange custom Reginald clung to the occasional oasis, like the English newspapers in the club at Malaga. He also warmed to the gypsy entertainment at Granada "presided over by the king of the tribe . . . a real nailer on the guitar". Almost the high spots were his solo outing to Jerez where he downed "a great deal of fine sherry" and a tour of the tobacco factory at Seville where he saw "the interior economy of a cigar and a lot of handsome gypsy girls". After a month Reginald was bursting with home thoughts: "Oh, what bliss to sleep in a really comfortable bed again, happy with the certainty of getting fresh butter for breakfast. England,

Montserrat, watercolour by Alice.

with all thy faults, I love thee still!" So Reginald returned to Cuffnells, safe in the conviction that he knew what he liked, and liked best what he already knew, and that was a world bounded by aristocratic country houses between Land's End and Carlisle.

While in the temperate greenery of home Reginald gleamed with a well-bred gloss, Spain's barbarous clime had dulled his finish and roughened his edges. Was Alice disillusioned? Boors had not been allowed often to plonk their uncultured elbows on the tables at the Deanery in Oxford. Had Alice gone to bed with a prince, only to wake up and find that she had a frog on her hands? In fact, Reginald's aversion to Spain, both its fine art and gross habits, did not prick the bubble of mutual enchantment. Six weeks back on the welcome soil of England, Alice and Reginald exchanged letters as husband and wife for the first time and they sang as ecstatic a duet in concert as they had done before in rehearsal: the thrill of anticipation had survived the fact of marriage. Reginald to Alice (May 9th, 1881) – "I found myself humming the duet in 'The First Fell[?] at Hull station, and I thought of that night at the opera when I won you, then the end of all my hopes, now the beginning of all my happiness, the result of which is that I can sign myself your most loving husband." Alice to Reginald (May 11th, 1881) – "I am glad to think I am something in your happiness – if I *could* tell you about myself, I would; half of myself seems gone again, the joyous happy half, dear, that you bring back to me with your love and care for me. Every night and morning on my knees I pray God to protect you from all evil and keep you safe."

Cuffnells.

Alice was to spend much of her time in such acts of genuflection; frequent separation from her husband was one price to be paid for marrying into inherited wealth, where perpetual leisure was an assumed birthright. At Eton and Oxford Reginald had been moulded to don the robes variously of a kind of Arthurian knight, feudal baron and sportsman, in a lifelong fete of social prowess. The roles fitted Reginald snugly. He and his sleek peers were the last generation to assert (and with wavering aplomb) an age-old principle of social order. Drawn as pyramid, chain, beehive or simple ladder, it amounted to the same canon – that each man, high or low, should know his place and keep to it, lest the whole ordained scheme of things should topple. Such thinking made the leisured and luxurious lifestyle an *obligation* on the rich man: "He has been placed by Providence in a position of authority and dignity, and no false modesty should deter him from expressing this quietly in the character of his house" (Sir Gilbert Scott, *Secular and Domestic Architecture*, 1857).

Another expert, Robert Kerr, voiced the same opinion in 1864, in advising gentlemen on the design of houses from "Parsonages to Palaces". First, he said, decide how many servants you can afford (as *the* token of your status) and then design a house large and complex enough to give them work to do. It was presumably on just such a formula that Mr Hughes of Kinmel Park, Clwyd, built a room exclusively for the ironing of newspapers. Those were the days (just) when liveried and pretty footmen were still engaged for show in matched pairs, like china dogs. A decade later at Cuffnells, Alice and Reginald compromised and settled for a single footman, but his looks were still a matter of concern: (Alice to Reginald) "He is five foot nine inches, twenty-three years of age. So I engaged him. Not very good looking, but he says he is very careful . . . Wages £20 . . . Shall he be measured for any clothes?" Later, the butler earned disapproving frowns: "Falconer has grown an ugly little pretence of a beard; I hope he will cut it off before dinner-time."

In the 1880s, as Alice and Reginald set up home at Cuffnells, the day of halcyon swank was waning. From the mid 1870s an agricultural recession made the largest estates increasing liabilities, expensive to maintain and often impossible to sell. By 1895 Oscar Wilde's Lady Bracknell could lament that "land has ceased to be either a profit or a pleasure. It gives one position, and prevents one from keeping it up." Cuffnells was more a large house in the country, with a modest and therefore less burdensome estate of about 150 acres.

Watercolour by Alice.

Servants, too, who until the 1870s seemed to be bred in endless abundance, chafed more and more at their caged lives. Young girls actually chose the appallingly privations of factory and mill (with free, if brief evenings and weekends) rather than the captive routine of domestic service. Securing suitable servants and keeping them proved a recurrent chore for Alice at Cuffnells. What with reproving the gardener and settling disputes between the maids, Alice found herself "giving 'snakes' all round . . . you see I am becoming something of a termagant." One of the cooks who moved on took with her a secret on which she prospered. At Cuffnells she had made marmalade to an old recipe of Alice's grandmother, Mrs Reeve of Lowestoft. The cook left to marry a Mr Cooper, and under his name – not Mrs Reeve's – they offered their famous "Oxford" marmalade to the world.

Although propped up by an army of hirelings, families in country houses generally expected the hewers of wood and drawers of water to live and work inconspicuously – the more menial, the more anonymous. So those who hauled the coals rarely met those who sat in front of the fire. While the housekeeper and butler attended daily audience with the mistress, they conveyed orders downstairs to the turnspits and scullions, who slaved, unseen by master and mistress for weeks on end. That, argued Robert Kerr, was just as it should be: "The family constitute one community; the servants another . . . each class is entitled to shut its doors upon the other, and be alone . . . what passes on either side of the boundary shall be invisible and inaudible on the other." The desire may not have been mutual, but the servants' quarters never overlooked the garden, or offered envious glimpses of the family at pleasure. In an ill-planned house, it was feared, the staff might constantly intrude on the family's privacy or, worse, threaten its purity. Housemaids' scandals were locked away in the laundry and the footman's dalliance in the broom-cupboard. (Fears of the laundry degenerating into a brothel prompted the owner of Hesleyside in Northumberland to install a new entrance. At all costs the family's sanctity had to be protected from the immodesty of its retainers.

Watercolour by Alice.

On principle, then, genteel records omitted the gross or foul play of the servants. Those who fell were dismissed as "unsatisfactory" and bundled out through the rear entrance. The letters at Tetbury, between Alice and her sister, Ina, offer more than a passing glance at one such ignominious departure. In March 1885 Ina's three children, Moncrieff, Elsie and Hilda, arrived at Cuffnells for a short stay, after what Alice referred to, with finger to her lips, as the "grand upset".

The protagonist was Ina's governess who, like all in her role, was expected and assumed to be the embodiment of earthly virtue (though not of wealth or position). Her name was Miss Pringle; in that respect, she shared with the Liddells' Miss Prickett and Oscar Wilde's Miss Prism a name oddly appropriate to her calling (through connotations of "Prim" and "Proper"?). But the comparison with Miss Prism is more apposite than that, and, beside the scandal of Miss Pringle, Miss Prism's sin of merely *losing* a baby in a handbag at Victoria Station, pales into an absent-minded peccadillo. Miss Pringle stumbled and fell over one of the bulwarks of Victorian rectitude.

The prologue to her tragedy is spoken in a letter from Ina to Mrs Liddell: "I continue to like Miss Pringle very much and she is so nice . . . in all little things she is so helpful. I wish she were well, though – going abroad this summer in June put her wrong and she has never come right yet. She has seen a doctor and is taking medicine and doing what he told her – but she looks so pale and gets such bad headaches, but she never gets cross with them, poor thing." Pity changed to horror, the "poor thing" became bête noire, as the cause of her lingering "malady" came to light in the most sensational manner possible. Alice related the circumstance to Reginald:

It is neither more nor less than that Miss Pringle – the "very nice" governess in whom Ina flattered herself she had found a treasure – increased the population by a female infant in Ina's house on Sunday last! Ina left her very suffering, but no thought of what was coming ever entered her head. She took the girls and Moncrieff to the zoo in the afternoon – most luckily it was all over before they got back – the children never got any idea of what happened most luckily and, of course, never will . . . The whole thing is so

Watercolour by Alice.

horrid and dreadful it makes me feel miserable. How Ina never thought, I can't imagine.

The rest is tight-lipped silence. Untold is Miss Pringle's growing wretchedness and the moment of blank horror when she herself realised what was amiss, and what the consequences would be. Reginald put it frankly, if brutally: "One does not know how she may have been tempted, but, of course, it is next door to ruin for her."

Such shameful moments were regarded as exceptions to prove the rule; life in the Victorian country house was cushioned by the comforting assumption that man was perfectible in the image of God and the English gentleman. Crucial to the image were lavish and frequent house parties, and, to judge from the letters at Tetbury, Reginald was often called away on this serious business of pleasure. He divided his calendar into man-made seasons – for fishing, shooting and cricket. He migrated from country house to country house, from moor and woodland, to river, to wicket, in earnest pursuit of quarry and runs. He sent back to Alice at Cuffnells a steady supply of grouse, partridge, venison, rabbit, trout, salmon and letters as full of statistics as a managing director's report to the board: "We got 138 brace yesterday, sixty brace in one drive, at which I got twenty-three birds." In one day Reginald despatched eighty birds himself and earned the respect of others in this skill of licensed slaughter: "They lay it on a bit thick about my shooting and talk about my being in a class above them all."

Shooting party, photograph from the Cuffnells visitors' book.

To be a "good shot" was the *summum bonum* in this male domain. It was a society which came close to using the adjective, "good", synonymously in the phrases "a good man" and "a good shot". In the 1890s, and under royal patronage, annihilating wild-fowl evolved from mere pastime into mystic ritual. At Eaton Hall in Cheshire, the Duke of Westminster's principal seat, the annual "bag" of pheasants swelled to almost countless numbers. Inside the country house, too, gentlemen retired to their sancta – the billiard and/or smoking rooms. Again, royal precedent set and sanctioned the style: the Prince Consort had smoked at Court, and the smoking room at Osborne, the royal retreat, was the only room with an exclusive "A" (for Albert), instead of the romantically intertwined "V and A" above the door.

Reginald excelled at most of the big business of country-house life: billiards ("I believe they think I am a semi-professional") and "games without end" – Coddlums, Hunt the Ring, Hunt the Slipper, Squeaky Voice, Shouting Proverbs and Dumb Crambo. It was an enclosed world where the rules of the game could be mistaken for moral absolutes; Reginald reported to Alice the mortal sin of "Meux" dealing two cards at a time at whist, with a feeble excuse that they were "too damned sticky". Such sins could always be atoned for at Matins on Sunday, unless wet weather forced the party to stay indoors and worship instead at the billiard and loo tables, fortified in spirit by hot rum and water.

Alice had been brought up in a world peopled by men of mental muscle and aesthetic grace, and she upbraided Reginald for his thin letters home. By return she was put firmly in her place: "I'm not sure you deserve a letter after the slighting way you spoke of my epistles a few days ago." But there was never a real crisis since Alice accepted the traditionally submissive role of loving, honouring and obeying. The Victorian home was *ruled* by the master, even though its daily life may have been *run* by the mistress. H.E. Gurney, banker, for whom Nutfield Priory in Surrey was built in 1858, put the mistress in her place in a motto carved on the library fireplace:

A good horse never stumbles,
A good wife never grumbles.

Although Reginald never metaphorically stabled Alice with the horses, she sometimes found acquiescence as effective as grumbling; it could sting Reginald to an agony of self-recrimination: December 5th, 1885 – "My darling, I got both your letters this morning; you blame yourself far too much; no man has a more loving and faithful wife than I, and, when I think of all my selfishness and thoughtlessness, I feel how little I have deserved such a blessing at God's hands; it is for you to forgive and not for me, and with God's help, I will spend my life to make you happy. I do think of the motto of my ring sometimes and, Alice, you must not think you can love me too well."

Any suggestion that Alice felt unfulfilled and isolated in a marriage to an intellectual inferior is not borne out by her letters and journals. Alice's feelings for Reginald went far beyond a faut-de-mieux comfort. After more than a decade, when Reginald would have long toppled from any shaky romantic pedestal, Alice could still write: "Best love, my husband of eleven years – if I have failed in much, I love you still with as tender a love as the day you took me 'for better, for worse'."

Being left alone at Cuffnells, however, to play the role of mistress never came easily to Alice, even after years of marriage, and with three growing sons to divert her: "It seems so lonely without you. I think you have been with me so much this year, I hardly understand being alone." A certain pride, however, led her to placate Reginald's conscience: "My dearest, though I turned it off with a scoff – I was very sad at your leaving this morning. I can't bear your going away . . . but then it is joyful when you come back, so don't trouble about me." Not that she wanted Reginald to *follow* that injunction; and there were flashes of pique if Reginald was less than duly troubled about her: "You seem to be having good times with all your lovely ladies. I believe Lady Herbert was always considered one of the most fascinating of women." Again: "I expect you had a festive evening with your old friends; how glad they must have been that I was safe in the country." Alice allowed herself an occasional gesture of independence: "I suppose we shall hear if you mean to honour the dance [at Cuffnells]. I mean to dance every dance and enjoy myself."

Oakley Park.

Alice was not exactly a prisoner at Cuffnells. People of her and Reginald's class measured their stature both in numbers of servants and in numbers of houses owned, leased or let to provide frequent change of vista. Reginald rented Oakley Park, Scole (in Suffolk) by the year from Lady Cavendish; he made it available, too, to the Dean and Mrs Liddell; they found it a "palatial abode". A *pied-à-terre* in London was also obligatory for reasons of both culture and fashion. On that point Oscar Wilde's Lady Bracknell was, as ever, adamant: "a girl with a simple unspoiled nature . . . could hardly be expected to reside in the country." London property a century ago, however, proved no easier for tenants to find than today; a footsore Alice almost despaired: "I shall hardly be surprised if we have to apply for rooms in Buckingham Palace! There seems no other empty house in London." In 1883 they found a place – empty and (only just) satisfactorily placed at 3, Stratford Place – the rent, 140 guineas. Alice and Reginald had already turned their noses up at a house in Eaton Square, on the Victoria Station side, as "rather low down" (shades of Lady Bracknell again, who lamented that suitor Jack's town house in Belgrave Square stood on the "unfashionable side").

The Dean, Mrs Liddell, children and grandchildren.

In his regular separations from Alice seldom in his letters home did Reginald stray from the straight and narrow report of his conquests with bat and gun, into more speculative and cerebral territory. When he did, the result could be unfortunate: "I should hardly say that Matthew Arnold was a national loss, his writings . . . had not real depth enough to last, at least that is my idea." Fortunately, Reginald's letters were for Alice neither a lifeline nor mirror to the world outside Cuffnells. The talents of her own family, fostered in the Deanery, were now scattered abroad and the family's compulsive need for letters constantly proved how thick was their blood – in the case of overseas ventures, somewhat thicker than sea- and swamp-water or monsoon rain. "Young" Lionel, with a first-class Oxford degree as springboard, was making his way through the lower levels of foreign service; he stretched the family network in a letter to Alice from a lonely exile: "Don't forget the inhabitant of the mud-hut in the swamps . . . I wear long galoshes half-way up my finely developed calves and can splash along with immunity. The only excitement is getting the post and that only twice a week; otherwise, one hears no news except occasionally some high-class Greek paper has some astounding news from Constantinople which naturally is never true."

Mont St Michel, watercolour by Dean Liddell.

From closer home than Lionel's distant postings, Alice

Henry Irving.

had a vicarious finger on the pulse of national and international affairs through her father's letters. The Dean's letters to his "Dearest Alice" turned up regularly among the boxes at Tetbury. In a chronological bundle they make a fascinating fifteen-year anthology, in which the Dean mixes humble and high, matters of the kingdom or of the kitchen, equally at home in the higher reaches of philosophy or the lowest bends of domestic drainage. He dismissed neither one as too abstract nor the other as too banal, though as he grew older his preference grew for the terrestrial over the ethereal: "I fear I share Montague Burton's opinion that, after forty, metaphysics becomes distasteful." In the same letter the Dean could discourse in adjacent paragraphs and with equal authority on the ecumenical spirit and the relative merits of stone and plank floors in an ironing room.

Over the years the Dean's letters to Alice provide a fragmentary commentary on public people and events, strained through the filter of his judgment. The Dean reduced some giants of public esteem to mortal stature, including Henry Irving whose one hundred and fiftieth performance of *Hamlet* (opposite Ellen Terry's Ophelia) he saw at the Lyceum: "Now you want to know what I thought of him . . . his words were hardly audible, and the language of Shakespeare disappeared . . . Mr Irving wants power, depth and flexibility of voice and he tries to make up for this by strange intonations . . . considering how exquisite the poetry is and how precious every word, I feel that you [Alice] have yet to see a satisfactory Hamlet . . . on the whole he cannot, as an actor of Shakespeare, be compared to the great actors."

One issue, the theme of two full letters, shows how closely and deeply the Dean and Alice felt for those who carried national burdens. In February 1885 they anxiously awaited news of General Gordon, "lost" at Khartoum. It is hard now to recreate the sense of a nation holding its breath, in an agony of uncertainty: had Gordon escaped? Was he a prisoner of the Mahdi? Or dead? The Dean wrote to Alice with a sense of real personal anxiety: since Gordon had boasted he would never be taken alive, he must be dead (in which case the Mahdi would have broadcast his triumph), or, more likely, executing a daring plan of escape along the Equator to the Congo. When the news of Gordon's death put an end to speculation, the Dean paid his tribute in superlatives: "My heart is woe for Gordon, and the feeling touches all my thoughts. It is the saddest, most dismal event that I have lived to see. When your Uncle Charles heard of it, he burst into tears, and my feelings were akin to his. What a true hero! I was sure he would never be a prisoner. Better, then, he should die sword in hand than that he should fall into the hands of those savages." It was an age which still worshipped the now obsolete breed of imperial hero.

General Gordon.

The rigours of winter rarely penetrate the veil of our nostalgic image of country-house living; what glisters through is almost all golden, an eternal summer that never faded. But even a regiment of servants carrying coal could only moderate the harshness of winter. For two consecutive winters the Dean and Mrs Liddell occupied Cuffnells, while Alice and Reginald moved to Oakley Park. For most of the time the house was ice-bound, though the Dean and his wife insisted on a spartan daily drive in an open carriage, braving a "frizzling north-east wind". A trifling inconvenience, however, compared to the memories of an arctic experience endured in 1881, when Mr and Mrs Liddell, Violet, Eric and Lionel, en route by train for Bournemouth, were stuck in a snowdrift for twenty-four hours near Radley, without food, drink, heating or light:

The wind howled and was so furious that the heavy railway carriages shook and rocked under its force. The snow drove in swirling eddies all round and round. It drove into the carriages through every crevice; we had no light, for no lamp was in the carriages; no warmth, for the hot-water tins were cold as ice; no food to create inner warmth. Twenty-two hours without food at that temperature was indeed a great privation. Your mother and Vio were our great comforters. They retained their spirits and to some extent their warmth, through all. I being held fast by gout was a helpless piece of goods, I fear, but I hope I did not add materially to the difficulties. I should not have cared half as much if I could have got about. I think I suffered most in

Alan, Rex and Caryl – Alice's sons.

being carried by soldiers for about two hundred yards from our carriage to the station, the snow driving furiously in one's face, and the poor fellows staggering with my weight through the deep snow. I wonder how they got me along at all. You would have been amused to see the motley party assembled about eleven on Wednesday morning in the little third-class waiting room at Radley Station, a stoker handing round tea from a kettle, and afterwards coffee in a bedroom ewer: all drinking in turn from the same tin can.

For Alice and Reginald at Cuffnells the 1880s were years of beginnings: marriage, a new home and the birth of three sons, Alan, Leopold and Caryl. (Was "Caryl" an echo of "Carroll"? Alice claimed it was merely a name from a novel.) But for Dean Liddell at Oxford the decade had rather the feeling of cadence. Even more than by the heroic death of General Gordon, the tone had been set four years earlier by the death of his closest friend, Arthur Stanley at Westminster, on the first anniversary of Alice's marriage. What that loss meant to the Liddells can be gauged from an earlier letter from the Dean on Stanley's departure from Oxford: "My best and dearest friend, Now have you torn open afresh all the wounds which the first news of your departure caused – I can scarce see to write – for tears." If there were unembarrassed tears at this separation, there was heartbreak at Stanley's death. The news reached the Dean at Ina's house at Pitlour: "Out of my own dear family no death could so rend my heart. Is there anyone in England whose loss would be felt by so many, by people of so different conditions, creeds and opinions . . . I cannot, I cannot bear to think that I shall never again press his hand, or be greeted by his friendly smile, or listen to the charm of his words." There followed a telegram asking the Dean to preach the funeral sermon in Westminster Abbey, but, at seventy, the Dean thought it would be too much: "I could not have got through a sermon in the Abbey – I am sure I could not."

Who was to succeed Stanley at Westminster? Influential eyes turned to Dean Liddell. Gladstone proposed his name and Queen Victoria urged it by letter: "How earnestly she hopes he will accept Mr Gladstone's proposal to recommend him to succeed our beloved and so deeply regretted friend, Dean Stanley . . . The Queen trusts he will not refuse, even if he only holds it for a few years." It would have been the last great honour of Henry Liddell's life, but, although he felt the Queen's wish almost a command, he refused: "The memory of Arthur Stanley is to me sacred. I would do all and anything to show how I feel his irreparable loss, except to attempt to wear his mantle."

The death of Arthur Stanley seemed at the time to tip the balance of the Dean's life: "Alas! if it were not for you, My dearest [Mrs Liddell], and my beloved children, and one or two others, I feel as if life were at an end for me. All with whom I had sympathy falling one by one. It is a sad privilege to survive." Such thoughts of decline were premature: Henry Liddell stayed Dean at Christ Church for another ten years, decorated by more honours: Professor of History at the Royal Academy, Trustee of the British Museum, and Honorary LLD at Edinburgh University. But the family doctor, Sir Henry Acland, was under strict orders to tell the Dean when he should move from driver to passenger. In the end, Acland had more confidence (or less courage), and the Dean made the decision himself to sever half a century's link with Oxford: "I feel that my work ought to be committed to younger and more vigorous hands . . . I wish if I am permitted to walk out of the Deanery rather than be carried out" (to Lord Salisbury, August 1891).

The Deanery at Christ Church was more than a home for Alice; visiting after her marriage always evoked memories of the days hymned by Charles Dodgson: "I am in my little old room, which I half asked for . . . there is a huge musical box come, a miniature orchestrion, with drums and cymbals etc. It plays quite loud enough to dance to . . . A few Beaux are coming to amuse the Belles."

At Christmas 1891 Alice left the Deanery for the last time: "I shall be glad to be home, but I can hardly bear to feel it is my last evening here as my own dear old home of many joys and sorrows; dearest, I think you know, if I talk of it it makes me cry."

As he had vowed, Henry Liddell walked out of the Deanery on his own feet – to a house among the pines at

Arthur Stanley.

Dean Liddell as Vice-Chancellor, contemporary cartoon.

The Deanery garden, c. 1890.

Dean Liddell, 1891, from the portrait by Herkomer.

Ascot: "There were no less than thirteen vanloads of furniture to be disposed of, and it has been disposed of – as well as possible." He lived another six years, with Mrs Liddell, Rhoda and Violet, dividing his time, as always, between the practical and the abstract – pottering with his rain gauge in the garden or revising the lexicon in the study "looking south down those pleasant vistas – such as might be in Switzerland or anywhere that is beautiful".

On January 19th, 1898, the great bell in Tom Tower at Christ Church tolled the death of Dean Liddell the previous day. He was buried at Christ Church near his beloved Edith. He lives on in the college, stonily in a statue and in portraits by Herkomer and Watts, and in rumour as a ghost. He haunts Oxford in august company: the decapitated Archbishop Laud walks in the library at St John's, and the Duke of Marlborough drives a spectral coach up Woodstock Road, while Prudence, a Puritan housemaid, carries devotion to duty beyond the grave, whisking away spooky dust from a house in Magpie Lane. Dean Liddell's spirit does nothing spectacular, only suffusing a wall in Christ Church with a damp stain in the supposed shape of his reverend visage.

9
MONUMENTS TO AN OLD ORDER

In January 1901, almost three years to the day after the death of her father, Alice travelled to London to buy suitable clothes for an event unique in the memory of most people alive – the death of a monarch. Queen Victoria had ruled for sixty-four years. At her accession Henry Liddell was a graduate fresh from Christ Church; Charles Dodgson was only a boy of five. In a sombre London Alice reflected on ends and beginnings – "everyone in deepest woe: the streets most melancholy and every shop filled with black clothes – cabbies with whips tied with black and small black shutters in nearly every window". A new century and a new king – "It seems so difficult to realise the immense change it will make." Although the family at Cuffnells, isolated from unrest, basked for a decade or so in the comfortable afterglow of the Victorian evening, the "immense change" Alice found it hard to imagine would first strike the family with a double tragedy and then reduce the house to rubble in wild grassland.

For once, the first years come not from records at Tetbury, but through the mind's eye of one who, as a boy, humbly watched the family's comings and goings from the lodge at the end of the drive. His father had migrated from Muggerhanger, a village in Bedfordshire, to work as head-groom and coachman at Cuffnells. Ernest Odell was delivered by the Lyndhurst village midwife, Mrs Purdue, in March, 1897, and his survival at all was in the first instance a triumph of will over medical opinion: the local doctor, eyeing the feeble newcomer, said he wouldn't live long anyway, as if it would have been redundant bureaucracy even to complete

Alice.

The remains of Cuffnells.

Ernest Odell.

a birth certificate. Ernest thwarted the doctor and survived what he nonchalantly referred to as "one or two spots of bother from time to time" later in life; they included being bitten by a cobra, being treed by a tiger and meeting a twenty-two-foot python at "very close quarters". He proudly unrolled the python skin for me across the carpet as almost endless proof of the encounter and its outcome. Exotic as the estate at Cuffnells might have been (a visitor in 1842 had remarked, 'many things here speak of other lands'), oriental game never roamed the park to prey on unwary pedestrians. Ernest's narrow escapes were in the foothills of the Himalayas, during thirty-three years' service in the army, twenty-six of them in India. Before the First World War took him away (in a less final sense than twenty other young men in the parish), for the first eighteen years of his life Ernest fought smaller game around Cuffnells: rabbits, schoolteachers, starlings and policemen.

During his long Raj army life Ernest earned a reputation for his stories. Prompted by his brigadier, he sat down to type out "everything of interest" he could remember in his life. The resulting hundreds of pages spanned a life summed up in his own words: "I was born at the end of a golden reign that had seen a kingdom become an empire; then I fought in the war that didn't end war but which destroyed a generation; and I served in India while the sun sank slowly on the British Raj. But I am glad I was there before the sun set." The details of his boyhood, intended only as prelude, focus on life at Cuffnells from a different angle: through eyes that always looked up – up the stairs, up the drive, up to his "betters".

Cuffnells, the lodge.

As befitted the little boy who hung on the gate, hurriedly tidied by his mother at the sight of stately pedestrians promenading down the drive, Ernest deferred to the grandees of the House. Like most of his class at the time, he did not begrudge ritual gestures of servility, demonstrating that he "knew his place" – even though it was expected of him. It was the foundation of a social order: "The position of a landed proprietor, be he squire or nobleman, is one of dignity . . . to him the poor man should look up to for protection; those in doubt or difficulty for advice; the ill-disposed for reproof or punishment . . . " (Sir Gilbert Scott, *Secular and Domestic Architecture*, 1857). In Ernest Odell's eyes Reginald Hargreaves cut an appropriately aloof and awesome image: "Mr Hargreaves was a stern-looking gentleman with a deep voice; a keen golfer, he played cricket for Hampshire and was a fine shot" – almost two-dimensional enough to have been cut out of card, but nevertheless the classic profile of landed gentry. Alice's silhouette, though softer, was stereotype too, full of grace and largesse: "Mrs Hargreaves had blue eyes and a charming manner. She was so thoughtful for others, treated her servants very well and was very popular in the village." Whether from goodness of heart or sense of duty, acts of parochial kindness were part of the *job* of being a country-house mistress. Over the years, Alice and Reginald acted as senior members or figureheads of local institutions: the Conservative Club, Golf Club, Parish Council, Boy Scouts and Women's Institute.

Reginald at Cuffnells.

The prescribed distance that separated master and servant as solidly as a wall prevented Ernest seeing much

through formal façades – except when "Miss Rhoda" and "Miss Violet", Alice's unmarried sisters, came to stay. They were different; they fussed over him like aunts and escorted him to the family pew in church clad in his sailor suit and straw hat. Crossing the fields one summer Sunday after Matins, the staid ladies were suddenly transformed into "Liddell sisters" again, larking among the pooks and ricks. The names of "Dodo" and "Ducky" were wistfully in the air, and talk of trips up the river by boat for a picnic. Ernest was puzzled and Alice asked him whether he knew the Mad Hatter. Expert in most local lore, Ernest knew all of Lyndhurst's fogies – like "Brusher Mills", the snakecatcher, who lived for twenty-one years in a charcoal-burner's hut and sold adder-oil to the chemist; or Mr Tizzard, the fishman, who could only be relied on to wheel around his shrimps, prawns and winkles (sold by the pint) until he had made enough and drunk enough to be put away in Southampton gaol. But as for a Mad Hatter – did Alice mean the milliner at the end of the High Street? They all laughed at Ernest's ignorance; Alice explained, became "Alice" in his eyes, and gave him a signed copy of *Alice in Wonderland*. She also did her best to re-create the spell of the river trips by punting him across to the island in the lake in front of the house, for an afternoon encompassed by goldfish and more stories.

With a boy's natural affinity for food Ernest made himself a favourite, too, with the cook, and spent enough time loitering around the larder to remember the intimate and appetising workings of the kitchen: the huge open coal fire for all the roasting, the clockwork spits and basting trays, the charcoal fire, hanging ranks of copper pots mustered according to size and shining like gold, and, in the middle, a table of three-inch-thick timber, 'forty feet by twenty'. Ernest had to cadge his morsels of food, unlike the postman, whom custom allowed to help himself with as much meat, bread and butter as he wanted, washed down with a pint of ale. The gardener who delivered the daily vegetables and the man who hauled up the coal from Lyndhurst Station shared the same privilege.

Outside the house Ernest remembered the ice-hole,

Cuffnells, the household staff, c. 1908.

concrete-lined, six-yards across and about twenty feet deep. Winter snow was rammed down hard and insulated with a cover of hay, bracken, leaves and earth. In the shade of surrounding trees, the well provided ice even in summer.

The indoor staff who kept the wheels of Cuffnells turning comprised a small army: lady's maid, housekeeper, cook, butler, footman and boot-boy, two kitchen-maids, scullery-maid, three housemaids and a laundry-maid. Where Alice and Reginald saw them only starched and on-duty, Ernest mixed with them at ease, cavorting to accordion and banjo in the servants' hall, or grouped around the footman's phonograph down at the lodge.

Within a decade of the turn of the century Ernest's father's title of coachman was to sound, if not obsolete, at least outmoded, vestige of a horse-*drawn* world of brougham, victoria, open four-wheeler and pony trap. Already in the early 1890s Alice had given notice of a slicker form of transport: "I went to see Mrs Grigg about the children and rode down on my bicycle" (December 1894). By then bicycles had passed the test of gentility for ladies but were still new enough to generate awful jokes: "Did you see the competition in *Truth* for the best text for a sermon on

Alice's chauffeur, Ernest Odell's father.

Mrs Liddell.

The Rolls-Royce.

The Thorneycroft.

bicycles? First prize: 'The Singers go before'; second prize: 'The race is not to the Swift'." But the bicycle hardly vied with the carriages; the motor car ousted them.

The horse-*powered* world is ushered in by Mrs Liddell's last letter to Alice in November 1910. She was eighty-five and still conscious of royal notice: "We had a splendid time at Windsor. I hired a *motor*! would you believe, and we flew there and back; and I was very proud for I was the only person the Queen and King shook hands with . . . " In the grave matter of choosing a motor car for Cuffnells image was crucial, as it was down to the tiniest domestic detail (like the poor butler's beard). Down in the lodge Mrs Odell spent hours with the Robin starch and blue-bag, iron *and* polishing iron to complete the white and smooth effigy her husband was expected to be when driving the carriages. Even the butter from the estate farm appeared in half-pound pats neatly embossed with the Hargreaves crest – a stag's head with a bough in its mouth. For a motor car nothing less than a Rolls-Royce would do.

Rolls-Royce, however, were as fastidious as their customers: they would not supply a vehicle unless the chauffeur had been trained by them, believing that the badly driven car would be an insult to its maker. In six months away Ernest's father learned to keep the car in the grand manner in which it was accustomed; even then, parts such as the gear-box were sealed against second-rate meddling. Odell drove back to Cuffnells the fifty-ninth Rolls-Royce ever built. Capacious and stately though it was, the car was not designed to carry anything as mundane as luggage. The family approached the marine firm of Thorneycrofts to build a car for that menial job. Thorneycrofts had no cars yet in production, but they installed a marine engine in a car chassis. This heavy and noisy compromise served as more than a makeshift, in daily use up to 1935.

By the time Ernest Odell made his obstinate entrance into the world in 1897, Alice's three sons, Alan, Leopold ("Rex") and Caryl, had made a partial exit from Cuffnells – to boarding schools: first, to Summerfields, near Oxford, then to Eton. Ernest Odell has no memories of them except at

Cuffnells, watercolour possibly by Caryl.

holidays; they had in any case lived two of the Seven Ages of Man. On the stage of their world they had played the parts of mewling infant and reluctant schoolboy. The records at Tetbury flesh out these roles in only a conventional way. (Alice oversaw the early stages of their education, with *Alice in Wonderland* an obligatory text on the syllabus, both for reading and dictation.) There are predictably, too, school reports, as there are in the dullest family archives; they seem to have immortal resilience to destruction, shadowing men's lives (even outliving them) and shouting out fledging faults or the confident misjudgment of teachers. The Hargreaves' reports from Eton run the usual narrow gamut of cliché and shine with the dull patina of sardonic wit: "I am pretty sure he [Alan] means to be a good boy and he succeeds in being a very nice one . . . he admits that he believes it beyond all human, or at any rate, Hargreavian, effort to attend for a whole week's school . . . English gives him an excellent opportunity of sitting wrapt in contemplation of nothing." By comparison his brother, Rex (nicknamed the "Mouse") was "all conscientious and painstaking"; while Caryl edited a magazine which earned the literary accolade of surviving to more than one issue.

Alice and her sons.

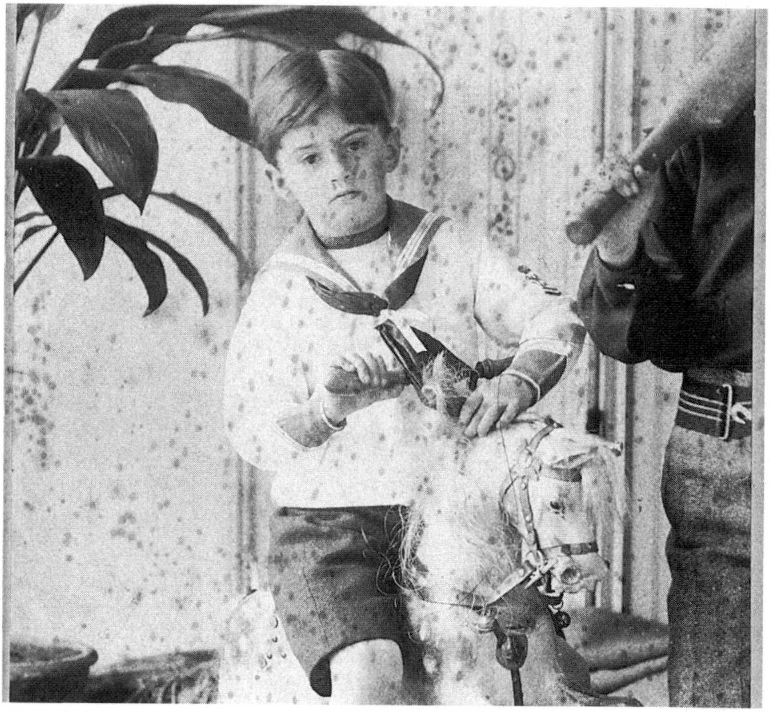

Caryl.

These are unimportant faint traces, but what lends them special poignancy is that they assume a future in which promise can be fulfilled and talent flourish. But Alice's three sons were, in Thomas Hardy's famous words, "Men Who Marched Away" to the war to end all wars. When war was declared under the glorious sunshine of August 1914, young men in their straw boaters and girls in calico dresses thronged Whitehall in an ecstasy of war fever, chanting and singing patriotic songs, envisaging a glorious (and swift) crusade to humble the German aggressor. In their hearts they believed, again in Hardy's words:

Victory crowns the just,
And that Braggarts must
Surely bite the dust.

None foresaw the exorbitant price of justice. For Alice and Reginald the cost was the lives of Alan and Rex. Their tragedy is played out in infinite detail in two black boxes at

Tetbury. There is, ironically, a hundred times as much record on the circumstances of the deaths of Alice's sons as on the years of their growing up, as if to emphasise by the dead weight of evidence the sheer waste of young lives, or to demonstrate, perversely, that nothing became them in their lives like the leaving of them.

That was not, one imagines, quite the reward the Dean had had in mind when he wrote blithely to Alice (before Rex was even at school): "Tell Rex he will do as well and bravely as the Black Prince, whenever he is called away to fight or act and that I hope he will be rewarded quite an munificently." The Dean's bland picture is matched by a letter of conventional piety from Alice in the same year, after Rex had been convinced that he would die of a bleeding nose – "I comforted him and told him he was not and even if he did, I did not think he would mind but be very happy – but when I said it, I felt how hard it would be to give him up, even to God who only lends us the children, as I always try to remember." Twenty-five years later that faith was put to the test.

When war broke out, Alan Hargreaves had already "fought" for fourteen years as a regular soldier, though compared to the hell of trench warfare, his army life before was snug repose. "Getting on" at Eton, in the "Army Class", had meant entry to Sandhurst, a filter which allowed only an upper-class trickle through to the regimental officers' messes. Between officer and ordinary ranks lay a great social divide. Respectable mothers would have bristled with shame at the idea of any son of theirs enlisting as a private: "What cause have you for such a low life . . . a refuge for all idle people . . . I would rather bury you than see you in a red coat." (Undeterred, the recipient of this letter, William Robertson, marched on and made it, uniquely, from private to field-marshal!) The officers on the other hand were a social elite; to live their life and uphold regimental honour a man needed to dig deep into his own family purse.

On August 11th, 1900 Alan Hargreaves was gazetted to the Rifle Brigade and embarked at the end of the next year for South Africa to face the Boers. In truth, the real enemies he faced were boredom, and the discomfort of spending one

Alice's sons.

Alan, dressed for polo.

Alan, in dress uniform.

Christmas Day "sitting in a tent with one lamp and the rain of a thunderstorm splashing through onto the paper as I write". The critical battles had been won, at Ladysmith, Kimberley, Bloemfontein and Mafeking. After a skirmish at Krondstadt, Alan found himself caught up in the tedious tailpiece of containing Boer guerrillas by blockhouses linked with wire. He saved the Empire at his lonely outpost, Blockhouse 21, by reading *Country Life* in a deck chair, playing polo, picking mushrooms, and, in the absence of Boers, shooting at hares and quails, while awaiting the solitary joy of the provision train:

They may call us in old England jolly Tommies at the front,
And the lads who will the Empire's honour save;
But we don't feel much like heroes in this corner of the hunt,
We are hermits with a blockhouse for a cave.

After playing this role of a kind of anchorite of the veldt, Alan spent a ten-year uniformed siesta in unperilous corners of the Empire. One letter from Malta in 1909 finds him playing polo, visiting the opera and planning a shooting trip up the Nile: "I don't think you need be in the least bit afraid of my getting blown up or coming to any harm."

In that nonchalant spirit he sailed with the Expeditionary Force as a captain in September 1914. With no hint of what lay ahead, he crossed the Channel in officer style – losing forty-five pounds at poker and chemin de fer on the way to St Nazaire. A fortnight later the games were over, though, in a darker sense, life became all gamble and hazard. After eleven days marching and miserable bivouacs, moving up to the trenches near Soupir, Alan found himself isolated with two others on a mound under direct German fire:

Well, here we were – three of us – self no arms better than a stick and Paul (hit in the leg) had dropped his rifle. Our mound was covered with brambles. Paul seemed to think that he couldn't get back. But seeing as it was useless to try and take the German trench, I started Paul off to crawl back . . . soon Churches and I started. A distinctly unpleasant crawl and I must say I wished myself at the end

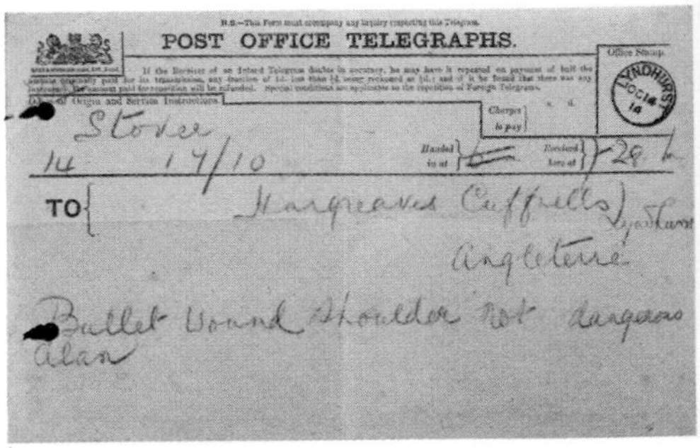
POST OFFICE TELEGRAPHS.
Office Stamp
LYNDHURST OC 14 14
Charges to pay
Stover
14 17/10
Handed in at
Received here at
TO Hargreaves Cuffnells Lyndhurst Angleterre
Bullet wound shoulder not dangerous
Alan

of it. I don't suppose it was more than fifty or sixty yards. Paul got hit in the thigh, Churches in the mouth and hand, the latter just as he fell over the bank. I got gingered up by two bits of earth and stone kicked up by bullets striking close. One tore a hole in my breeches and in myself, but not worth even dressing.

Two weeks later a telegram arrived at Cuffnells tersely announcing a closer brush with death: "Bullet wound shoulder not dangerous, Alan". He detailed the event in his diary for the day (October 13th) with amazing and characteristic coolness:

During an advance of, say, eighty yards I got hit. Ran on the last twenty or thirty yards but then told them to go on and remained lying there for over two hours on my back and it rained a lot of the time. Pretty miserable. I didn't know exactly where the wound was and at first wondered if I was going to die. More nervous about this than I might have been if I had not seen the wounds of the two Germans bagged by C Company. When I saw them, I did not think they were immediately mortal but they both died in less than half an hour. I lay quite still on my back to avoid haemorrhage and could hear all the firing – occasional bullets struck near me.

In fact, the bullet passed through his lung and he was shipped home to convalesce. There his "chums" wrote to him of the mud and the blood, mixing the appalling deaths of their friends with words like "fun" and "great sport". These were still the early days of the war, but the regular army had already been decimated by casualties. The real blood-bath of slaughtering thousands for sixty yards of cratered mud lay just ahead, when, in the words of the song, you could find the old battalion "Hanging on the old barbed wire", and men, supping with death, mastered a grim brand of humour: "Dear Aunty, hoping this finds you as it leaves me. We are wading up to our necks in blood. Send fags and a lifebelt."

Alan returned to the front for the attacks in May 1915, on the Aubers Ridge, only to be hit again. This time the telegram which carried the news back to England lacked the reassuring suffix. A fortnight later the company sergeant major chronicled for Alice and Reginald what he called "that most eventual Sunday morning, sir, I can tell you that it was the most frightful twenty-four hours that I have ever spent". It was one of those fatal days which recurrently disproved General Haig's belief that, after enough artillery bombardment of the enemy positions, the infantry could calmly walk up to their objectives without needing their rifles:

I am very sorry to say that our own artillery did more damage to our own men than what they did to the Germans . . . they killed or wounded over fifty of our poor chaps which I can't say was very creditable of them . . . The captain [Alan] led us over the German trench but no sooner than we started we came under a most galling fire and I am sorry to say that the captain was one of the first hit. He received a bullet in the stomach and he knew as soon as he was struck that he was mortally wounded. We made him comfortable in the bottom of the German trench . . . I asked him where he was hit and he told me he was finished; I asked him if I could do anything for him or if he wanted anything and he asked me to get some morphia from the doctor. But he seemed as if he had taken something already and was going to sleep and I was called away then. In the afternoon the artillery opened up another bombardment so we shifted the captain into a dugout for safety but he gradually got weaker and weaker but remained conscious even until the stretcher bearers came over during the night and took him back to our own trench where he died early in the morning without complaining.

Rex.

Rex Hargreaves crossed the Channel two months after his brother, in November 1914, as captain in the Irish Guards. Mud was his first enemy: "A Belgian road consists of a strip of cobbles down the middle, wide enough for only one thing, and directly you get off the centre strip you get into the mud. I believe Napoleon is credited with the statement that in Belgium he discovered the fourth element: air, fire, water and mud – and he is not far wrong." He fought at Ypres,

Rex and Alice.

Bethune, and survived the early massacres of the Battle of the Somme (in which, on the first day, July 1st, 1916, 60,000 troops, half the force, fell). By the end of November, after months of suicidal frontal attacks, the allies had made a maximum of seven miles, the route paved with the corpses of over one million men. In that incomprehensible carnage lay Rex, killed in the attack on Lesboeufs on September 25th: "He was hit as we got to the German trench . . . we got him into the trench and he lay there all day and he was so patient and confident about himself that I had hopes that he might recover although we knew that he was hit in the stomach. We got him away as soon as it was dark and I think he had a possible chance but he died next day in hospital" (letter from his CO).

Relatives paid respectful obsequies to Alan and Rex: "They both fell in the most glorious death one can imagine, at the head of their men in attack . . . It only remains for us the survivors to consecrate ourselves to that example and be inspired in a humbler sphere, by that record." Such lofty sentiment urged two and a quarter million men to enlist in a

The commemorative plaque in Lyndhurst Church.

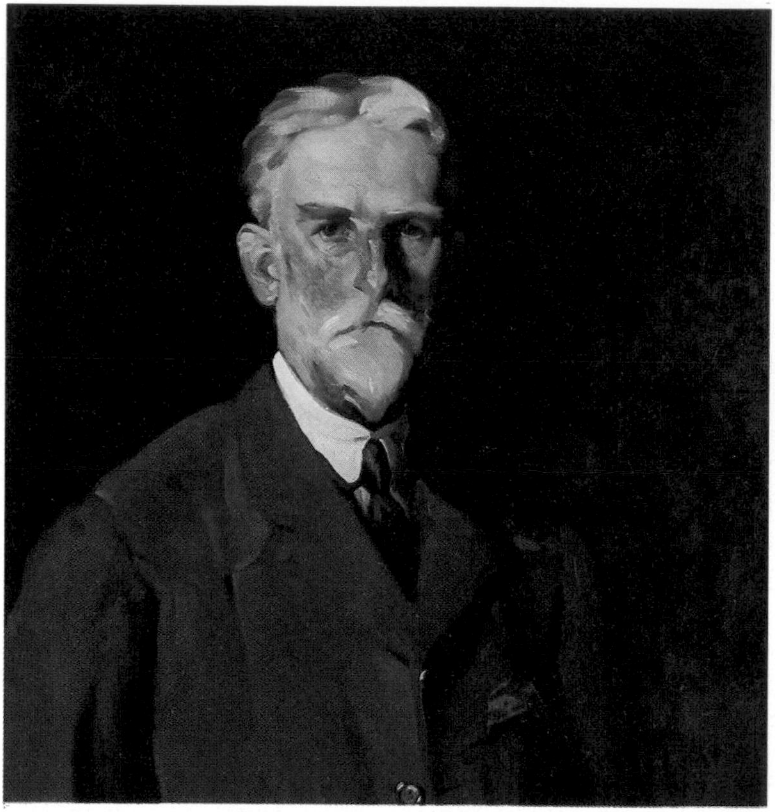

Reginald.

delirium of patriotism; some, their dreams haunted, would soon dismiss it as the "old lie": *Dulce et Decorum est pro Patria Mori* ("It is a glorious and fitting thing to die for one's country").

The double loss of Alan and Rex maimed, if not fatally wounded the family at Cuffnells, though they clung to the consolation of the survival of their youngest son, Caryl, a captain in the Scots Guards. There was scant solace that several families in Lyndhurst had lost more than one son. As if to mark the devastation of the family, there is a blank gap in the records at Tetbury for eight years after the end of the war. They were, in a real sense, empty years and, for Reginald, a slow, invalid decline to his death in 1926. His spirit died long before with Alan and Rex, and lay buried under foreign soil in military cemeteries so vast that individual crosses are reduced to impersonal statistic.

When Reginald died in 1926, among the letters of condolence, one from Alice's brother, Eric, understood that he was a lingering casualty of the war: "It is so easy to write that life had become such a wearisome burden to him that no one could wish it prolonged . . . His was a very happy life till the all-devastating war played havoc with it, and left him as part of the wreckage it had caused." In a small blue envelope, to be opened after his death, Reginald left his tribute to Alice: "God bless and keep you for all your love and care for me. No words of mine can express what you have been to me."

Rex's grave.

After Reginald's death Cuffnells died its own slow death, though it had been chronically ailing. The turmoil of war and the upheavals of society had left the house high and dry on a foreign shore, monument to an old order which had rapidly changed. Caryl was now master of Cuffnells, though he played that part only at weekends, living mostly in London. Alice spent summers at Cuffnells, but hibernated to a house leased in Westerham, Kent, where she had the close companionship of Rhoda.

There is no truth in the suggestion that Alice now felt a "lonely old lady", trapped by geriatric dullness. She had infinitely more spirit than in the listless picture of her sitting at home in maudlin reminiscence, gazing at Richmond's portrait of the "Three Sisters", and, like Dickens' Miss Havisham, stopping the clock of her memory. Her Liddell appetite was as sharp and catholic as ever, digesting news and events, big and small. She followed the fortunes of Roosevelt, bewailed Parisian riots ("It's rather inappropriate to have the worst of the fighting in and around the Place de la Concorde"), and threw up her hands at Lady Oxford's published "candid" memories of "all these unlucky people – Balfour, Rosebery, etc. – all dead and cannot disclaim these innuendos and stories". Alice busied herself with local meetings, encouraged to use her influence to stop the advance of civilisation on the New Forest – "I'm not sure one is justified in stopping the spread of electricity." Theatres, concerts, exhibitions and dinners still punctuated the social routine, if less frequently. Not once in her letters did Alice even hint that she felt time heavy on her hands; she

Westerham.

Cuffnells as a hotel.

The remains of Cuffnells.

only regretted her distance from Cuffnells: letters to Caryl constantly refer to the place: "It's good to hear of the bluebells in the Wilderness – with the azaleas, they are a dream." But in reality Cuffnells was a burden, expensive to keep up, difficult to sell or to lease; its scale and lavish splendour deterred rather than encouraged tenants or purchasers. But the house outlived Alice and flourished, briefly, as a hotel which tempered the "glories of the past" with modern "necessities", such as *heated* garages.

The last and least glamorous act in the story of Cuffnells is played out in a long estate agent's letter to Alice's son, Caryl, in June 1944. It is a far cry from Reginald's boyhood when his parents imported pictures, marbles, even Italian painters themselves. A solitary straw from the past refused to be blown away: Odell was still nominally on the staff, "working occasionally", and drawing five pounds per month, an arrangement that was to last another seven years. But there was also squalid litigation with a lessee over rent arrears, dilapidations and the disappearance of the fridge and Aga. In April 1941, the War Department requisitioned the house; they removed the carpets and furniture and replaced them with Royal Engineers. The Pompeian and peacock walls were covered with ten-foot boards; but the precautions were unnecessary: after the war only the bulldozers moved in, whilst Ernest Odell stood and watched. Then in furtive invasions, shrubs disappeared from the garden to root in other soil; and the "Wilderness" reverted to wilderness.

10
IN MEMORY OF A SUMMER DAY

Before the First World War romantic tourists from Bournemouth could jolt and clatter through the village of Lyndhurst in four-horse stagecoaches, decked out as in old prints, a man with post-horn perched at the back. He did blow the horn – for effect, but found it more useful to swipe at local urchins clambering onto the bottom iron step for a free ride down from Swan Green. Besides repelling these unwanted boarders, the hornblower directed the passengers' gaze to "noted places of interest", en route to lunch at The Crown. Approaching Lyndhurst, all heads swivelled to peer fleetingly into "Cuffnells Park on my right, the home of the original Alice in Wonderland".

A passing wonder for visitors and a distant warm memory for the family – those were the niches occupied by "Alice" in most of the life of the real Alice. In her mind the fiction never supplanted the fact or threatened to walk in her shoes; Alice could always distinguish between the rhododendrons at Cuffnells and the gaudy tiger-lilies in Wonderland. Sometimes, perhaps, the fictional shadow might be an embarrassment: "I went to a meeting yesterday and after it was over the lady who addressed us came up and said, 'I must shake hands with the real Alice,' and after a few inane remarks she asked, 'Did you know Mr Dodgson?' Well, I ask you . . . " Occasionally "Alice" might be a useful credential: "I have been wondering if I should buy a new Morris, and write and tell him [ie W.R. Morris himself, later Lord Nuffield] who I was and come from Oxford, and so ask him to pick me out one of his best. It would not be wrong, would it?" But for most of Alice's life Wonderland lay beyond the looking-glass of memory.

After Reginald's death, the rest of Alice's life in seclusion at Westerham might well have been silence – an unsung death following obscure retirement: "We had wild dissipation yesterday – a collector of old tabbies to see Rhoda, and today she has a bridge party." Instead, in the last six years of her life Alice made as many headlines as all

Hall Barn, former property of the Hargreaves family.

the preceding generations of Liddells. She was thrust into the glare of public renown, harried by newspaper reporters tracking down big questions and trivia: Did Charles Dodgson really love her? Was Dinah a real cat? Alice was feted on both sides of the Atlantic; the wife of the American ambassador conceded, without begrudging it, that Alice was, momentarily, the "most famous woman in America". How did it happen? Ironically, it was through a simple strategem devised to ensure Alice a quietly comfortable old age.

The Hargreaves family had basked on the greener grass of the great social divide between those obliged to work and those obliged only to live in style. They had made their money among the mills of Lancashire, then flushed away the taint of commerce by investing in land and property. But as landed estates became as much a burden as a badge of rank, the family was forced to clip its own wings. In the 1890s Reginald sold Oak Hill, the family seat in Accrington, to the local authority, and found himself both £10,000 richer *and* acclaimed as public benefactor. Then in 1912 he sold off part of the Lancashire estate – houses and farms valued at £24,000. That shored up the family and staved off until Reginald's death any altercation at the bank. Thereafter,

Alice, aged eighty, at Cuffnells.

Facsimile of original manuscript of *'Alice's Adventures Underground'*.

lack of money was for Alice an insistent fact of life that would not go away, though she wrote of fiscal bureaucrats with the blue-blooded hauteur of one who had never really had to count pennies: "How about the income tax? The man seems a little excited."

In November 1928, with huge maintenance costs whittling away resources and with death duties still owing, Alice decided to placate the Inland Revenue by auctioning some of her mementoes of "Alice": several autographed editions of *Alice in Wonderland,* an "Alice" postage-stamp case, and an ivory Tweedledum and Tweedledee in a box. Not enough, in themselves, to guarantee solvency or to set Sotheby's alight – but at the top of the list sat an item which had reposed for years in a window-seat box at Cuffnells – "A Christmas gift to a dear child in memory of a summer day", a ninety-two-page illustrated manuscript in Charles Dodgson's hand, the original three-chapter version of what had since become one of the most famous children's books in the world. (It had sold over a quarter of a million copies before Charles Dodgson's death.)

There is no sign that the manuscript was any longer so precious in sentiment to Alice that she had any qualms about parting with it – apart from wanting a good price. It was sixty-five years since the sun had allegedly shone on that golden river trip to Godstow, and twenty years since

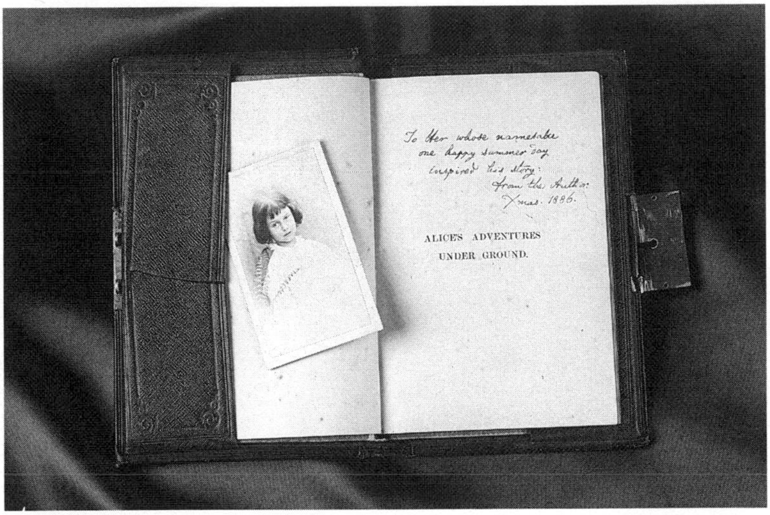

Charles Dodgson's death. Anyway, after Alice's marriage, she and Dodgson met only across the gulf that divided a cloistered and celibate Oxford common room from the fashionable and family drawing room at Cuffnells; they wore their contrasting mantles snugly enough as to pre-empt any serious debate as to whether *he* could have made a husband for her.

Biographical storms have been brewed in the tea-cups of Charles Dodgson's not mentioning Alice's wedding in his diary (he was at Eastbourne at the time), and his giving up photography in the same year. A year later, in effect, he "retired", resigning his lectureship, but by right continuing to enjoy the privileges of a Life Fellow; he dedicated himself to a "new life" of more literary projects, managing the common-room wine committee, introducing the institution of "afternoon tea", and advertising his brother's marmalade at "10d (possibly 9d) per lb". In 1886 he borrowed the "Alice" manuscript from Alice for a facsimile edition, and wrote, in ignorance of even the simple facts of her family: "May I also have the pleasure of presenting one to your eldest *daughter* (even if she be not an 'Alice' – which I think unlikely)." In return, Alice asked Dodgson to stand godfather to a son, but he refused. His last letter to Alice (a note while she was visiting the Deanery for the last time) stretches formality into awkwardness:

My Dear Mrs Hargreaves,

I should be so glad if you could, quite conveniently to yourself, look in for tea any day. You would probably prefer to bring a companion: but I must leave the choice to you, only remarking that if your husband is here he would be ~~most~~ very welcome. (I crossed out most because it's ambiguous; most words are, I fear.) I met him in our common room not long ago. It was hard to realise that he was the husband of one I can scarcely picture to myself, even now, as more than seven years old!

Always sincerely yours,
C. L. Dodgson

In a letter to Mrs Liddell on the family's departure from Oxford, Dodgson identified himself with the parents rather than with Alice: "Now I am an old man, already beginning to feel a little weary of life." He was twenty years younger than Henry Liddell but died within four days of him. After

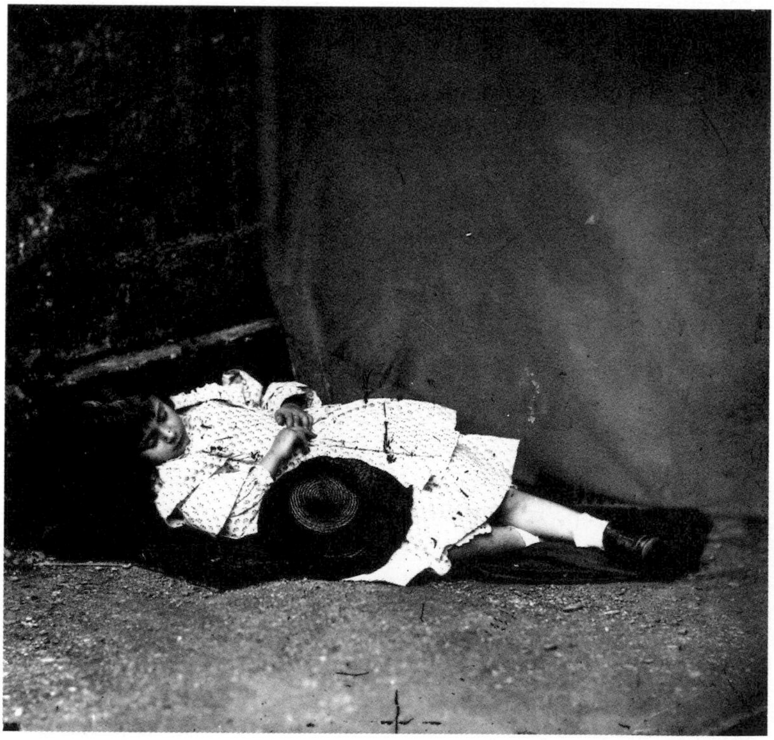

Alice, photograph by Charles Dodgson.

Dodgson's death in 1898, Alice wrote to Macmillans (publishers of *Alice in Wonderland*) asking to buy Tenniel's original wood-block illustrations. They told her, in a canny, if needless, untruth, that they had been "inevitably destroyed" in the process of engraving. "What, then, shall I have as my legacy?" wrote Alice to Reginald. Whether she wanted keepsake or investment, Alice had already had for thirty-five years the richest "bequest".

By 1928 the original manuscript had acquired more value than anyone could guess. One adviser, consulting the "best judges", decreed not less than £2,000. Sotheby's, having sold a single letter by Robert Burns for that price, suggested a reserve of £4,000, adding, "We feel sure that your manuscript will make auction history." April 3rd was the date set for the sale. Backstage, lobbies were formed and deals proposed. Should the manuscript be offered at all on the open market, inevitably to be swallowed up by a rich foreign collector? The issue burned in the correspondence columns of *The Times* and even made the third leader. The last few days before the sale concentrated the minds of interested parties as wonderfully as a capital sentence. Stanley Unwin, in "One Last Appeal" to Alice (March 31st) offered to buy the manuscript for the British Museum – "Whether Mr Dodgson's manuscript goes to America thus rests with you. It is still in your power to prevent it." The Director of the British Museum asked for a price so that he could appeal to the general public. Two days later came a telegram from the London dealers, Quaritches: "Will you accept five thousand pounds for the Alice manuscript from an English gentleman who undertakes to present it to Christ Church College, Oxford?" Alice referred all enquiries to Sotheby's. Less than forty-eight hours before the sale, an offer of £10,000. Sotheby's demurred and Alice wavered: "At one moment I very nearly took it . . . in the end, I said no, let it go on."

On Tuesday, April 3rd three hundred spectators crammed into Sotheby's dark-oak and burlap auction room in Mayfair (where, in the words of the *New York Times*, "sleek motors roll, lovely ladies walk in sables") to share in a moment of auction history. All eyes focused on the protagonists, ranged

around a U-shaped table: Dr Rosenbach, of Philadelphia, backed up by the muscle of an American fortune; the President of Quaritches of London, representing the British Museum; and B.D. Maggs, another London dealer. In a preliminary sparring bout Rosenbach beat Maggs to a first edition of *Alice in Wonderland* at £5,000.

Among the reporters busily absorbing or embroidering the event, Allen Raymond, *New York Times* correspondent, best recreated the climax:

"No 319," says the auctioneer quietly.

"Five thousand pounds," comes a firm voice from the horse-shoe.

"Ah," exclaims the gathering.

Then ensues breathless silence, while the air tingles with electricity.

"Six thousand, 7,000, 8,000, 9,000, 10,000," the bids jumped a thousand pounds at a time till £10,000 was reached. That is $50,000. The bidding slows down. "And a hundred," says the agent for the British Museum quietly. "And a hundred," says Mr Maggs. "And a hundred," whispers Dr Rosenbach . . .

So it goes. Once in a while there is a jump of £50. At one round of the fighting trio there are three bids of £10.

Necks are craned, ears are strained . . .

The British Museum drops out at £12,500. It is Mr Maggs or Dr Rosenbach.

"Fifteen thousand two hundred pounds," says Mr Maggs.

"Fifteen thousand four hundred," the Philadelphia dealer persists, and victory is his . . .

It seemed as if everyone in the room relaxed together. There is a sigh that is almost like a moan. Then the auctioneer says:

"Dr Rosenbach wishes to announce that he is prepared to sell the book to the nation at the price for which he just bought it."

A few hands clap. Then the crowd starts melting away. Over near the rostrum an old woman, once little Alice, brushes a handkerchief across her eyes. Then she, too, vanishes.

Dr Rosenbach has bid the highest price ever for a book in a British auction, nearly a thousand pounds more than he paid

WHAT TO WEAR AT EASTER: By LADY DUFF GORDON IN PAGE 9

DAILY SKETCH

INCORPORATING THE DAILY GRAPHIC

No. 5,922. WEDNESDAY, APRIL 4, 1928. ONE PENNY.

£20,000 FOR EMPIRE TRAVEL ENTER NOW

"ALICE IN WONDERLAND" AS SHE IS TO-DAY

Chapter I

Auction of the 'Alice' manuscript.

for a first folio edition of Shakespeare. He seemed unabashed: "I think I got it reasonably enough, as precious things go nowadays." There would have been no ceiling to his bidding; his brief was simply, "Buy it." (At the posthumous sale of Charles Dodgson's effects in 1898, his whole library, drawings, photographs, furniture and effects realised only £729 2s 6d.)

The British nation did not respond to Dr Rosenbach's offer to sell back the manuscript which, according to the British Museum's Director, had "won so unique a place" in its heart. It crossed the Atlantic, where it immediately changed hands again, for double the price, and graced the library of Eldridge R. Johnson, founder of the "Victor Talking Machine Company", which enriched him by $30,000,000. (Eventually, the manuscript did find its way "home" to the British Museum. It came on the market in 1948, devalued at only $50,000; well-wishers bought it and presented it to the United Kingdom "as an expression of thanks to a noble people who held Hitler at bay for a long period single-handed". With due solemnity the Archbishop of Canterbury accepted the gift as an "unsullied and innocent act in a distracted and painful world".)

As Mrs Hargreaves vanished from the auction room, the eyes of the world followed; they had "discovered" the real Alice. Patsy Bess-Irene Fahy of Tulsa, "Your Little Friend", penned the typical response: "When I was a very little girl I used to wonder what you were like and not until a few days ago did I know you were real and honestly alive, as much as I am today." The press hurriedly added flesh to the bones of the story, making up in sentiment what they lacked in factual accuracy: "Today, she lives alone – poor, widowed and childless. Before the lodge-keeper's gate of her old country place is a sign reading: 'To rent furnished, this historic mansion'." The laurel for downright fabrication sat on the brow of the *Daily Mail*: in its garbled version of the story, Charles Dodgson fell in love with Violet, the Dean's "eldest" daughter; he asked the Dean's consent to marry her, and was refused; thereafter Violet pined away and died of a broken heart at the age of eighteen, while Charles Dodgson became a "solitary, hopeless, old bachelor". Such

Alice's belongings.

was the publicity following the sale (which brought a total of £19,000) that even letters addressed to "The Original Alice, England" found their destination easily.

The avalanche of mail ranged from the impertinent to the pathetic, and Alice learned what it meant to have newly-acquired wealth advertised in public. Sun Life Assurance cunningly took up a wide-eyed remark of Alice's, reported in the *Daily Sketch:* "It is a large sum of money and I do not know what I shall do with it." Sun Life assured her *they* had the answer. So did a vicar in Staffordshire who asked for a donation towards new toilets. A "poor widow" in London begged "just a wee bonus of your percentage" to support her and her "ailing" mother. Others appealed to Alice as an arbiter in the matter of valuable books: one lady hoped to sell to Dr Rosenbach "a French book . . . a friend has translated most of it and it cost nineteen shillings for typewriting"; an American who hacked stories for children's magazines bewailed not taking care of her own manuscripts (they had come to grief in a cousin's cellar); and there were letters galore from those hoping that their unexceptional copies of *Alice in Wonderland* would bring in an income for life. Among all the nonsense one, only one letter – from Lord Montagu – took Alice back over seventy years: "Of course you will not remember me out of the hordes of undergraduates that used to invade the Deanery at breakfast-time . . . but I remember you well, in spite of the years."

Since Alice had lived among Oxford's distant ivory towers, it might not seem surprising to find an academic hood in the cache at Tetbury, except that it denotes a degree not conferred at Oxford, nor, indeed, anywhere in the country, but a Doctorate of Letters at Columbia University, New York. The recipient of the degree was Alice herself. It was at once the highest and most singular public accolade paid to her for being "Alice", ensconcing her in august company, with James Balfour, Marie Curie, Guglielmo Marconi, Albert King of the Belgians, Jan Smuts – and another eighty or so non-Americans honoured by the university since the turn of the century. The solemn event exudes an

THE WALDORF-ASTORIA
Park Avenue, Forty-ninth to Fiftieth Streets
NEW YORK

unconscious whimsy worthy of Lewis Carroll, and all played out against a grim social backcloth of the Depression, Prohibition and the rule of the gangster underworld. A *New York Herald Tribune* leader hit on the inverse connection: "Is it inconceivable that her [Alice's] presence might remind a host of worried Americans of how much more there is in the world than economics and how scant a relationship wealth has to fun?"

The whole pageant of Alice's visit grew like a gaudy inflating balloon from an innocuous request in November 1931 that she should write an address to mark the opening of New York's celebrations of the centenary of Lewis Carroll's birth. At the heart of an exhibition of Carrolliana at Columbia University would lie the original manuscript – on Dodgson's own mahogany dining table, which, too, had crossed the Atlantic. Within weeks Alice's minor role swelled to the stature of a state visit, with all the accompanying razzmataz – press receptions, police escorts through New York, a private suite six-hundred feet up in the Hotel Astoria, a "talkie" film and radio broadcast to the western world. Alice would walk only on red carpets through doors that would open to her; she would be spared the democratic inconvenience of ever having to queue or to wait – and any other obstacle that might deter an old lady of nearly eighty from visiting New York. Even the hotel would slow down its elevators to minimise her discomfort, and hide her behind an impenetrable wall of security, to protect her from gate-crashers, hand-shakers, well-wishers, autograph-hunters and some grim, violent facts of life in New York. Only flowers filtered through the net; they transformed Alice's hotel suite into an ornamental garden. Outside, in the eerie silence of the deserted corridors snaked a mass of cables, lifelines to the moment when the Real Alice would speak.

Alice arrived in New York at the end of April on board the *Berengaria*, with Rhoda, as observer, and Caryl, as manager. As the ship nosed past quarantine, thirty or forty reporters embarked and roamed in search of Alice; they chased Caryl on to the sundeck and pursued him into the lounge; he turned at bay, with Alice, in the palm court and

Lewis Carroll's Alice, Now 80, Visits U. S.

Alice Liddell at the age of 7½ years, photographed by Lewis Carroll. Upper right: Mrs. Reginald G. Hargreaves, the original "Alice," as she appeared last week. Lower: Lewis Carroll, from a photograph taken by himself. (Published by courtesy of the Century Co.)

answered an agreed number of prepared questions. The press, however, seemed to take away different answers and even disagreed on what Alice was wearing; was she dressed "appropriately in a frilled and beflowered frock, relic of a period known as mid-Victorian", or in "a dark, printed silk gown, with blue polka dots"?

With happy communal disregard of some ugly facts in the city around them, the press concurred in one great fantasy: the fictional "Alice" incarnate was setting out on another volume of adventures – "Alice, she who has run down a rabbit-hole and sat at tea with the Mad Hatter . . . began her adventures today in a *new Wonderland.*" They thrust a giant copy of her first adventures into Alice's arms and expected this "ageing lady of pert manners and whimsical face", "placid, sweet, immobile, with wise old gently smiling eyes", to be exactly the sort of lady "Alice" (not Alice) would have grown up to be. The New World (or Wonderland) hung on her first words. But they came out more humdrum than droll: "How often do they dredge the river so that ships of deep draught may pass into port?" In like prosaic vein she then expressed interest in the ventilation shafts of the Holland Tunnel.

The newsmen were undeterred: the *New York American* actually reported Alice as saying "curiouser and curiouser" on her arrival. Others indulged in lame Carrollese:

"What are all those tall things?" asked Alice, landing in America.

"Those are sky-scrapers," said the Mad Hatter. "The country is full of them."

"What good are they?" asked Alice.

"That's what some of the mortgage-holders want to know," put in the Carpenter.

Alice's son, Caryl, joined in lucratively in the game: for the *Herald Tribune* he wrote "Alice in a New Wonderland". "So in a minute they found themselves in a smooth, silent car going up to the thirty-first floor, where Alice was to live while she was in New York. She soon began to wonder whether they would reach heaven, and, if so, whether New

4 New York Herald Tribune

"Beautifuller and Beautifuller!" cried Alice, "The Buildings Are Opening Out Like the Largest Telescopes That Ever Were!"
Drawn for the Herald Tribune by Robert Lawson

Alice *in a* New Wonderland

The Same "Alice" Who Fell Down a Rabbit Hole 70 Years Ago and Landed in "Wonderland" Has Visited America and Written This Added Chapter on Her New Adventures

By Alice Hargreaves—*the* Alice *of* "Alice in Wonderland"
As Told to Her Son, Captain C. L. Hargreaves

York was a good place to start from . . . 'When I was young,' Alice said, 'I had to grow my neck long to get to these heights.' "

They were all playing a game tinged with pathos, a new version of fiddling in the midst of a burning Rome. Overleaf from Caryl's article, beneath the banner, "Shall the Underground Rule?", the *Herald Tribune* thundered against a new aristocracy spawned of brothels, prisons and gambling dens, and ruled by the "law of club, torch, bomb and machine gun". The helplessness of the republic in the face of this regime of crime was epitomised by a national hero, Charles Lindbergh, hiring gangsters to rescue his

NEW YORK
Herald Tribune
MAGAZINE

Section XI | Mrs. William Brown Meloney, *Editor* | *Twenty-four Pages* *1
Sunday, June 5, 1932

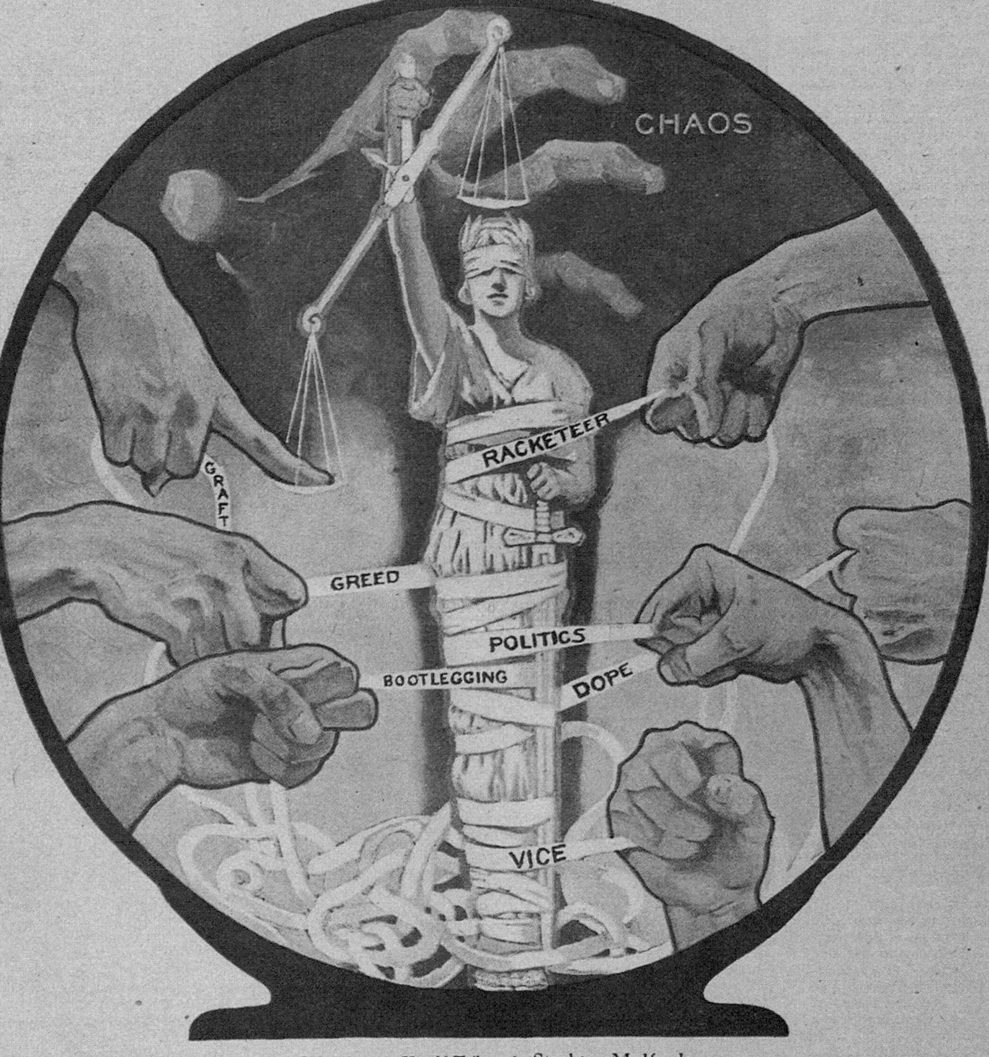

Painted for the Herald Tribune *by* Stockton Mulford

Shall the Underworld Rule?

The First Article of a Series on the Rising Power of Gangdom—a Warning to the United States

By Denis Tilden Lynch

Author of "Boss Tweed—the Story of a Grim Generation," "Grover Cleveland—A Man Four Square," Etc.

IN THE last ten years an aristocracy has arisen in this country.

Its leaders, in the main, are the spawn of the brothels, the gambling dens and the corrupt political machines of the big cities, and the prisons. Their followers are drawn from all walks of life.

Its law is the law of terrorism—the law of the club, the torch, the bomb and the machine gun.

Like all aristocracies, this aristocracy within the republic is a drain on the wealth of the nation beyond definite calculation.

Its annual cost to the American people exceeds, by far, the expense of maintaining the Federal government in any twelve months of the last decade; and the appropriations of Congress in the ten years beginning with 1923 averaged $4,329,684,210.10 annually.

The main source of income of this ruling class—the phrase is not an empty one in some of our larger cities—is extorted from legitimate business. This highly organized, well armed horde of racketeers is commonly called gangdom.

The racketeer—to use the popular designation—has been with us for many years, especially in the building trades; but the gargantuan growth of racketeering and the golden masks of respectability worn by its leaders are the gifts of prohibition.

It was not so long ago that the underworld signified the slums and the dives of the cities, the offspring of poverty and ignorance. But in this country, for the last

Alice's eightieth birthday.

Alice and President Murray Butler.

kidnapped son. Al Capone was now in prison, after a four-year federal battle to convict him; a new film, *Scarface*, played to packed houses and there were brawls among the queues for the late show.

Alice was scrupulously protected from any visible sign of villainy, and for her America made lavish gestures, as if an interlude of dreaming would make harsh economic facts more palatable. The two acts of the dream were the degree ceremony and Alice's eightieth birthday celebrations. They might well have been played out in Wonderland, invested as they were with all the grave pomp of real nonsense.

Two days before her birthday, and clad in gown and mortar-board, Alice processed to the huge circular reading-room at Columbia University, flanked by Professor J. Enrique Zanetti (Chairman of the Centenary Committee) and Dr Nicholas Murray Butler (President of the University). There, in front of a huge bank of flowers and with soft music from a gallery above, the President from his throne draped the hood of a Doctor of Literature around Alice's shoulders. His dedicatory speech aimed at solemnity but hit only a clumsy verbosity, celebrating Alice as a "moving cause". "Awaking with her girlhood's charm the ingenious fancy of a mathematician familiar with imaginary quantities, stirring him to reveal his complete understanding of the heart of a child as well as of the mind of a man; to create imaginary figures and happenings in a language all his own, making odd phrases and facts to live on pages which will adorn the literature of the English tongue, time without end, and which are as charming as quizzical, and as amusing as fascinating . . . " He opened with a fanciful genealogy that took even Alice by surprise: "Descendant of John of Gaunt, time-honour'd Lancaster . . . " "Please, where did the idea of my being descended from John of Gaunt come from?" wrote Alice later to Caryl.

Shortly after 3 p.m. on Wednesday, May 4th, Alice's birthday, two thousand invited guests saw and heard the real Alice in the university gymnasium as the climax of the celebrations. Thousands more heard the proceedings broadcast across America, Canada and Europe. The time might have been 3 p.m. precisely, had the bandleader not been the last in the hall to see his cue. Belatedly, he struck up "Rule Britannia", and amid much curious neck-straining, Alice processed again. She sat on a stage with other dignitaries beneath a "Wonderland" frieze. Dr Butler introduced Alice; she hesitatingly paid tribute to Lewis Carroll as the "ideal friend of childhood"; the audience gave her an ovation; a "special chorus" of 120 from college Glee Clubs and the university orchestra performed an "Alice in Wonderland" suite. Then, as if to put a cerebral seal on the occasion, there followed a lengthy allegorical analysis of the book by the university Professor of English. In Caryl's opinion the opening seconds promised much more than the later long minutes delivered. The audience had, anyway, satisfied their real curiosity.

For ten more days Alice relaxed and travelled to see notable sights: the Empire State Building, Stock Exchange and the rich men who had bought Carrolliana and wished to meet and entertain the "real thing". Photographers were always present to provide lasting proof of the event. On April 14th, with newsmen still in tow, Alice left New York on board the *Aquitania*, which, to the captain's embarrassment, flew an absurd Cheshire-Cat flag (Zanetti's

The Lewis Carroll centenary celebrations at Columbia University.

Alice and Eldridge Johnson, new owner of the manuscript.

The 'Alice' biscuit tin.

suggestion). To the end, then, Alice's hosts worked hard to preserve the illusion of a new Wonderland, but Caryl travelled more freely than Alice and could not avoid the beggars on the subway steps in Times Square. Though he, too, dined in privileged circles, the banquets were garnished by tales of erstwhile millionaires wondering where their next meal would come from. At the Stock Exchange he saw the slack economic tide: brokers and clerks were throwing paper darts at each other. On his return to the United Kingdom Caryl published his impressions and his remedy. In view of the imminent nightmare in Europe, it has a sinister ring: "And so at last we come to the root cause of the world's trouble, and that is Democracy. Democracy as in force today is incapable of producing good government. It cannot produce leaders, it cannot control crime, it cannot but squander. It is, after all, government by the inefficient. How long shall we put up with it?"

In honouring Charles Dodgson's centenary, the United Kingdom reversed the principle of catching a cold from a transatlantic sneeze: by comparison with the delirious fever in New York, London merely succumbed to a slight temperature, with an exhibition of Carrolliana at Bumpus' bookship at the end of June 1932. There was no original manuscript, but among the singular accumulation were *Alice in Wonderland* (chapter seven) in shorthand, a "rare" Alice in Wonderland biscuit tin (a limited edition made for Messrs Jacob and Son), Tenniel's original wood-blocks (miraculously restored), and, inevitably, the "real" Alice herself. J.C. Squire paid tribute to this central exhibit at the opening ceremony in rhymed couplets:

Till recently I thought Miss Alice
Coeval with the Crystal Palace,
Prince Albert and the Albert Hall,
And not a real girl at all;

In replying, the girl who, "standing at life's portal,/Induced a man to be immortal", insisted on her common mortality by describing herself as a very old person who got tired very easily. An even older lady (of ninety), who doubtless tired as

easily but could remember playing tirelessly with Alice as a girl in the Deanery garden, presented a bouquet. For the press there was an incidental immortal moment (and headline): beside Mrs Alice Hargreaves stood Mr Peter Davies, also famous in a juvenile role, and this meeting of Alice in Wonderland with Peter Pan was a collision of fancies not to be missed.

Having occupied time and space solidly for eighty years, it was odd for Alice to face a wide-eyed world surprised to find that she was a *real* person at all, a world quite ready to ignore the last seventy years of her life, her fulfilment as a wife and mother, and the tragic deaths of her sons. For many she was literally the girl who tumbled down a rabbit-hole and passed through the looking-glass. A lonely lady in Norfolk asked Alice to be patron of a society she and a retired colonel had founded "to prove to the world that fairies exist". After all, she wrote, if Alice had been to Wonderland, she must have seen fairies.

After the glare of New York and London Alice's postbag was swelled with letters to her alter-ego, mostly from autograph hunters and which, under strict instructions, she despatched to Caryl. He acted as manager in a growing "Alice" industry, limiting the supply of autographs as if minting a rare currency. He scoured newspapers with the assiduousness of a press agency for the slightest mention of

Alice's belongings.

his mother, and filled several scrapbooks with the gleanings. Even her non-doings made news: "Alice not at wedding" (of her niece). Caryl combed bookshops at home and abroad to amass a collection of some 250 different editions of *Alice in Wonderland*. He liaised with purveyors of "Alice" trifles for tea-towels, tiles and trays. He corresponded with advertisers using the "Alice" motif to peddle wares from cigarettes to laxatives – a spoonful of "Alice in Ficoland" is the sugar to help the "Ficolax" down.

Three months after the centenary celebrations Alice wrote to Caryl in the fond hope that she might revert to plain Mrs Hargreaves again: "Enclosed is a letter which I should like to answer. There surely can be no reason that I should not do so now – so long after the celebration. Probably most people have forgotten all about me, as an individual." That was wishful thinking. Requests still showered in for her patronage of schemes as worthy as children's hospital wards and as pathetic as lunatic societies. In the end Alice found the constant attention not flattering, but tiresome: "But, oh, my dear, I am tired of being Alice in Wonderland. Does it sound ungrateful? It *is* – only I do get tired!"

One public event therefore had to do without the real Alice – the unveiling of the White Rabbit statue at the West Bay in Llandudno. From heaven knows where, the civic dignitaries at the resort (where the Liddells' holiday home, Penmorfa, had become Gogarth Abbey) had spun the legend that Charles Dodgson was a frequent guest of the Liddells there, that on his sea shore rambles with young Alice he dreamed up her adventures in Wonderland, and read his manuscript at the fireside in the evening. Alice categorically denied it: "Your mother's breath was fairly taken away . . . I have not the faintest remembrance of it." Undeterred, Llandudno leaned on the fading memories of its fading residents, who remembered a man who knew a man . . . Failing Alice, Llandudno turned to Lloyd George to do the honours, leaving most observers guessing as to the connection between him and Charles Dodgson. The *Sunday Times* conjectured a link – "the child has never died in Mr Lloyd George." In his address at the Pier Pavilion he praised Lewis Carroll's books in vacuous hyperbole – "a bubbling fountain of perennial delight . . . pure joy . . . a limpid, exhilarating joy in every sentence". He also gave political edge to the fanciful proceedings by drawing a parallel between the current practice of a "great European country" and the Queen of Hearts' rule that punishment should precede the crime.

Before her death, Alice was caught in the net of one more great "Alice" event – the making of the first *Alice in Wonderland* film. In the quest for the ideal heroine Paramount Studios rejected all famous (and therefore worldly) actresses – including Mary Pickford – in favour of the unknown. The real Alice would be asked to approve the choice. Seven thousand applicants on both sides of the Atlantic hoped to satisfy Lewis Carroll's severe test of "a child of pure, unclouded brow and dreaming eyes of wonder". In the event, Hollywood decided that girlish innocence lurked in its own ranks, in nineteen-year-old Charlotte Henry, who, in her four years at Hollywood, had lacked even the worldliness to secure more than one day's work a year. The *Daily Mail* drew her ingenuous profile: "She likes pies, pastries, ice-cream and Rudy Vallee." The real Alice was, fortunately, not asked to say how far this sugary compendium coincided with *her* image of "Alice", nor what she thought of the heroine's Philadelphia accent.

442 — The Sketch — December 6, 1933

ALICE IN FILM WONDERLAND.

Lewis Carroll enthusiasts are looking forward to the Paramount Picture "ALICE IN WONDERLAND." MISS CHARLOTTE HENRY IS ALICE. Here she has got too big to get through the door into the lovely garden.

Alice was introduced to the LEG OF MUTTON by the RED QUEEN.

It will be remembered that Alice met the LEG OF MUTTON at dinner—but, having been introduced, was not allowed to cut it!

EDWARD EVERETT HORTON is a most convincing MAD HATTER.

HUMPTY DUMPTY makes a superb appearance in the screen "Alice in Wonderland."

(Left) The SHEEP SHOP-KEEPER is played by MAE MARSH. Alice is the customer.

Stills from the *Alice in Wonderland* film.

The finished product was the first American film to be premiered in this country. Charlotte Henry was surrounded by bigger names: Gary Cooper as the White Knight, W.C. Fields as Humpty Dumpty and Bing Crosby as the Mock Turtle – all anonymously behind masks. A special showing was arranged for Alice at home; she said, or was reported to have said, the "right" thing – "I saw Alice and her adventures exactly as I pictured them many years ago" (*News Chronicle*, December 27th). The *Sunday Times*, however, dismissed the film on the two basic criteria of neither telling a story nor moving. Young filmgoers were struck enough by Charlotte Henry to adopt her hairstyle in a short-lived vogue that had everything to do with Hollywood coiffure and nothing to do with Charles Dodgson or Alice. The latter would have smiled at the irony of Charlotte Henry's claim that the character destroyed her: "I no longer

existed as Charlotte Henry. With that costume I was transformed . . . to the creature people had read about as children. My identity was gone."

Early in November 1934 Alice Hargreaves was taken ill while out for a drive in the car. It was her last illness. For ten days the world, metaphorically, camped on her doorstep, followed the vicissitudes of her decline with a fascination little short of morbid and reserved only for those (like monarchs and football players) whose coughs and colds are matters of public concern. Alice shared the *Daily Telegraph*'s list of "notable invalids" with the Earl of Powys and Sir E. Farquhar Buzzard. Besides the neutral and dignified reports of her condition – "about the same", and "slightly worse" – one stands out for its indulgence in the kind of sentimental myth-making that hounded Alice in the last six years of her life:

> The Alice who wandered in Wonderland seventy-two years ago is dying. In an old white house overlooking the green of this peaceful Kentish village she lies, a woman now eighty-two . . None of those who saw her in those days are beside her in these last hours: she has outlived them all . . . But in the house are a group of figures that bring back the days when she was in Wonderland. One wears a top hat. Another is a cross between a footman and a frog. A third is obviously an angry Duchess . . . Now "where childhood's dreams are twin'd", Alice of Wonderland is dying . . .
>
> *Daily Express*, November 3rd, 1934

Alice's grave at Lyndhurst.

Alice died on November 16th, commemorated by headlines in all the national newspapers, and an obituary in *The Times* which ranked her with Beatrice, Laura, Stella, Lucasta and other happy women made immortal by contact with literary genius. Even family and friends at Westerham who lamented the passing of plain Mrs Hargreaves, the "old lady who got tired very easily", saw her burdened to the last with the mantle of "Alice": one of the floral tributes at the funeral service bore the inscription, "To Alice, in her New Wonderland".

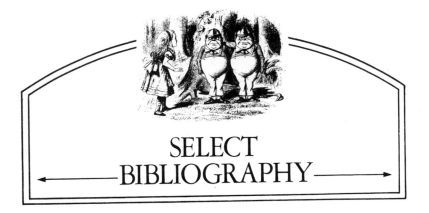

SELECT BIBLIOGRAPHY

Carleton, John D., *Westminster School*, Hart Davis, 1965.
Cooper, Derek, *Skye*, Routledge, 1970.
Courtney, J.E., *An Oxford Portrait Gallery*, Chapman and Hall, 1931.

Forshall, Frederic H., *Westminster School Past and Present*, Wyman, 1884.
Franklin, Jill, *The Gentleman's Country House and its Plan*, Routledge, 1981.

Gardner, M., *The Annotated Alice*, Bramhall, 1964.
Gattegno, Jean, *Lewis Carroll— Fragments of a Looking-Glass*, Crowell, 1976.
Gernsheim, H., *Lewis Carroll — Photographer*, Parrish, 1950.
Girouard, Mark, *The Victorian Country House*, Oxford University Press, 1979.
Green, Roger Lancelyn (ed.), *The Diaries of Lewis Carroll*, Greenwood Press, 1970.
Green, V.H.H., *Religion at Oxford and Cambridge*, S.C.M. Press, 1964.

Hollis, Christopher, *Eton, Hollis*, 1960.
Hudson, Derek, *Lewis Carroll— an Illustrated Biography*, Constable, 1976.

Lennon, Florence Becker, *Lewis Carroll*, Dover, 1972.
Lyte, H.C.M., *History of Eton College*, Macmillan, 1877.

Markham, Capt. F., *Recollections of a Town Boy at Westminster, Arnold, 1903.*
Morris, Jan, *Oxford,* Oxford University Press, 1978.

Ruskin, John, *Praeterita,* G. Allen, 1885.

Stirling, A.M.W., *The Richmond Papers,* Heinemann, 1926.

Tanner, L.E., *Westminster School,* Country Life, 1936.
Thompson, H.L., *Memoir of Henry George Liddell,* J. Murray, 1899.

ACKNOWLEDGEMENTS

The author would like to thank the following for help in preparing the book:

Mrs Mary Jean St Clair, without whom, literally, there would have been no book. She provided most of the Liddell material (now preserved at Christ Church College, Oxford), and proved an inexhaustible source of information, hospitality, patience and thankless hard work in deciphering illegible documents.

Major Ernest Odell, who kindly lent the manuscript of his autobiography and allowed the author to use its contents.

Dr John Mason, of Christ Church College, Oxford, who unearthed extra documents relating to the Liddells, and cleared up several uncertainties.

Mr Derek Phippard, of the Brantwood Trust, Coniston, for help in securing material on John Ruskin.

Mrs Dorothy Ashe, for picture research in Suffolk.

Thanks are also due to many at Hodder and Stoughton for their continuing enthusiasm, encouragement and expertise: especially to Ion Trewin for his manifold involvement, not least as editor; and to Sharyn Troughton for her sensitivity in design.

The author is also grateful to the following for kind

permission to reproduce pictures:
Messrs Macmillan Ltd: pp 5, 9, 13 (top), 16, 23, 51, 79, 88, 91, 108, 109, 152, 169, 209, 212, 225, 226, 247, 249, 251
Oxford County Libraries: pp 11 (bottom), 36, 37, 39, 82, 83, 100
Bodleian Library: pp 12 (top) Minn. Neg. 11/26
Newcastle City Libraries: p 24
Charterhouse School: pp 30, 31
Avon County Library (Bath Reference Library): p 34
Colonel Charles Liddell and Mrs Mary Liddell: pp 41, 49, 134
Balliol College, Oxford: pp 46, 95
Mansell Collection: pp 48, 207
British Museum: p 52
Norwich Castle Museum: p 53 (top)
Suffolk County Library: pp 53 (bottom), 54, 184
Christ Church College, Oxford: p 63
Westminster School: p 65
Illustrated London News: p 67
National Portrait Gallery: pp 70, 122 (top), 133
The Trustees of the Estate of the late C.L. Dodgson: p 86
Lincoln College, Oxford: p 96
The Ruskin Galleries, Bembridge School, Isle of Wight: p 101 (bottom)
Bassano and Vandyk: p 104 (bottom)
Punch Magazine: p 105
The Trustees of the Ruskin Museum, Coniston: p 106
Brasenose College, Oxford: p 118
BBC Hulton Picture Library: pp 167, 172, 204, 205
MCC: p 166
Major Ernest Odell: pp 210, 212, 213, 214

INDEX

Pictures are indexed by both subject and, where appropriate, by artist or photographer.